Geor

It was a pleasure to end 2007 by sharing a wee drink with a true Scotsman! We'll have to fee it up on your next tripoire!

Enjoy the book,

Patrick

PM
1st Sgt USMC

# STREET FIGHT IN IRAQ

***What it's really like over there***

**By**

**GySgt Patrick Tracy**

LEATHERNECK PUBLISHING
Oceanside, California

Published by Leatherneck Publishing
A Division of Levin Publishing Group
http://www.leatherneckpublishing.com

Publisher: Lt Col H. Neil Levin, USMC (ret)



Edition: 10 9 8 7 6 5 4 3 2 SAN: 256-8799

Library of Congress Control Number: 2005938954.

ISBN-13: 978-0-9771431-1-5
ISBN-10: 0-9771431-1-2



Cover Photo: Patrick Tracy

Printed and Bound in Ann Arbor, MI 48106
United States of America.
This Book is printed on Acid Free Paper

## DEDICATION

To the Marines of this great nation who made the ultimate sacrifice for their brothers in arms, especially Shane Folmar, who was born a Texan and died a Blackheart.

Semper Fi, Folmar!

**PFC Shane Folmar**

# PROLOGUE

Among the thousands upon thousands of books about combat, you can choose your war, conflict, action, battle or skirmish and discover how these events shaped continents, countries, states, cities and the world and changed history. I love these books and am an avid reader of them. I consider myself to be part history buff and part military student. I firmly believe history repeats itself and one can learn a lot about skills and tactics from them. I am fascinated with the evolution of warfare and the men, and now women, who fought in the battles that made history. However, I believe the major flaw in most of these books is the actual people who pull the triggers rarely, if ever, write them. Sure, every general throughout history had something to say when it was all over and done, but I wonder if the average reader even realizes most generals, then and now, aren't the ones on the front lines, fighting and dying. Another flaw I see, most of them contain politics, policies, ideologies, explanations, excuses, or even worse, complicated tactics on a command level that most people don't understand or don't care to understand.

Lately, we receive our books, pictures or documentaries by "embedded" journalists, reporters, photographers, analysts, and "experts" who often have their own agendas or opinions. Therefore, with that in mind, I intend to keep a journal throughout my experience in combat. I won't delve into politics or advanced tactics but try to keep my journal focused on my actual thoughts and experiences as I see combat "up close and personal" from the viewpoint and language of the Marine "grunt." I will write it as it happens and sure to hurt the feelings of some, probably many, if my thoughts are ever published. What I will not do is, edit my thoughts to spare any feelings and I most certainly will not ever try to be politically correct. Friends, family, acquaintances, and people I have met in classrooms, bars or any manner of social occasion often ask one or all of the same four questions when they discover I am a United States Marine.

"What's it like over there? What do you actually do in the Marines? Were you scared?" And my all time favorite, "Did you kill anybody?"

Even if people don't ask that one, they think it. That last question is the one most Marines, except those youngsters who don't know better, hate to answer. I'm never sure of the motivation behind that question. How are you supposed to answer? Will the person think more or less of you if they find out they're in the presence of a killer? Does killing people in combat make you a better or worse person? A better or worse Marine?

The other three are fairly normal questions, but only the one about fear is easy to answer. You show me someone who does not get scared when bullets impact all around them and bombs explode everywhere. Either that person has never experienced combat or they're full of shit. The brave man acts with honor and professionalism despite the fear. I hope if anyone reads my journal, they understand what it's like to be in the war in Iraq. What it's like to be an infantry Marine.

* * *

Usually, you know when you're going to deploy. Even if you're going to war, there's a schedule. Sometimes, you might only get a few days or weeks notice, but usually you have plenty of time to prepare. In the case of Fox 2/5, we knew our battalion, therefore our company, would head back to Iraq for Operation Iraqi Freedom (OIF) 2 B. OIF 1 was the big war President Bush declared back in 2002/2003. I'm not exactly sure when the war was declared, but Fox 2/5 deployed in January of 2003. The actual fighting began in March of 2003 and Fox 2/5 came home to Camp Pendleton in August of 2003. A battalion of the Royal Dutch Marines relieved them during a relatively peaceful time in Rumaytha, Iraq. The U.S. Marine battalions that made up OIF 2 subsequently deployed between December 2003 and January 2004. Our re-deployment was scheduled for the summer of 2004 as part of OIF 2B. Many people might not understand the Fox 2/5 that fought in OIF 1 is almost a completely different unit than the Fox 2/5 of this deployment.

A company of infantry Marines consists of four platoons and the headquarters section. In a perfect world, this is nearly 200 Marines and a handful of Navy Corpsmen. Marines continuously come and go within a company. The average life cycle for any infantry Marine in any one company in the Marine Corps is three years or two deployments, whichever comes first. Normally, a company will go through a six-month training cycle and deploy to Okinawa as part of a standard Unit Deployment Program (UDP) or to somewhere else as part of a sea-going Marine Expeditionary Unit (MEU). These deployments last for approximately six months in duration.

Upon return from either a UDP or MEU, the company will have 18 months of training before doing one or the other again. This two-deployment cycle covers approximately three years, give or take a few months. After being with an infantry company for that length of time, a Marine can change duty stations, take time off from the infantry in a "B" billet such as Drill Instructor, Recruiter, Security Guard, Infantry Instructor, or simply leave the Corps at the end of his enlistment. It just so happened OIF 1 was at the end of the second cycle of deployments for about 80% of the Marines in Fox Company. Everybody knew the next deployment would return to wonderful Iraq and this greatly decreased the number of volunteers to stay on or "extend" for another deployment.

As a result, the Pogues (non-infantry personnel) at HQMC in Washington D.C., whose job it is to staff units for deployment, had to fill our company with experienced Marines from around the world who were due orders back to the infantry, such as myself, and with brand new Marines fresh out of infantry school. In time, a very long time it seemed, we had our team put together and did all the training we could in order to prepare us for our next deployment into a very different type of combat in Iraq. I'll not bore you with all the details of our constant training exercises in 29 Palms, March Air Force Base and Camp Pendleton in California, but we spent more time away from our homes and families because of our training than we did at home. That is the number one reason for the longevity, or lack thereof, of the grunt's time in an infantry unit and probably for the 50% or more divorce rate.

This company is ready to once again go into combat and fight a man's fight. We watch the news, read the papers and get word from our brothers in combat right now. A lot of Marines are being hurt and too many killed by a cunning, adaptive and ruthless enemy. Although he is also a cowardly piece of shit it doesn't make him easy to beat, only hard to find. If you ask any Marine, past or present, what is the most difficult and scary type of combat, they will tell you it is MOUT, Military Operations in Urban Terrain, fighting house-to-house, street-to-street, and block-to-block.

This is *his* house, *his* street, and *his* block. He has lived here all his life and knows all the houses, streets, places to hide and where to hide things. He has many advantages in this regard. But, he doesn't have the most evolved and proficient fighting force in the history of armed conflict. He is not and could never be what we are.

Many people fear the radical Muslim extremists that come from a culture and society taught to hate us and to hate everything we stand for. Many think these guys are crazy sons-a-bitches that will stop at nothing to kill us.

The terrorists and fanatics think they can scare America into capitulation. For the most part, they have done a damn good job of frightening nearly everyone in America. As Americans, we all have the lasting images of the 9/11 attacks burned into our hearts and minds.

We have seen years of mindless, crazy violence on television perpetrated on others in the name of religion and terrorism. But, there are a few hundred thousand or so of us who are not scared. A few hundred thousand who still remember, and are more angry than scared. A few hundred thousand, who have never been scared of anyone or anything. What many Americans and certainly every crazy, American-hating piece of shit in this world, the French included, needs to realize is America has its own group of radical extremists. We're called United States Marines and we invented crazy. Trust me, you really, really do not want to piss us off.

General Mattis, God bless his warrior heart, came up with the slogan "No better friend. No worse enemy." Those six words sum it all up better than any poet or writer ever could. You could never find a better friend or a worse enemy than us, not even if you had access to Hell.

The choice was theirs and I'm sure history will record they made a huge mistake when they decided they wanted an enemy. I am in the midst of warriors who are ready to fight. I know I'd willingly give my life for any Marine in this company and they all feel the same as I do. It really is a beautiful thing. If I could grant one wish to every person I know, it would be for him or her to have one day in their life where they are in the presence, and a part of, a company of Marines like Fox 2/5. Then they would know what it's like to believe in and be a part of a cause and way of life that defies explanation and description. All I know is there is no one on earth who I'd rather be with, or have stand and fight beside me in combat than these Marines.

# WHAT IT'S LIKE OVER THERE

19 Aug. 2004

Departure day! Any Marine will tell you the hardest thing about deployment, especially if it's to a combat environment, is not related to the mission like the enemy, climate, operational tempo or anything else. The hardest part is the last goodbyes; the last phone calls to friends and family and then the torturous last hugs and kisses for the wife and kids. Saying goodbye always sucks. It doesn't get any better or easier no matter how many times you do it.

**Farewell**

This time it's even harder because the harsh reality of this last, little, sad goodbye in a dark parking lot full of crying women and children may be the last time you will ever see them and they will ever see you. At this point, you regret every wasted moment and every stupid little fight you ever had with your wife and children. Now I know why the Spartans forbade their women from crying when seeing them off to battle.

No matter how hard I try, I can't keep a flood of morbid thoughts from my head. Will this be the last memory they have of me? Was I a good enough man, husband, father? Do my daughters and wife know how much I love them? I can't stand to see my wife and daughter in tears and broken hearted. It cuts me to the bone and makes me contemplate why I continue to do this for a living. Many hardships come with a life in the military. Constant separation from your family is definitely the hardest one of all.

When all the last minute hugs and kisses are over, the last assurances everything will be OK, we load the busses and head off to Miramar to await our flight to Germany. Normally, a pretty boisterous and raucous crowd, we Marines ride unnaturally quiet, not even little snippets of conversation. Each Marine, alone with his own thoughts, has no choice but to clear away the sadness and store it deep in the recesses of the brain. It's time to change gears and focus on what's over there, not what's left behind.

20 Aug 2004

One day just rolled into the next as our flight lumbered across the Atlantic. For a big treat, us Gunnys took it upon ourselves to go sit up in the 1st class section. What a difference a seat makes. This one reclined into a bed as comfortable as any chair I ever had beneath my ass. We arrived to our terminal in Germany and had to wait around for a few more hours until ready to fly to Kuwait. At this point, we were just anxious to get over there and get started. We're part of the advance party, about fifty of us on this trip. Advance parties deploy about ten days to two weeks prior to the whole unit for our battalion. For Fox Company it's just me and my Police Sergeant, Corporal Swartz, better known as Dirty Steve. The Police Sergeant has nothing to do with police shit, as in law enforcement, but he's the guy in charge of all gear and everything else, plus he's my driver. Our job is to get familiar with the camps and start the process of turning over all of the gear, weapons, vehicles and equipment from the unit already in place. Although a big responsibility and an important one, I know it's going to be boring as shit. Oh well, that's the job of the Company Gunny. And who knows, maybe amidst the paperwork and counting, I might have an opportunity to send some rounds down range.

21 Aug. 2004

We reached Camp Victory in Kuwait in the middle of the night and went right to our tents for some much needed sleep. This camp is absolutely massive and looks like any tent city on any base in America. I guess letting us stage here is the least the Kuwaitis can do to show their appreciation for us saving their asses back in the first Gulf War. Maybe they should give the French some lessons on gratitude.

When we awoke in the morning it was *Hot*! No shit hot! The temperature today ran somewhere around 120 degrees. You actually have to experience that kind of heat to even comprehend what it feels like. I don't know why, but the endless sand, stretching to the horizon and beyond freaked me out. They said Ramadi, Iraq is mostly urban with some river-type farmlands and not this vast desert. I hope that's true because all this sand is a Gunny's nightmare. I see this as a more destructive agent than the enemy.

Our only mission is to pretty much hang around and anxiously wait for our next flight to Al Asad, Iraq. From there, we'll drive in a Marine convoy to Ramadi. That's when the war really starts for us.

22 Aug 2004

Ready to depart Kuwait comes the time for payback for the 1st class ride from the States and Germany. In 110 degrees in the shade, they packed us into a piece of shit C-5 in the customary asshole to bellybutton fashion. We sat for an hour and a half in full fuckin' gear and the inside temp of the plane approached about 140 degrees while the Air Force jackasses tried to fix an electrical problem. Finally, somebody asked, "WTF," and then they explained the problem. Well, do you think those morons could unload us back into the hangar until they get their heads out of their asses? Or does the Air Force really think we're like cattle to shuttle from one place to the next with no regard for our comfort? It's not like we ask for much because we pretty much know we aren't getting shit anyway. Even among our fellow service members, Marines are treated in a very standoffish manner. It seems to be, part fear of us because of our psycho reputations and part fact, the Air force sees us as little more than cargo to deliver. Finally, we had enough, walked off the plane and told the flyboys to call us when they pulled their heads out of their asses

Two hours later, we got airborne and in Iraqi airspace. Thanks Assholes!

24 Aug. 2004

We arrived at our new home, Combat Outpost ar-Ramadi. Even the name sounds tough. Not Camp Victory or Blue Diamond or any of that shit, no sir! You're going to the Combat Fuckin' Outpost and you better bring your A-game. Our convoy from Al Asad to Hurricane Point took forever to get moving but once it did we got there pretty quickly. We drove down the highway of fifty or more vehicles and as Iraqis passed us, I wouldn't exactly call their demeanor friendly, not once did we get a single wave or even a smile. I wasn't looking for the last vestiges of the victory parade but neither did I expect indifference or downright hostility. What a weird feeling to drive in a military convoy on a highway in Iraq. I wonder if the average soldier throughout history felt like I do as they traveled down a highway of a conquered nation.

Finally, we got to Hurricane Point and hitched a ride to the Outpost with Golf Company 2/4. Although we did not encounter any enemy, the ride was nonetheless educational because we had to keep our heads below the metal side of the 7-ton to avoid being sniped or blown up along the way. Wake up call number one.

**Combat Outpost**

As for first impressions of the Combat Outpost, this camp is a shit-hole by any measurable standard. I guess it's as good as 2/4 could get it, considering the conditions they faced when they started, or they are a bunch of complacent shit birds. I won't throw stones their way 'cause I haven't walked a mile in their shoes yet, but already I can see a shit-ton of work. In case you're wondering, a shit-ton is somewhere between two ass-loads and a fuck-ton.

I'm taking over from Gunny C. (Echo 7), who's a good man, but he's more than ready to depart due to the stresses of not only losing a lot of his boys, but moreover, the command situation here, which I won't discuss because it ain't my place. But I will say this company is not a happy place. I hope whatever their problem, it does not affect my company, the turnover or me.

My first day at the Outpost and with the exception of a few sniper rounds, or poorly aimed potshots, fired into the compound, I didn't see much action. I didn't expect to get here and immediately go knuckles, but I'd be lying if I said I didn't want to. I can't explain the warped thought process of most Marines. We want to be here, because *here* is where the fight is. Fighting is what we do, what we've always done and what we always will do. Perhaps that's another thing most people don't understand. Hell, I don't understand it myself. I can't tell you what's in me that makes me want to strap on my boots and whip some ass. In the world we live in now, where terrorists target innocent American civilians in our own country, I hope what we do and who we are does not go unnoticed and unappreciated by those for whom we do it.

25 Aug. 2004

My second day on deck, I learned we had no water for the boys to shower. Why? The Iraqis paid to provide it, don't exactly come here regularly or, at least, on an exact schedule. The air conditioning went out in some places, the Internet got blown up by a mortar, the plumbing is so bad it's not half-ass, but quarter-ass, only three washing machines function, most of the sinks were plugged up or not even hooked up to the plumbing lines and the trash is piled up. All of these things fall under my realm as Company Gunny. Shit that I'm supposed to provide myself or take care of with the assistance of our S-4 section. S-4 is in charge of logistics, and in case there are any history buffs out there, I guarantee some logistics asshole promised Napoleon that the supplies would be there. Does anyone remember Napoleon's S-4 Officer? I'll bet Napoleon spent his last days on that island cursing that prick. And any grunt who ever relied on an S-4 throughout history, and especially now in Iraq is already feeling my pain. All logistics pogues quickly go into pogue denial with their usual complaints that we ask for too much unreasonable shit. Unreasonable because for us to have it, some pogue has to not have his own personal back-up shit in case his primary comforts go down.

The funny thing about being a Company Gunny for an infantry company is you are not judged or evaluated, either fairly or unfairly, by your ability to get these things in the first place. Rather, you are judged conversely by your ability to fix, maintain or get better shit than what you already have. In other words, you're not a good Gunny if all these things are there and taken for granted as natural, god-given shit like the dirt and dust. But, if that shit is not there or if it is broken and unfixable, then you suck.

The old-timers would get a kick out of me mentioning things such as showers, the internet, and fuckin' A/C in a combat zone. But, first of all, it's 2004, you old bastards. Secondly, when you operate out of a firm base, and when every other firm base and fuckin' pogue in the country has this shit and more, then it becomes not only a comfort item and a morale boost, but a necessity. In fact, it burns my Irish-American ass that we have to ask and beg for shit like this.

As the story goes right now, the Iraqis won't come

to the Combat Outpost for fear of their lives. Truth be told, most have been shot at coming, going or both. Even worse, a few have been killed and made examples of, for working with any coalition forces.

So, here's a great idea! Somewhere in this fucked-up, bullshit country there are water making and transporting Marines, Army or Navy guys. There are mechanic guys, electricians, plumbers and probably every thing else we need from within our own system without having to rely upon the indigenous persons who are too scared to help us help them, but more on that later.

Just now, Echo 2/4 has gotten a frag order from battalion. Movement to Contact! The word has come down and Echo Company will go out on a mission in an area where the bad guys have been known to hang out and cause trouble.

"This is a nasty part of town, Gunny We'll probably see some action," one of the boys said.

I went to see the Captain and asked, "Hey sir, can I tag along?"

"Yeah, Gunny," he frowned and reluctantly agreed, "but you better put down a shit-load of water before we go, and you better not get fuckin' killed or I'm fucked."

He has a right to worry because I'm not acclimatized and I'm here for turnover from his company to mine. What happens if I get injured or killed? Anyway, I'm going and I'm pretty pumped up. This is the real thing and there is no feeling like it.

"What about me, can I go, too?" Swartz asked.

"Naw, not on this one. The Captain will only go so far," I hated to say.

Swartz thinks it's his job to look after me because he never lets me out of his sight. Basically, he's the power behind the throne, so to speak. When things need to get done, I tell him and he makes it happen. A good Police Sergeant and headquarters element is the key to having a well-run company and Swartz is worth his weight in gold. I never told him he has to shadow me but he always seems to be right there every time I need him.

This started at Combined Arms Exercises (CAX) in 29 Palms, but to be honest, I like for him to be around. That way I can also look out for him. Even though he couldn't go on the mission, he scored me a shit load of 40mm rounds for my grenade launcher. Just walked in and handed me a 12 pack of 40s like giving me a coke. Then he proceeded to give me my instructions on how to act without him.

"You better not get killed when I'm not there to look after you. You better not get any kills either."

Sometimes I wonder if he works for me or if I work for him. That's the second guy to warn me not to get killed. I don't know how I can stand so much optimism and encouragement.

As we pulled out, I loaded up next to Habib, the interpreter, an Iraqi-American from Chicago. We pulled out of the Outpost and onto our route and then into an alley to start our movement. One platoon on each side moved up the backside of the houses and our vehicles moved right up the road. The Iraqis hung outside, lots of men and children standing around is usually a good sign of no explosives on the road. They kept asking for footballs. Most of their knowledge of English is: "*Futebol meestah*!"

We didn't have footballs today but we did have a bunch of pencils we handed out to many of the kids who seemed pretty fuckin' happy to get a pencil.

**Football Handout**

This went on for about two miles up and two miles back down the road. No contact. Not even a sniff. Nothing at all, but you could tell from a whole lot of those people they did not like us patrolling their street. In fact, I got stares that would get the starer an ass-kickin' back home. What the fuck you looking at? Huh, mother fucker? But not here my friends; orders are to smile and wave back.

26 Aug. 2004

Not much went on today, just turnover of camp.

The Marines still came and went from the Observation Posts (OPs) but this is an every day occurrence. Mostly I was involved with boring paperwork and continued to ask many questions about what goes on around here so I can get my boys ready. We went on a convoy to Hurricane Point, which turned into the proverbial milk run.

I get the feeling this stretch of road can be a wild ride if the enemy chooses to ambush us at any of 100 side streets and alleys. There is no way we can cover or observe every one of them. If I was an insurgent with an RPG, I could do some serious damage. I hope our armored vehicles are as good as advertised. I know sooner or later we'll end up, slugging it out on this street. Maybe they know I'm here and are waiting to arrange a proper welcome or maybe they know the Blackhearts are coming and they don't want an ass kickin' of epic proportions. I, for one, will believe the latter!

With nothing for me to do, I decided I should call home and let my wife know I was still alive. There are no pay phones or phone center here like every other camp so each platoon has a satellite phone. They share it among the thirty or forty Marines to make a ten minute call home every fourth day or so. That's the good news. The bad news; for it to work and receive a signal, you have to be outside. The worse news; mortars, nasty bombs the enemy launches with alarming regularity, land in the area where you must stand to get a signal. Most Marines take their chances and I figured so would I.

Just as my wife answered and we got the initial greetings out of the way, explosions shattered the calm night, similar to an earthquake and having someone fire a shotgun next to your ears. There wasn't even time for a goodbye because when mortars land near you, the survival mechanism kicks in and you run for cover like your ass is on fire. I didn't get injured but my ten minutes were up so I guess four days from now I'll try again. War really is hell, just ask my wife.

27 Aug. 2004

More boring turnover. I don't delude myself I'm here for any other reason, but I always have been a man of action and not paperwork. To sit around all day and count shit drives me crazy. I will end up op-checking and signing for hundreds of thousands of dollars, no, millions of dollars worth of gear in my Captain's name. Therefore, I don't take it lightly, but damn, I can't wait until my boys get here so I can operate out in the Ville.

Tonight we went out and inspected all the OPs. One good thing, this company has good, defendable positions set up that won't require much work on my part to make them better unless we change them or move them, but that will be decided much later and by others higher up the chain than me. I took Swartz and two of my guys from the cargo-watch flight along with me. Their job was to guard the gear I packed to bring over and now that it's here, I have myself a Fox Company fire team. At least, they take this shit seriously. I talked to them before we went out and they had that look in their eyes. Not fear, not craziness, but the look Marines get when they have a shit-load of ammo and really believe they may fire some or all of it at their fellow human beings. I like that look and what it tells me about the readiness of my boys. *I Like it a Lot!*

29 Aug. 2004

As we rolled out on a Cordon and Knock mission, I tried to memorize the streets and routes, although very difficult to do in the dark from the back of the Hummer. While the cordon was being set up, one of the platoons set up a blocking position to seal off the front and rear of the convoy. It's funny the things you never think of in training. For our own protection and to maintain tactical superiority, the boys either unscrewed or broke all the outside lights on all the houses or shops. We can see in the dark and Haji cannot.

The concept of a cordon and knock is to roll up on a group of houses, form a tight, defendable perimeter, and then gain entry either the easy way or the hard way. It all depends on how much these particular people like their doors and windows. We had intelligence (intel) these particular assholes distribute weapons and conduct mortar attacks in our area. We hit them in the wee hours when they least expect it. That probably means little to no shooting, but a boy can hope.

Different squads from different platoons reported over the radio they found stashed weapons or explosives and had eight detainees from four different houses and the evidence required to take them to the detention facility. Although we did not find any huge caches, we did find wires used in making explosives, a mortar sight and a few weapons. By the time I made it to one of the target houses, the Marines already had the detainees cuffed and blindfolded. Another bit of a wake-up call for me concerning my duties on certain operations involved taking responsibility for all detainees and any evidence collected. I took over and properly tagged the detainees and their contraband. Once I ensured all the details in order, we headed back to camp where the processing of detainees took place.

The Corpsman gave them the once over and then the intel guys saw what they had, if anything, on some or all of these guys. After we finish all the paperwork and processing, we transport them to the main lock-up later in the day. And guess who gets to take care of all that shit while everyone else gets some sleep? That's right my friends, the Company Gunny.

One point of interest; this was my third time out the gate and so far not a shot was fired by either side and no Improvised Explosive Devices (IED)s were found either the easy or the hard way and this is very, very unusual for this area. Something big is coming. I can feel it in my old bones the same way I feel a storm coming on. Like I always say; "Bring it on motherfuckers!"

01 Sept. 2004

Still waiting for my company to get out here. Two things I hate: I'm not in charge of Jack or Shit and it's driving me crazy not to be running this camp. There are so many things I want to do but I can't get started until my boys get here and their boys leave. Two, I really need some Marines to yell at. Not that I needlessly walk around yelling for no reason like a complete jackass, but a Gunny without a company is like a bachelor party without strippers. The mission gets accomplished but it's boring as shit. Echo's CO just got relieved. Great fuckin' timing guys! Two days before my own CO gets here and now this. Plus, they took the acting company Gunny away for questioning or who knows what. I guess I'll do the fuckin' turnover by myself.

I have never seen a company with as much disdain and downright dislike of their CO. I have worked for my share of jack-off, egotistical retards over the course of my 18 years in this green machine, but one thing is almost always true. Even if Marines dislike or even hate their Commander, they usually grudgingly respect the guy, or, at least, understand where he is coming from. Not this Company. Not this guy! I don't know him and have not really seen anything myself but I learned long ago that if you are in a room with 200 people and all 200 think that you're a horse's ass, guess what? You're probably a horse's ass. Unless maybe, they're all wrong and you're right. Then again, if that's the way you think, you probably are a horse's ass.

04 Sept. 2004

Golf Company's CO got here yesterday and I was under the impression my own Captain would be with him, but I just found out the plan changed and my CO will not arrive until Monday. I guess that's information I didn't have the need to know. Not that I had a convoy ready to go pick him up or I might have done anything to prepare for his arrival, but how fuckin' hard would it be for someone to call someone else and let me know? Oh, I know, the fuckin' e-mail is down, which is how we pass word nowadays so if I can't get on the computer to check my e-mail then I'm not privy to what's going on. I swear if Dan Daly or Chesty Puller ever came back from the dead, they would lose their fuckin' minds if they ever saw how much all this new technology makes us a *better* and more *efficient* Corps. At least all this bullshit with the gear turnover is coming to a close. What a pain in the ass! The funny thing is I sign for all this gear but the 2/4 Marines need to keep using it until we completely take over. That way they get to break and abuse my shit. But I'm sure they will take extra good care of the shit now that it belongs to someone else. Oh well, just one more reason to look forward to the Blackhearts showing up.

A funny note: Today they needed an extra body to stand post so I sent PFC Florez to help out. In fact, I woke him up and told him he had five minutes to get his shit together and leave with the convoy. He wasn't too happy, but he knew better than to complain. Wouldn't you know, he comes back all smiles because he got to shoot at the enemy while on post. He's not sure if he killed the fuckers who launched mortars at us but nevertheless he is the first person from Fox 2/5 to shoot his weapon during OIF 2-B. He already has his war story to tell his buddies when they get here. Of course, by then he'll have had the time to make the necessary embellishments in which, at the very least, he killed a squad or so of the bad guys before, of course, going hand to hand to kill the rest.

06 Sept. 2004

My Captain finally arrived and at least now I have much shit to do. First off, I organized a convoy to pick up the key leadership from my platoons because the S-4 took the time out of their busy lives to once again fuck me in my ass.

"Hey Gunny, we'll bring everybody in with the CO," the lieutenant said the day before.

"Are you sure I don't have to get involved?" I asked, knowing full well if I didn't it would be a complete cluster fuck.

"No Gunny, we got it. You just get ready to move them in here," he replied confidently.

I knew they'd fuck it up but they have their job and I have mine. It turned out there are not enough vehicles for them to get everyone here in one trip. Do they pick up a fuckin' radio and call me or any goddamn body else to inform us their master plan has gone to shit? We all know the answer to that now, don't we? You know how many trucks you have, how many people need a ride and how many fit on each truck. Maybe we should bring in a third-grader to run the S-4. So instead of getting my guys here early, we had to travel down Route Michigan around high noon at the busiest part of the day with me in the lead vehicle.

We went right through the heart of the marketplace with people and vehicles everywhere. A fuck-ton of both! And we all remember how much a fuck-ton is, don't we? That's correct! More than an ass-load and more than a shit-ton. This was actually kind of fun, if you're insane.

Swartz drove his ass off. He cut people off, bumped them with this big, armored Hummer and laid on the horn like a New York asshole. I stood out there yelling at people and directed traffic like I owned the fuckin' town. And considering I held the ole' M203 Grenade Launcher, my M16A2, a 9mm pistol strapped to my leg, two hand grenades, 12 rounds of HE 203 grenades, and the other sixty pounds of gear strapped to my body, I damn do own the town!

Of particular note, any time I am out of the vehicle and surrounded by all these people, most of whom hate my American guts, and don't let anyone fool you they don't, there is a very likely chance I make myself a very inviting target for any jackass brave enough, or stupid enough, or crazy enough to try to remove my physical being from the planet.

Nevertheless, it was not fear I felt, but more like the nervous anticipation I used to feel before a wrestling or boxing match. I'm not sure if this is normal or crazy or how most or all Marines feel, but I'll tell you one thing, it is a Rush!

We got to Junction City with no incidents and

reunited with the Blackhearts. I can't describe how good it felt to see the 1stSgt and ole' Mikey (SSgt Roy) and all the rest of my boys.

The convoy went back through the marketplace, without a person in sight. Bad! Real Bad! We know we're going to get hit and hit hard. It made me nervous because I worried about all my Marines in those vehicles. As we progressed, the ole' asshole puckered more watertight than a bullfrog's super-glued ass. The hair stood up on my neck and arms and I couldn't help but yell "Bring it on Fuckers!"

The Captain let out a war cry of his own as Swartz swerved around an odd roadblock of stacked tires and I braced for the explosion … Nothing happened. We pulled into our firm base without incident.

Later, when a small convoy from Weapons Company headed out in the other direction, they got hit and hit hard. They had small arms fire, RPGs, and IEDs. Luckily, no one was hurt or killed due to the armored Humvees and I'm here to tell you those things are worth their weight in gold and save a lot of Marine's lives.

09 Sept. 2004

I spent the last couple of days trying to get all of our shit moved from Junction City to this camp and to complete the training and turnover from Echo 2/4 to Fox 2/5. It's been smooth for the most part with the minor problem of only having enough gear and space for one company on our half of camp. Thankfully, we just have to tough it out for a week or so and then the firm base and AO belong solely to us.

Tonight we go on a raid with Echo so they can show us how they do business and we can learn from their expertise—Cancel that! This Operation was a cluster fuck combined with a goat rodeo.

They entered a house and an Iraqi soldier "accidentally" shot off two rounds, one of which hit an Echo lieutenant in the arm. If these guys are the best Iraq has, we are gonna be here for a long time! They had to search a Mosque and brought an Iraqi soldier to do it. He took off his shoes. I'm all for respecting someone's religion, but do we really have time to stop and take off our shoes in the middle of a combat patrol? I watched him go barefooted inside for all of 30 seconds. There is no way this guy searched in any kind of detail in that short period of time.

I hate to bag on another company but these guys want to go home and have achieved a dangerous level of complacency. Even their acting CO sounded pretty pissed off at the way his Marines operated, especially that one of their officers got shot by one of the Iraqi Special Forces soldiers.

The operation achieved its objective in a backward kind of way. We learned what not to do and how not to act on a mission.

I would be professionally ashamed if my company ever looked or acted that way on an operation. I hate to say this, but if the enemy was out tonight and ready for us, there is probably a very good chance we could have gotten a shit load of Marines wounded or killed. And the real kick in the ass, it wouldn't have been attributed to a well-trained enemy force. If tonight went badly, then the finger of blame pointed squarely at their leadership. And if this is not how these Marines operated during their time here and they did fight a good, hard, professional fight, then why did they wait until turning over with us to become so unprofessional? I can't begin to explain how much that pisses me off!

12 Sept. 2004

The Army and Golf 2/5 planned a Joint Operation to sweep through the area where Haji had attacked our re-supply convoy. We were supposed to stand up our company and be prepared to reinforce. As we monitored the mission in the Combat Operations Center (COC), we heard a lot of yelling over the net and we could hear pretty serious gunfire right outside of our compound. It seemed as if the whole area was engaged in the fight.

Then an Army tank commander screamed about how he is getting lit up and I quote, "We are getting the fuck out of here."

"We," being the Army tanks, exactly what they thought the enemy could do to their tanks with small arms fire is irrelevant because they sure as shit took off and left Golf holding the bag. But first, they ran their tank over one of my vehicles the Navy Seabees welded up with better armor to be delivered to me when Golf finished with the mission. The Seabees figured a convoy of Army tanks would have no problem escorting a vehicle down the road.

Whereas I hate to speak poorly of any Marine unit, let me tell you I have no such qualms about saying any such thing about the Army. I worked with the Army in Hawaii on a regular basis and occasionally in Colorado, and to be perfectly honest, they have never impressed me. I have however been shocked, awed, dismayed, bewildered, and freaked the fuck out. I don't know how we continue to whoop ass on a worldwide level with them as our major force. I truly cannot comprehend how they make it all work. Maybe the Norman Schwarzkopffs and Colin Powells really are geniuses because if they can get these guys organized and win battles then they really are military Einsteins.

How do you run over a Humvee with a tank? Really, who does that?

Meanwhile, I was called to Post 3 on camp where my sentry just shot an enemy carrying a rifle. When I got there, I found out this guy popped out of a trunk 200 meters from our gate with a rifle in his hands. Either he was the enemy or the most completely stupid idiot in Iraq. Either way, he was on the wrong end of a well-aimed shot and now he's dead. I tried to get permission to take the car out with a 203 grenade but there were too many of our own Marines in the area.

After a few minutes, I got called back to the COC because Golf called for reinforcements. That's us! They were in heavy shit and low on ammo. We geared up and got ready to move and since so many of my vehicles are down, as in broke like the one the Army just fuckin' ran over, the no good sons of bitches, I was forced to ride in an armored Humvee with an L-shaped door.

This means little things like bullets, shrapnel, rockets, gasoline bombs, you know, fun shit, can get through that huge opening and ruin your day. Most Marines (GRUNTS) will scoff at this because totally armored Humvees for us infantry guys is a new concept, but when you see an RPG bounce off one of these without killing everybody inside and without much damage, trust me, you'll become a believer.

We headed out and as we turned onto the road we heard the gunfire and explosions and headed right into it. I had more ammo in that vehicle than I ever hauled because I didn't know what Golf needed so I brought a shit load of everything. As we moved down the road, we stopped for no reason I could make out from my position as third vehicle from the rear. I called forward on the radio and they told me an enemy vehicle and possible, Suicide Vehicle-Borne Improvised Explosive Device (SVBIED) blocked our path. I'm hunched down damn near on the floor and Swartz rode lower in his seat than the coolest Ghetto Pimp of all time.

"Shoot the bastards and get me off this fuckin' road," I screamed.

The lead gun trucks opened up and I could hear the impacts and then we hauled ass down the road toward Golf Company. We passed the vehicle and I saw one dead guy lying across the front seat and the other dead in the middle of the road with blood pooling all around him. I processed this sight with almost complete detachment. We pulled up to Golf and I looked for Golf 7 to get ammo to him.

"Where the fuck is Golf 7?" I called to nearest Marine.

"Fuck, Gunny, over there somewhere," the young

Marine quickly pointed and immediately resumed firing his weapon.

We drove a bit further down the road and turned left on a side street. As Swartz turned onto the street, Golf's gun trucks fired at this building and shit flew everywhere.

I noticed one of the enemy peek quickly over the rooftop and then he let loose a little spray and a round actually hit my door. I got out and returned a few shots and once again the 50 cal. let loose and punched holes right through the building.

I thought, this is some intense shit. Combat resupply at its finest.

We holed up with Golf for a few hours and slugged it out right in the streets. We fired AT4s, SMAWs, 203s, the 50 cal, the MK-19, 240 Golf, SAWs, M-16s… bottom line, if we had it, it got fired.

I've been to many training evolutions where a lot of different ammo gets fired at the same time but nothing in my 18 plus years of experience comes close to compare with the reality of no-shit *CLOSE COMBAT*. Eventually, we decided to break contact, why I don't know, and our two companies foot patrolled back toward our firm base. We had small resistance in some spots on the way but we pretty much dealt with it as it came and returned to base. We got back at 2100 and were immediately told to prepare to go back out at 0400 so it's rack ops, boys and girls. Oh, the good news, no casualties on our side and a whole bunch of dead insurgents.

13 Sept. 2004

Rather dull after yesterday's excitement, Bruce and I tagged along on a night patrol around our compound and found lots of people on the streets, once again, a good thing. After we patrolled through the sector, we came upon the subject house of some of yesterday's action. After our Marine shot the Iraqi with the gun, the wounded/dead man was dragged inside this house's perimeter, which gave us reason enough to pay a visit. There are two ways to go; knock and wait until they answer and tell them why you are there and what you want or kick the doors in and hit the place hard. We went with the easy way, since it seemed pretty quiet and unthreatening. This is the part where you run into shit you just never expect in combat.

A no-shit bull stood tied to a rather flimsy looking rope in the yard and this fucker was pissed. How do you search a compound with a rampaging bull running around the yard? I often say, "Sometimes it's good to be the Gunny." This was one of those times.

I assigned a PFC to distract the bull while we went to the door.

"Gunny, how do I distract a bull?"

"Ever watch a rodeo, boy?"

"Yes, Gunny."

"Well, now you're a fuckin' clown."

Way up high on the list of the funniest shit I ever saw was that bull chasing the PFC around the yard.

Meanwhile, we knocked on the door and introduced ourselves. We had the interpreter question the owner but, of course, he knew nothing. In fact, every Iraqi we ever ask anything seems to have no clue as to what goes on in or around his own house. They act like the old time New Yorkers who were afraid of the mob or even modern day inner-city dwellers that are either corrupted by those around them or too scared to speak up or help out. There was no way to prove they harbor terrorists and had nothing at the house to warrant detaining anyone so we wrapped up the mission and went back home.

No matter how many times you do a patrol in training and no matter how seriously you train, there is just no way to replicate the feeling of a combat patrol. The biggest difference and the one factor you cannot put into training is the knowledge you can be shot at or blown up at any time along the route or engage in shooting and killing of your own at any minute. I don't know if I'm crazy enough yet to call it fun, but it's as exciting as hell and that's a fact!

14 Sept. 2004

We went out to occupy a series of blocking positions while Golf Company swept through a sector to our south. Attached to 3rd platoon, we went to our position and entered a series of buildings and occupied positions on the rooftops. Our mission was to make sure no reinforcements could come in from the north and impede Golf Company's mission.

After a few hours, our company was called into action to help take over a sector where Golf encountered heavy resistance. For my disparaging remarks concerning the leadership of this platoon, I hope we all learned some lessons because we were very lucky we didn't take some serious casualties today. It's not only truthful but also a lesson for anyone who wants to know what actual combat with a young, inexperienced, and at the time, overwhelmed lieutenant is like.

As we prepared to pull out, the lieutenant said to get back on Route Michigan and make a left on Canal Street. He had his map out but we were literally one street over from Canal so I didn't offer to look at his shit or ask if he wanted me to take lead vehicle. When we pulled down the road, he passed Canal St. and flew down Michigan while I screamed over the radio to turn the convoy around. He stopped his vehicle in the middle of another platoon's position and we just sat there. I felt sure an RPG was about to kill me.

He came over the radio, "Fox 7, do you know where Canal Street is?"

In shock and awe, I yelled, "Yeah, it's way the fuck back there."

We still sat there and Fox 6 came on my net, "What the fuck?"

The lieutenant turned around and instead of going to the circle to head down Canal, he stopped right in the middle of the road again and began to dismount.

In his defense, he tried to get his Marines in the fight but leaving the gun trucks in a position where they could not support the movement of the troops was a very bad start.

The CO told him to send his platoon south down Canal and the lieutenant pointed north, back across the street from where we just came, and told them to head that way. By then, I had enough and figured since he was momentarily lost and bewildered, things were about to get deadly for the wrong side. Not one to stand around with my thumb up my ass, I directed his troops in the direction the CO wanted us to go.

The shit truly hit the fan as I tried to get them headed in the right direction. I failed to remember I stood in the middle of the street when suddenly rounds impacted all around me. I quickly jumped behind a vehicle and I could see this no good bastard shooting at us from between two buildings. Dumbfounded for a second as I could actually see this guy firing at us, I had a brainstorm of my own. Wait a minute, I have a grenade launcher. I sighted in and let one fly.

I watched the round fly 200 meters down the road, which seemed like slow motion. Then BOOM!

Wouldn't you know, this round landed directly between the two buildings? I couldn't have drawn a picture any better of where I wanted this round to land. One minute an asshole fired a rifle at me and the next, parts of this asshole spread around a ten meter area.

Now, let me tell you something. I don't claim to be great at too many things but if I were to brag about being great at something, I'd say, shooting the M203 grenade launcher. I carried this weapon since I was a Lance Corporal and technically should have long since quit carrying it but why fix what ain't broke? Don't think I'm talking shit because I have a road full of Marines as witnesses.

Then I reloaded my baby, and ole lieutenant still didn't move his people.

Although it may have been only a matter of about

ten or fifteen seconds as I dealt with my own problems, that's a lifetime in a fire fight.

The CO came back on my net and directed me where to move this platoon. I heard him tell the lieutenant what to do and where to go, but this guy just didn't respond. Plus, would you goddamn believe it, he still had his fuckin' map in his hand.

Here's a fuckin' news flash! If the enemy is shooting bullets and RPGs at you, you can put the fuckin' map away cause whether you're where you're supposed to be or not, you're finished with the land navigation part of the operation. All we had to do was move down the street, gain some rooftops and continue to shoot these fuckers so 2nd platoon could move through our position. Then they do the same and we move through them and continue like this until the CO says so. Definitely not advanced tactics or brain surgery, my friends.

I screamed and yelled and got the debilitating D.I. headaches from lack of oxygen while I tried to tell this platoon where to go. I couldn't pass it over the radio because mine was continuously clogged up with too many people trying to talk at once.

Finally, Fox 6, the CO, linked up with me in person and told me the circumstances. I told him the lieutenant seemed overwhelmed.

"What's his problem?" he asked.

"Fuck, sir, he's still running around with his map out."

Fox 6 called him over. "Calm down and put the map away."

That took a lot of cool on the Captain's part. He looked him right in the eye and said, "We're going to head west, your platoon on the left and 2nd platoon on the right."

No shit, the lieutenant looked east, over an impassable canal. In utter disbelief, I looked at Fox 6 and if we weren't about to get killed, I would have laughed my ass off.

The Captain took a deep breath, no-shit pointed west. "That way."

When the lieutenant ran off to gather his platoon, Fox 6 looked me straight in the eye. "Keep this platoon moving and don't let the lieutenant fuck it all up."

To be honest, I was real worried about trying to get some vehicle support and I had much more things to do than move one infantry platoon around but the Captain made it pretty clear where he wanted me for the rest of this fight.

On the move, we entered houses and seized the high ground. Sun Tzu would be so proud. Occasionally, we stopped and put suppress fire on targets downrange.

Something I never considered in our training was the noise of combat. It's not really shooting your own weapon that makes your ears ring. It's other people shooting near you.

During one bit of laying down some heat, I fired from a kneeling position next to a Humvee and Sgt Davidson, one of my Goons, crouched down behind me and fired just to the right of my ear. It felt like my head came apart and I actually turned to see what the hell just made, not just my ears, but my whole head ring.

He just gave me this maniacal smile, shrugged his shoulders as if to say, "Sorry, Guns," and then he

popped a few more shots. So much for passing the next hearing test!

The fight progressed along without any damages to men or equipment until someone decided to use my Humvee as a battering ram to open up a locked gate. But first, they forgot to raise the MK 19 grenade launcher, or at least turn it around, and as I watched helplessly, my big gun broke off its mount. This sucked in a multitude of ways and on many different levels. Mainly, I no longer had the best possible weapon for this environment. Oh well, there's no crying in a firefight, so I called Fox 6 and asked him to send me another gun truck with a machine gun. He moved with 2nd Platoon and I could see him on the rooftop one street over to my right.

He sent a truck on its way and all of a sudden we took fire from the buildings directly in front of us. The forward elements of 3rd and all of 2nd started laying into this building and I looked for my gun truck. I turned around and way back there I saw the lieutenant with the new gun truck and much needed machine gun, driving behind the broke-ass truck with half his platoon in front of both of them. I was way beyond pissed off at more than just the lieutenant because some combat experienced NCOs right there didn't take charge or make any kind of decisions.

At that point, I lost my mind and all of my military decorum and went ape-shit right there on the street.

"Orient the fuckin' gun west!" I screamed at the gunner.

The gunner no shit turned the turret to face north and it was aimed in on 2nd platoon. "Get the fuckin' truck up here now!" I shouted.

"Where's the enemy?" said the lieutenant as he ran up near my position.

I couldn't fucking believe it. "Do you see the fuckin' building getting hit with all the fuckin' bullets? Pull your fuckin' head out of your ass and get in this fuckin' fight!"

And if I'm lying I'm dying, he said, "Calm down, Gunny, I got it under control."

If nothing else, I can say he seemed calm and eager and ready to fight. And it probably didn't help that his psycho Gunny yelled and screamed at him in the middle of a fight in front of some of his men but there is a time and place for calm mentoring and tact. This was not the time or the place, not when two companies were heavily engaged with bullets and rockets impacting.

Finally, we got the gun truck back up front and began to move again. Then, as Murphy would have it, my comm. went down and the lieutenant had the only working radio. I knew Fox 6 passed info over the net, but at the time, the lieutenant, all butt hurt, wouldn't pass any of the info to me or anyone else in his platoon. I could have chalked up his bewilderment to inexperience and a good Gunny ass chewing/counseling could fix that. But now I realized the lieutenant had unwarranted, foolish pride and was willing to risk the lives or well-being of everyone around him because I hurt his feelings.

That made me mad as hell because as a Gunny, I may have to jump in a lieutenant's ass from time to time. They all know this from their training up to this point in their young careers. The time for anger and pride is not during a no-shit life and death firefight.

What I will do is talk to Fox 6 about all of today's actions to ensure he has a long talk with the young lieutenant.

Eventually, we got to our limit of advance and suddenly the sons a bitches opened up on us with a big gun. A real big gun! I always wished I were taller, maybe 6'2" or so, but if I were, I'd be tall and dead because a round went through the wall I took cover behind like it was made out of paper. This gun punched fist-sized holes through all the walls in our area. We unloaded with everything we could but he was tucked in pretty good. Then this jackass with an AK opened up from a not so well-covered position.

"He's on that big dirt pile, Gunny. I can see him," said the young PFC who was with me.

I couldn't see shit but aimed the grenade launcher, let a round fly, the 40mm grenade landed and BOOM!

"He ain't gonna be shooting at us no more, Gunny."

SSgt Flann pulled up in the gun truck with the machinegun, let loose down the street and silenced that big gun. I don't know if we got him or just scared him off, probably the latter of the two.

**Gun Truck opens fire**

We waited for word from 2nd platoon and Fox 6, but, either the lieutenant wouldn't pass any info or more likely the comm. crashed yet again so we hunkered down for a couple of hours. After linking up, we dug in for a few more hours and then we headed home.

For most of our Marines this was their first firefight and first taste of real life and death combat. I'm proud as shit of all of them because they fought their asses off and had plenty more left in them.

Most people could never comprehend what it's like to be in a situation like that but our boys acted like it was just another day at the office. Most of them don't even have a clue how good, tough and professional they are. I wish some of the old-timers could see what we're like when the shit hits the fan. They often think we're getting soft and spoiled. But I'm here to tell you we carry on the proud traditions handed down to us. We may have it a lot easier and our technology gives us

certain advantages, but pound for pound, we measure up and then some to any generation of Marine before or after. You can bet your ass on that.

15 Sept 2004

I guess everyone reacts differently after being in a serious fight with the very real possibility of being killed. I knew I'd be in some hairy situations over here and as a Marine and leader, I'm ready for the challenge and responsibility. After getting home yesterday, I had to go find a quiet spot and wind down from the adrenaline. I suppose my journal may be full of realizations by the end of my tour but one I can state with absolute certainty is never in training do you get that kind of rush or high or whatever you want to call it.

Once I calmed down, I came to a second realization. Instant Messenger on the internet is the greatest invention in the history of mankind. Bruce got our e-mail working and downloaded messenger onto our computer. Thousands of miles from home and in need of a serious sanity check, I talked to my wife without worrying about being blown up. I didn't talk about the fight or give her any indications about how bad this place really is. I think we talked about the dog, our daughters, and a whole bunch of other stuff some might call unimportant but I call it life saving. After we signed off, my world was back to normal and I spent the rest of the night thinking about anything other than Ramadi.

I met Janet one night in a bar in Scotland when I was stationed there in 1987. Big shocker there, huh? It was not love at first sight. It wasn't even like at first sight. She didn't tell me at the time but she came over to me and pretended to like me because some creep was giving her a hard time. She used the tried and trusty girl tactic of finding someone bigger and uglier than the jerk bothering her to scare said jerk away.

Her original plan was to ditch me as soon as old boy got the hint. Unfortunately for her, I don't ditch that easily when I'm drunk enough to think the most beautiful girl I ever met is digging what I'm shoveling. She laughed at all of my jokes, gave that female touch on the arm when talking to me and even asked me to slow dance with her. I'm glad there weren't any other guys hanging around who were bigger and uglier than me because I'm pretty sure I would have taken a pretty serious beating before letting this one get away.

**Wouldn't let this one get away**

Needless to say, I talked or mumbled my way into a second date and eventually convinced her I wasn't so bad. Eighteen years later, she saves my sanity, thanks to the internet. Maybe I should have voted for Al Gore after all.

16 Sept. 2004

Today I experienced my first IED and realized certain portions of the insurgency have their shit in one bag. In fact, if they weren't cowardly bastards, they could have really handed us our ass. Operation Hurricane, a joint operation with the U.S. Army was today's special treat. If you think the enemy is scary, try hanging out with the army.

I traveled with 2nd Platoon. Mikey is the Platoon Sergeant so I felt pretty confident I was in much better company than the last operation.

Pulling out of the firm base at 0200 and darker than three feet up a bear's ass, we moved down the road and met problems from the get-go. The rear vehicle seemed broken down or stuck. It was hard to tell from the scratchy comm. We finally got that sorted out and we were on the way. As we headed down Michigan, we were supposed to go down No-Name Road and then up Apple but due to a tricky little turn we missed it and went on the wrong street. I was about to call forward to the lead vehicle… BOOM!!

Two IED's hit us; one near the lead vehicle and another in the middle and right in front of me. The explosions kicked dust and smoke everywhere and nobody could see shit. The 7-ton driver yelled over the net his vehicle was disabled, and the lead vehicle reported they crashed into a barricade and the lieutenant was hurt.

I got out of my vehicle, got everyone out of the 7-ton, and headed toward the lead vehicle when two rockets and automatic weapons opened up on us in the middle of the road. Like sitting ducks with nowhere to take cover, the enemy had us where he wanted us, which is very bad for business. If he fired those rockets and small arms from any of the nearby rooftops, he could have inflicted serious damage to our platoon. But, coward that he is, he fired from the next street over, and due to having to aim high enough to clear the walls, he fired all his shit well over our heads.

During the failed rocket attack, I tried to get the vehicles turned around and hitch up the disabled vehicles to the ones that still worked. Of course, I didn't have a tow bar for the 7-ton because today it was Golf Company's turn to have the only one our battalion provided for us two companies to share. Imagine how fuckin' funny it was to me as I sat and waited for a whole other convoy to come out and hitch up my 7-ton. Then, I remembered the Army tagged along and those guys don't fuck around and usually have two of everything whether they need it or not. Sure as shit, they had two tow-bars and we successfully rigged up our vehicles. When the rescue team got there, we changed out bad vehicles for good, drove to the rest of the company and set in and waited for the enemy to come at us.

Ten hours later, we still waited for the big no-show enemy. He's not about to come out and face an entire Marine Battalion and an Army Battalion or whatever it is they call themselves.

Of particular note, the quick actions of SSgt Roy (Mikey), and Lt. B. Mikey had things under control and his boys got away from the vehicles and into better positions right from the start. Despite breaking his nose and despite he had us on the wrong road, Lt. B didn't lose his cool and got back into the fight pretty quickly, without spazzing out. In addition, he was all ears for any suggestions on what needed to be done. All in all, the operation lasted for about 13-14 hours. We only had action and contact for about ten minutes.

**Close Call**

That's the funny thing, and the dangerous thing, about combat. You have to do your very best to stay disciplined and focused and then stay on your men to do the same. As far as being a leader goes, that's probably the biggest challenge out here. Most people probably think it's the heat or the daily grind or even the fact Haji shoots at us or tries to blow us up, but that's the easy part of combat. We all know what to do and how to act when the shit is going down. In addition, we're pretty damn good at it, too. But it's not constant action against an easily identifiable enemy. It's small, localized battles being fought where and when the enemy chooses. If this is how we continue, it's going to be a long seven months and when it's all said and done I'm not too sure what, if anything, we will have accomplished. Semper Fi, Mac!

18 Sept. 2004

Operation Hurricane II. Only this time, instead of sitting in a blocking position all day, we left that bullshit to the Army while we did the shooting and moving.

With a mosque as our first target, we must have a Showani squad, Iraqi Special Forces that are anything but special, attached to us. We had to bring these guys along because it's okay for a Muslim to enter and search these particular buildings. But to be honest and fair, these guys suck. Not only that, I honestly believe some of them work for the other side.

We have pretty good intel that one of the most wanted insurgents in Ramadi hides out in this mosque or the living quarters adjacent to it. Because this is "holy ground" and due to the huge political element to this war, we cannot enter this mosque, or any other mosque for that matter, unless we are attacked from the mosque. That chafes my ass beyond description.

Orders are orders and who am I to second-guess the politicians who want to be generals or the generals who want to be politicians. I'll tell you who I am. I'm the guy who gets shot because these assholes can't handle their own weapons. I'm the guy who gets to leave his wife and kids and family behind because some assholes in D.C. who never even served in the military want to make nice-nice with our Muslim "friends."

One note for the record: I'm not referring to President Bush, who I voted for once and would do so again. I refer to all the anti-war and anti-administration types who sit around and second-guess all decisions so they can push forward their own agendas.

As we departed the firm base, I was in the lead vehicle with Lt. J. I like traveling with him and 1st Platoon, largely since he's the only lieutenant that hasn't gotten me lost, shot at, or blown up, so far. He's a former enlisted guy and even though he has a lot to learn as an officer, he doesn't forget where he came from. Sometimes that's a problem but mostly it's a good thing.

We could see the night light up with tracer rounds. Believe you me, this gets the heart pumping! Through the gate and then down Michigan, Swartz made a left on Canal and sped toward our objective and we rolled past the mosque. We stopped the convoy and as Lt. J got his boys into position to set the cordon, we took fire from the objective.

This was both good and bad for us. Bad because the jig was up and surprise lost. Worse, these assholes were shooting at us. Good, we no longer had to worry about the Showanis 'cause these assholes just gave us a free pass to dick stomp all over their little mosque.

We entered both buildings and found one asshole in the mosque, not THE asshole, but nonetheless had a giant bag of ammunition with him. Standard Operating Procedure (SOP), when we find an insurgent or suspected insurgent with illegal contraband is to get real physical real quick. Within seconds, one of the Marines had this guy down, subdued, handcuffed and blindfolded. Then we entered the other building which seemed to be a living quarters for the Mullah and his family. Naturally, this "Holy Man" was in possession of more than the one weapon he's allowed. Not to mention, he had a shit-load of rounds and other military-type gear.

On most missions we bring interrogators and other intel types along so they can start the questioning and usually pretty effective because loyalty to one another is apparently not taught at insurgent school. After questioning by the intel rep, guess what? None of these assholes knew anything. They were sleeping and didn't even bother to look out the window while a firefight raged in their yard. Yeah, sure, I'm a fuckin' idiot. Sorry for waking you up, dickheads, but let's see how you like jail. We cuffed and stuffed both of these assholes, dragged them to the truck and carried on with the rest of the mission.

All three platoons moved simultaneously about a mile from south to north and searched every house in our sector. As we progressed, Marines shouted out from whatever house they were in or called over the radio if they found anything or ran into any trouble. My job was to get to each house, assess the cache and determine whether or not to detain or question anyone.

We searched a lot of houses, took eight prisoners

and got a bunch of weapons, ammunition, and from one house, a shit-load of bomb-making material. The scariest moments occurred when Marines yelled about finding explosives or rigged devices.

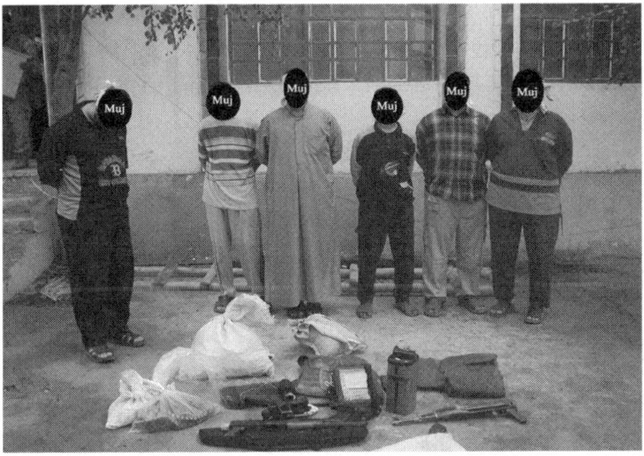


**2nd Platoon Muj multi-grab**

Most Marines are not too well-trained on foreign weapons and explosives. That's why they yell for me. Guess what? I know exactly jack and shit about foreign explosives! But, the Marines figure I know everything so it becomes my job to handle this shit. In most cases, the trigger devices and explosives are not hooked up. Then it's no big deal to confiscate the shit and send Omar to Abu Ghraib.

On other occasions, the explosives are wired to blow and that sucks big time. On this mission, we did not have to deal with any wired explosives and all detainees went down without a fight. Our battalion as a whole rounded up 25 of these pieces of shit altogether and ran a good operation. Finally, a good day for the home team. No injuries, no accidents, and no drama. We all went home feeling pretty good.

This day's side note concerns one particular Iraqi family. At the end of our sweep we were secure as you can ever be in combat. The Army covered our Six, and the other three companies had our right, left, and front. We holed up in about three different houses, rooftops, and a bunch of us sat on this guy's porch. He invited us inside to meet his family; three wives, eleven kids, and his little baby brother. The interpreter did the introductions.

This guy did a stint in the military and knows the whole deal, so he's not all hostile, angry, indifferent or pissed-off like everyone else. The little kids gave candy to all the Marines. You can tell these people don't have much, but what little they did have, they shared with us. Next thing you know, the wives cook us all flatbread and soup and made tea. We didn't want to seem ungrateful so we all took pieces of bread which tasted pretty damn good. It seemed like every kid in the house wanted to give every Marine a present. I got a flower from one of the older girls. What can I say? Chicks dig me! It's the cross I bear, you know?

We didn't have much to offer them so I gave Papasan $5 and told him to restock the candy and the rest of the Marines busted out the Meals Ready to Eat, (MRE)s and shared them. The one item that went over real well was the chem-lites, the glow in the dark light sticks we carry for marking certain things in the dark. The little kids thought they were the coolest things ever. They went into dark rooms and closets and we heard them whoop and laugh. When it was time to leave, the people actually appeared sad to see us go. The guy said if these were better times, he would invite us back in friendship. Just when you're about to start hating every Iraqi equally, you run into a family like this.

I guess people are people everywhere: Some good, some bad, most somewhere in the middle. All the Marines learned an important lesson today. I hope they all remember that not all of these people are the bad guy.

23 Sept. 2004

We began the serious planning for Operation Longhorn I. Battalion has eased up on the constant every day operations for the last five days and the boys are well rested. They continue to stand guard and OP watch, but that in and of itself is not too taxing. The Morale, Welfare and Recreation (MWR) fund came through big time and scored five large TV's and a play station for each TV. If you ever want to feel true love, walk into a Marine's hooch in Iraq and give them a big screen TV and a play station.

Today marks one month of living in Ramadi. Although the time has gone by in what seems the blink of an eye, I've spent a lot of time reflecting on my life before combat, especially the long and crazy road that brought me here.

Unlike most other Marines, I had no intention of ever joining the military. One night outside a bar in beautiful downtown Pittston, PA, I was minding my own business when a fight broke out in the street.

Where I grew up, this was not unusual, but an everyday occurrence as regular as the rise and set of the sun. For some reason, I felt compelled to break it up and send the two drunks home. After separating the combatants, I let my guard down and one of them picked up a beer bottle, christened my head and immediately ran up the stairs to his apartment above the bar. Since I was mildly upset about having my head broke open, I proceeded up the stairs and kicked in his door to discuss the matter. Not being a student of the law, I didn't realize this was breaking and entering and burglary. Nor did I realize the follow-on discussion would be classified as felonious assault.

I went to my arraignment prepared to appeal the judge's common sense and compassion. He told me to get out of his courtroom and come back in one week with a Philadelphia lawyer or a Marine Recruiter. It was four for the Corps or eight for the State. Nineteen years later, I'm in Ramadi with no regrets. Hell, that judge did me a favor.

We're ready to go on another sweep of our area. Once again, Fox Company is the main effort, why is somewhat perplexing, for the entire Brigade in Golf's Area of Operations (AO). After all, it is Golf's AO and we should play the supporting role. I wonder if this pisses them off. I know it would bug the shit out of me. The funny thing is, prior to coming over here they really thought they were "King Shit." They even went so far as to claim themselves the "Senior Company" in our firm base, although there is no such thing, and even if there were, it wouldn't be them. There are always rivalries and differences of personalities between companies in an infantry battalion. Golf and

Fox are miles apart, more so than most. We get along professionally and manage to coexist in our camp but it always warms my heart when they get knocked down a peg. Like when we get to be main effort in their AO. Eat Shit, Evil Empire!

24 Sept. 2004

We lost a Marine on today's Operation. His name was PFC Folmar, one of the new guys who we got from SOI around May, if my memory is correct. I wasn't there when it happened. We were doing two simultaneous raids on two different objectives. One was in a library, the other a bakery. Apparently, two honchos running ACF Operations own and operate out of these two establishments. 1st Platoon went to take down the library and 4th Platoon hit the bakery. I asked to go with 4th Platoon because this was the first operation where they would actually operate independently of the company and I really thought this would be where the heaviest action would take place.

We hit the bakery hard and it went off without a hitch. No politeness and knocking on doors, we stormed in and had everyone on their faces in the first ten seconds. Then we searched the entire place from floor to ceiling and wall to wall. 4th Platoon did a good job and their leadership did all the right things. I was pretty happy with their performance throughout the day and into the night.

There are always things to complain about, and at times I had to tell various Marines to "spread out - take cover - get behind your gun sights" things of that nature. But, to be fair to the Marines, it's easy to get complacent at times on operations like these. Once again, we had the entire battalion out there and a whole bunch of Army dogs.

At the end of our sweep of the AO, we had Golf Company to our right, fifty feet away, and 3rd Platoon to our left, twenty feet away. 1st Platoon was at our Six and the Army had the buildings to our Twelve. Literally speaking, we could not aim our weapons in any direction without flagging our own people. Around this time, I decided to head back to my vehicle and listen to the radio traffic to see if I could figure out what was going on with the link-up and extraction plan. I heard Fox 6 say we had a routine medical evacuation (medevac) and we would talk about it later.

There are three categories of medevacs: routine, priority and urgent. Urgent is no-shit life and death, get a helicopter now! Priority could be life and death but definitely serious enough to need attention right away. Routine is just that, routine. No big hurry but someone was injured in some way.

Earlier on, we heard a pretty serious gun fight but we assumed it was our heavy guns firing from the strongpoint positions along the road. Now I found out 1st Platoon was in the fight. Then I heard battalion call 1st Sgt and ask for info on the KIA. This knocked the wind right out of me like a sucker-punch to the belly. KIA? How could there be a KIA? Then I remembered a KIA is also a routine medevac.

It sounds pretty shitty, but the truth is, if you do

die in battle, you won't get any more dead so there is no hurry to have you flown out of there or risk others by running the body back to the rear in a vehicle convoy. What made matters worse, they didn't say the name over the radio so I could only sit and wonder who it was. I can't think of a worse situation. I love every one of these guys, especially the younger ones. They are all younger than my daughter Sonia, and I sort of feel like they're my sons in a way. I'm the Company Gunny, and responsible for getting them their food, water, equipment, mail, bullets, comfort items… you name it, if they have it, I got it for them. This makes me a bit of a father, or at least, a big brother figure to all the Marines. I know how I felt about my Gunny when I moved up through the ranks. Now one of my boys is dead. No one who hasn't been there can imagine the overwhelming feelings of anger or helplessness at a time like this.

A little while later, Bruce (1st Sgt) linked up with me and without even a greeting "Who is it Bruce?" I asked.

"It's Folmar, we got ambushed from a balcony."

The first thing that came to my mind was that time back in Pendleton on a field op when Folmar didn't pack any sleeping or cold weather gear because we were hiking home. I gave him a hard time over that one. But you could tell he genuinely felt bad about fucking up and would never do it again.

"1st Platoon came out of the library, got ready to move up the road and two guys popped out on this balcony and started spraying with machineguns," Bruce said.

"Did we kill the mother fuckers?" I asked. It was important to me that we did.

"I don't know, they popped back inside and we couldn't get to the second floor. Maybe. We poured a shit-load of ammo through that building."

**Folmar at the Barracks**

The fact the one round hit only one Marine was a minor miracle, but the one round got through the back of Folmar's neck, between his helmet and flak jacket, and killed him nearly instantly. Doc Chavez was on the scene in a minute, running to the fallen Marine while bullets still whizzed past, and less than a minute later, Folmar died.

"Did he have a chance, Doc?" I asked later.

"Naw, Gunny, nothing anyone could have done. I got to him in a minute and he had no vitals," said Doc with a most somber expression I've ever seen. Doc actually looked deflated, like something sucked all the air out of him.

All Marines have nothing but love and respect

for the Navy Corpsmen who are attached to our units. Doc Chavez is the best I've ever been around. When he hears a Marine is down he goes right after him without even a second thought for himself, even if it means running through bullets. I could never say enough about Doc or any of the Corpsmen in our battalion.

As we finished the operation, the body of PFC Folmar was transported to the BAS. The Battalion Surgeon and all the corpsmen looked him over and tried to determine the exact cause of death. The CO, XO, 1stSgt, Lt. Jones, SSgt Flammang, SSgt Garza, who was also his recruiter in this small Corps of ours, and myself just stood there and stared. We had the Doc hand over his dog tags and personal effects and then the surgeon asked us all to leave so they could zip up the body bag and have him transported to the proper base for preparation for his flight home. I asked them to hold on a minute. We all wanted to pay our last respects in some small way. I held his hand and silently told him I was sorry I wasn't there. Maybe it wouldn't have mattered even if I was, but damn sure I felt sorry I wasn't there and then I crossed myself and asked God to look out for our boy.

Everyone else then paid their respects in their own way and we left the Docs to do their job. Then we went back to have a mission debrief with all the leadership and talked through this thing a little bit. Every Marine in that room felt deflated. We knew this would come someday, but never wanted to think about it and damn sure, never talked about it. We had a reporter from USMC.mil with us. After the operation, he interviewed me. He asked me to explain the mission and exactly the point of it, why we did it and if the mission was a success. I could only respond that we merely accomplished the mission. We never feel a mission is "successful" if we come back with fewer Marines than we started with. Period!

27 Sept. 2004

Operation Longhorn II. Unlike Longhorn I, where we did a raid and then cleared, knocked on every door and searched every house in an entire sector of the city, this mission only consisted of a raid on two houses. Supposedly, a couple of assholes are out of prison and up to their old tricks. I had the feeling we were on another goose chase. Intel hasn't been exactly on the money and we never know until the mission is over if they were right or wrong. Well, the mission is over and Intel sucked as usual.

We went out with Weapons Company, who did raids a bit north of our position. Our initial portion of the operation went well if you call getting there, getting in, and getting out without any glitches, a successful raid. We were right on the money with the navigation, cordoned off the two houses, stormed through the doors and had both objectives secure within five minutes. Then again, if you factor in that all we did was scare the shit out of some women and children and sat around waiting on Weapons Company for way too long, then the mission ended up a complete abortion.

The point of a raid is to get in, do the job and get out before anyone knows you were there. The insurgents, of course, were not there, only several women and children in each house. It makes you feel like a complete asshole when you kick in doors and come through rooms violently and all you have at the end is crying women and children. The only good thing to come out of this mess, the company got up from being knocked down.

We needed to get back out there. Losing Folmar hurt us, especially 1st Platoon. That's another of those lessons that you can only learn in combat. Bottom line, you have to keep going on and keep staying focused no matter what happens on any previous mission. Easy to say, damn fuckin' hard to do. But the Blackhearts will prevail because there ain't an ounce of quit in any Marine in Fox 2/5. Damn proud to say that.

29 Sept. 2004

No Marine dies and is just forgotten. We had a memorial service for Folmar today, complete with a 21-gun salute, eulogies, prayers, readings and then a final farewell by each Marine in attendance. When Bruce and I had to go out there, take care of the practice and all the details, I kept thinking, this is for one of *OUR* boys. We set up the memorial with the upside-down rifle with the helmet on top, the boots at the bottom and the dog tags hanging from the rifle. It's a sobering and sad sight. I can't tell you how hard it is at times.

Most people think we deal with death differently because of who we are and what we do. It would probably shock most people to learn how deeply affected we are when one of our own dies.

**Memorial Service**

The service went well and we gave Folmar the best goodbye we could under the circumstances. At the end of the service, each Marine approached the memorial and had a moment alone. Everyone saluted, even the highest ranking officers present, most took a knee, and some touched the helmet, tags, boots or all of the above.

For my own part, I took a knee and grabbed hold of his tags in my right fist. I told him I was sorry once again and unlike many others who probably prayed for his soul, I made him a silent promise. I won't forget about you and move on, Folmar. And if I get a chance, there's gonna be some payback! You can bet your Texas ass on that!

30 Sept. 2004

I went out on Quick Reaction Force Alpha (QRF/A), with 1st Platoon. QRF responds to any call from any unit that gets into a situation and need more bodies and more bullets. We have a QRF/A and a QRF/B. I always go out with the QRF/A, which is on a ten-minute alert at all times. No matter where you are or what you're doing; you roll out in ten minutes. This could happen any time and often several times a day or night. We join up with the on-scene commander, and get our orders from there or get right into a fight and play the hand we're dealt. Usually, the enemy runs off long before we get there but sometimes it's a day long fight. I always go out with the Alpha but it has nothing to do with bravery or foolishness. Swartz and I still know the area better than anyone and not getting lost is a big part of getting there when they need us most.

Today we were called out to assist Golf Company. They swept through an area and ran into more than they could handle. Not that they couldn't handle the enemy, man for man. The problem in Ramadi, and most of Iraq, is that you get so penned in because of the walls and streets that you just can't get to all of the assholes that need killing. Therefore, you call out for a QRF and you let them handle one area while you handle another.

How's this for Deja fuckin' Vu? We went to the same exact street as with 3rd Platoon when we went out on the QRF that turned into our longest street fight. We got down there without incident and set up in our area. I was in the no-shit *same* spot behind the same wall with the big hole about six inches above my head and I talked to Fox 6 on the radio. All of a sudden, a car stopped on the road I pointed my weapon down, known in the business as covering the twelve. A guy jumped in with a weapon in his hand and they drove toward us.

"Hold on sir," I said and let two shots go to warn them not to drive any closer. I put both rounds right in the grill of the car so there was no mistaking my message.

The guy sped up and headed right at us. I had one second to contemplate their intentions and make a decision. Plus, SVBIEDs have increased all across this shit-hole country in the past few days.

I put one right through the driver's window and right through the passenger window. The car stopped and both guys fell out on the street. The driver crawled about two feet and stopped. I thought he was dead. The passenger with the gun tried to crawl away on his belly. Unfortunately for him, Garcia opened up with the MK19 40mm Grenade Launcher right after I took my two shots. I could only watch as about five or six grenades impacted all around the vehicle. Bad time to choose crawling as a means of escape.

No time for reflection right then and there because we had a job to do with more enemy all around. Plus, it's hard to philosophize with gunfire, rockets and people screaming all around you.

We fired up a building across the street and down another and all the while Fox 6 and Golf 6 both tried to contact Lt. J and transmit info and orders. As usual, comm. went down on one of the radios. Luckily, the one in my vehicle still worked so we could still communicate.

We strong-pointed our area, grabbed the high

ground for good observation, and hung out there for a few hours until it was time to go back. Whiskey checked the car we took out and found two more AK-47's and several magazines. That doesn't make them 100% guilty but it doesn't exactly make me think they were innocent either. If they weren't up to no good they damn sure shouldn't drive around during a firefight with weapons in their car. Today was a small microcosm of what this place is like on a daily basis.

* * *

We decided to play a game of Texas Hold 'Em to combat the boredom and also because there are some real pigeons here with nowhere else to spend their money. I dominated the table as usual when the word came down to mount up. Ten minutes later, I'm killing some guy on a street, and a few hours after that we go right back to our card game, picked up right where we left off with me holding queen seven in the hole when a queen and seven stare at me on the flop.

Later that evening, I contemplated what a way of life the Marine lives. I always wondered if killing people would bother me a whole lot. Especially like today when I'm not 100% sure those guys had to die. I asked a few other Marines for their perspective and we all seem in the same boat. It really doesn't bother us or affect us in our daily lives right here and now. There is a job to do and a mission to accomplish and if we have to take lives in order to get that done, then that's life, or death. That's just the way it is and in the long run, better them than us. I hope that doesn't sound too callous or indifferent but these are my thoughts in my journal and I hope anyone who disagrees can try to see it from my perspective.

03 Oct. 2004

Eighteen years ago today I went to boot camp at Parris Island, South Carolina. It may sound like a cliché, but the time has flown by. Sometimes I can't really believe I not only joined, but stayed this long. Usually, I have a bunch of cold Coors Light and think back on my time in the Corps. What I remember most, and miss the most, are the friends I've made along the way. Great friends who I don't really keep in touch with and will probably never see again. I don't know why we never stay in touch, we just don't. The funny thing is when I do run into one of these guys, it's like we've never been apart. We just pick up right where we last left off. To be honest, more people I call friend are back home in good old Pittston PA. But there are those few I will never forget who are as close to me as brothers. J.C., Joe, Travis, Gerry, Mikey and Ozzy, just to name a few. I don't know where these guys are for the most part or what they may be doing but I hope they're all OK. I wish I could hoist a cold, cold brew with them right now. To my brothers, and you all know who you are; I hope this day finds you well. If you're in contact with the enemy, I hope you're giving them hell and if not, I hope you're getting ready 'cause I think we're all going to take a bite out of this shit sandwich.

I guess if there's no one to throw a party for

you, you throw one for yourself. 2nd Platoon observed suspicious activity behind the house from our observation post. Their platoon commander asked the CO for permission to raid a few houses near there to see what might turn up. This sounded like a good mission. I was all excited to go and then their Platoon Commander came to my room to tell me he only wanted 2nd Platoon on this mission and the usual HQ element (myself included), that always travels with any platoon going out, would have to sit this one out.

"Why is that?" I asked.

"This is a mission just for 2nd platoon," he replied in his very best big boy voice.

This made absolutely no sense but rather than argue with yet another genius lieutenant, I said, "Fuck it, go ahead."

I probably should have gone to the Company Commander and asked why the latest version of Rommel is making decisions based on such advanced tactics as "I only want my platoon," but I am so sick and tired of some of the bullshit I figured I'd just sit back and wait because if they found anything we would have to call out a QRF. Why? Because Rommel Junior is not bringing enough vehicles for detainees, medevacs, or any seized gear. My biggest worry was the medevac issue. If they started a raid and got even one severe injury, they would have to stop right there, mount up and return with the injured Marine. The amount of time this could take, especially if they ran into trouble or came across a big find, could mean the difference between life and death for one of the Marines. We have what we refer to as the Golden Hour when a Marine is severely injured. If we can get him into surgery in the first hour he will probably survive. We always bring enough vehicles to evacuate any wounded without undue risk to any medical convoy. This was a perfect example of half-ass planning that can get Marines killed.

Fortunately, none of the bad shit happened and 2nd Platoon hit the jackpot. As soon as they dismounted vehicles, several Iraqi's started running away. They captured as many as they could and secured three houses in the immediate area. Every house they entered contained multiple weapons, rockets with launchers, and IED making materials. It looked as though the insurgents were staging weapons and personnel for a major attack. 2nd Platoon immediately called for a QRF and by the time we arrived they already rolled up nine detainees and found a bunch more weapons, bombs, grenades, RPG's, money, fuses, and automatic weapons in the houses and yards.

**Our first Big Cache**

While I thought about how to manage all this gear and prisoners, I saw two cars and two big trucks in the yard. I thought these guys were dirtier than hell so why let them use these vehicles as car bombs in the future? I called Swartz over. "Grab Reyno and Crazy Mike, and do some fuckin' vandal ops on those vehicles."

The Goons got these big smiles, broke out their knives and started going to town.

"Make it so no mechanic can ever make those fuckers run again."

What a way to spend your Marine Corps birthday. All in all it was a great raid and a great catch. We took a lot of shit from the enemy and locked up a bunch of bad guys.

I will talk to Fox 6 about these lieutenants and their brilliant plans. Actually, it's a bit unfair to paint them as dumb-asses, but just young, immature and over-enthusiastic, like most lieutenants. I realize they want to run their own show and do their own things without the 1stSgt or me or the CO breathing down their necks every time they go out.

However, it's our job to temper their enthusiasm and inexperience with our judgment and experience. That's pretty much the job description of every CO, 1stSgt and Gunny in the fleet. I hate to say it but someone can get hurt or killed for no reason other than their lieutenant makes some hasty decision and no one puts him in check. I will especially talk to my SNCOs. I honestly believe we have some really great SNCOs but they don't seem to keep these lieutenants in check. A young lieutenant needs a good SNCO in his ass pretty much all the time. They know it, I know it, the young bucks know it, and so does every other Officer and NCO, past and present. If we accomplish no other task in our lives, we train these officers on how to lead Marines. If not, then guess what folks, we're the fuckin'Army.

04 Oct. 2004

I hate to keep picking on a platoon and from reading my own recollections, I see I'm disgruntled with certain officers and one platoon in general so unless they do something completely stupid, I'll avoid any criticisms of their leadership. I realize these are my own thoughts and I should say whatever I feel, but if someone ever reads this for a learning experience,

I don't want to seem like one of those old, idiotic enlisted men unsatisfied with their station in life. I really do understand how the whole system works. I realize the Corps is unique in how we operate and I not only understand my role, but also wouldn't change it even if I could. I love the Corps with all my heart and I think we have the finest young Officer Corps of any branch of any military. However, there are always those few who just rub you the wrong way and who also just never learned how to listen. They're often those who had privileged upbringings and are either spoiled dickheads or just plain tools for lack of a better word.

Somehow, I got paired with 3rd Platoon again and we were the main effort. The first part of the mission consisted of raiding two houses in which a known terrorist hides out at night. The hits on our target houses went well despite the fact we drove a little too far past them and had to backtrack. This continues to happen and it pisses me off. The bottom line, we just don't know our area well enough. Add to this the fact, the maps aren't completely accurate and drivers are inexperienced and vehicular land navigation becomes a nightmare. We have handheld GPSs, but they don't work inside a vehicle. In the future, I will plug the waypoints into my GPS and have the turret gunner track it. I hope this works next time.

Even though we shot too far, we still got into our target houses with relative quickness. Of course, as is almost the norm on these night raids with Intel from higher, we got exactly jack and shit! We were on the objective and we had 15 minutes to kill before moving. The Platoon Commander decided to take down a few more houses in our area as we needed the high ground. If we have to be stuck in area for more than a few minutes, taking positions on rooftops is the safest way to hang out.

We went to the biggest house in our area with this massive iron gate we just couldn't open. We pounded on it for him to come out and open it, but of course, he wouldn't so we got the engineer attachments to put a donut charge on it. I guess we had extra C-4 just begging to be used because it caused a massive explosion that blew the entire gate apart and sent most of it flying into his yard. Oops! The moral of this story is; if you like your gate you may want to open it when we knock.

**Oops!**

A contractor or supplier apparently owned the house, and he had a three ring binder of correspondence and dealings with all kind of U.S. military personnel. Mostly work orders and orders for gear and equipment but since we couldn't be sure if the guy was legit or not, confiscated it.

In his yard sat a large shipping container with spray painted graffiti that read "Long live the Mujahadeen," or some nonsense.

What it said to me? "Please cut off my lock and take all my shit." I'm not sure of the exact translation but it's pretty damn close.

We opened the box and what did we find? A few flak jackets and bulletproof armor plates. A few thousand that is! A few minutes later, the lieutenant gave the word to move out but I thought it was a bad idea. If we left and conducted the rest of the mission, the Muj would move in and get outfitted with some nice bulletproof vests. I tried to tell the lieutenant we couldn't leave and in doing so I partially figured out his problem. He gave the order to move out and in the cartoon land that makes up his brain we should all have said "Aye, Aye, Sir!" and moved out. That's when I stepped in.

"Sir, we can't leave here and give the enemy a chance to get all this gear."

"Gunny, we have to move out and continue with the original plan."

In his mind, if we stayed because I said so means he is not the leader and I'm taking over his mission. Perhaps he feels by listening to me, he doesn't show good leadership and is not "In Charge." The answer could be that he is just a complete and utter jackass but I can't believe that any educated, intelligent man, however young and inexperienced, could actually be this stupid.

In order to avoid wasting any more breath and frustrating myself, I called Fox 6 on the radio and gave him a SitRep. "Sir, Fox 7 here. We got a container with about a thousand flak jackets and bulletproof vests and the lieutenant wants to move out and leave it."

"Bullshit, hold firm, Gunny," he ordered.

We held firm until guidance from battalion came over the net. The Captain often claims he's no genius but he's smart enough to know we shouldn't leave the stash unprotected.

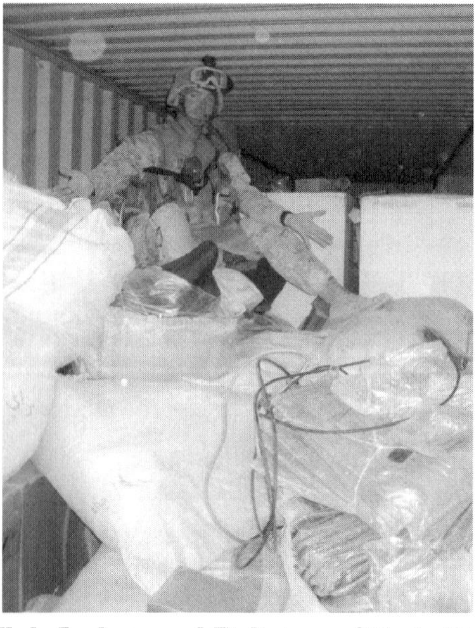

**Flak Jackets and Bulletproof Vests Stash**

Sure enough, orders came down to confiscate all the shit, which meant we lost two vehicles to load all this shit up and the rest of our mission was cancelled.

After taking down these houses, we were supposed to push through and clear a sector of that part of town. We do this for three reasons on most missions.

Reason number one; to provide a presence and show these jackasses nowhere is safe, and we're willing to go into any part of town and into any house we want. This lets the good people know the terrorists need to fear us and we don't fear the terrorists. That's big over here. Let's not forget who we're dealing with. Of all people on earth, the Iraqi's understand and respect that power resides with the most aggressive, committed, and ruthless person or group. Don't for a minute think anyone forgets the last 30 odd years under Uncle Saddam. Guess what? There's a new Sheriff in town. That's us!

Reason number two; we look for a fight. If the terrorists don't come to look for us, then we look for them.

Reason number three, simple and obvious; maybe we'll confiscate a bunch of weapons and other nasty stuff and if we're lucky the assholes who own them.

Needless to say, this is some pretty scary and hairy work. Every person could be the enemy, every house full of armed terrorists, every car packed with explosives and every step you take could be your last.

07 Oct 2004

A strange catch phrase has taken hold of my company. I'm extremely proud since the originator is none other than myself. In a few of the fights, I've been known to yell, "Your mother's a whore and your father's a cocksucker," while maniacally laughing and shooting at the enemy. I've yelled this phrase at various times in my life in every unit I've been in, but it's never been adopted by any other psycho. I usually reserve it on up-hill runs and hikes or whenever I need to motivate myself to accomplish a difficult task. The origin of the phrase is one of the funniest memories of my life.

When I was fifteen years old, a small group of my demented friends and I decided to play a practical joke on Paddy McHale. I guess every town has the local, burned-out, drug addict that everyone knows and sort of learns to live with. Paddy was harmless, but his claim to fame was to get all whacked out on alcohol or whatever drug was handy and scream obscenities, gibberish or lines from movies and laugh like a maniac. Every time our group hung out in front of the pool hall, he would come up and panhandle for cash and beg us for a joint. Even if we did smoke pot, or had any on us, we certainly wouldn't share it with Paddy.

One day, I put four rolling papers together and cut the heads off four books of matches and rolled them up. This made for one huge looking joint. As Paddy came over, I took it out and pretended to light it. Of course, Paddy begged for a hit.

"C'mon just one hit. Just one hit ya' greedy bastard, hahahahaha."

"Okay, you can have the first hit but that's it," I relented.

Paddy was so happy he was ready to elect me mayor. He rubbed his hands together and chomped at the bit to get it started. With much grandstanding, I handed over the joint and pulled out the Zippo. Paddy exhaled because of only one hit, he wanted to maximize the intake.

As I lit the Zippo, he sucked in as hard as possible and a giant fireball erupted and engulfed his whole head and face. A bit more than I planned, it scared the shit out of me. Paddy lost his entire mind after putting out the fire in his moustache and hair. He was double fuckin' mad because not only did I light his face on fire but also he didn't get any marijuana.

"Your mother's a whore and your father's a cocksucker!" he screamed, cursed and yelled, among other expletives.

He seemed to like that one best because he soon settled on it exclusively.

There was no way to convince Paddy this was a funny practical joke, and with all my buddies bent over double and laughing so hard they cried, I decided to get out of Dodge.

A few weeks later, I went to the bus stop to meet my grandmother. From about three blocks away Paddy saw me and picked up right where he left off with "Your mother's a whore…"

Gramma looked at me. "Patrick, who is that dirty man and why is he yelling about your mom and dad?" she asked with the most innocent, grandmotherly voice.

To this day, I laugh my ass off when I think of that.

Now I have a company of Marines who have no idea of the whole story, but love to yell the catch phrase, day and night.

It's been three days with no QRF and no operations. Of course, we still have the ever-present guard and OPs but we'll have those until the day we leave this shit-hole. We have an operation planned for tomorrow. I like to think of it as tonight since we leave after midnight but technically it's on the eighth. We go way north of where 2nd Platoon did their raid and move all the way south through that area again. This has the potential to be another big one because we cover a huge area. I don't expect much gunfire because this is a two-company movement. Fox and Golf together again. We noticed one trend; the enemy does not want to meet us man for man, even if we walk through his backyard. So far, we have not had any engagement whatsoever when we go out in a two-company or larger sized force.

My personal belief is the enemy has this delicate balance of intelligence and cowardice. He's smart enough not to take us on because he knows he will get his ass handed to him. Despite all of his posturing, rhetoric and bullshit the media shows on TV, what we really have here is a piece of shit coward who hides behind innocent citizens, especially women and children. They terrorize their own people and risk the lives of anyone, Iraqis or us, with their hidden explosives and car bombs, but they won't ever try to come out and fight and die like men. My biggest worry is the Marines will start to get complacent and expect not to fight on these big operations. As soon as the Marines let their guard down, will be the day when these gutless bastards decide to grow balls and come out and fight.

08 October 2004

Operation Money Pit: If we got lucky, like we did on October 3rd with 2nd Platoon, then we might take in our biggest haul yet. We used the GPS to guide us in to our dismount point and it worked real well. We tracked our route with the turret gunner monitoring the checkpoints on the GPS. However, as luck would have it, we pulled up way short of where we wanted to stop. We headed down the road and saw a bunch of Iraqi guys wearing man-dresses, walking along the side of the road. At 0430, we thought this pretty unusual.

I popped out of the vehicle and motioned for them to stop. They got all scared and walked toward me and jabbered away about who knows what. I wasn't overly threatened, but I couldn't let them walk right up on the vehicles so I fired a shot over their heads. Suddenly, they started to understand English like Queen Elizabeth. We searched them for weapons, such as guns or suicide vests, and they came up completely clean. Turns out they were walking home from wherever for whatever reason so we told them to get inside and stay there until we were out of the area.

Once again, I was in the lead vehicle with Lt. B. I knew the route and once there, I needed to take control of all the vehicles. The entire company dismounted off the vehicles and I moved the vehicles down the company's right flank, another slightly unusual tactic but we learn and adapt as we go. There was only one passable road to move the vehicles on and it coincided with the extreme right flank of the movement. The vehicles acted as a screening element and covered everything to the south and west. We moved through the area clearing houses, knocked on doors and looked around while the engineers checked the yards with metal detectors. We turned up a little bit of stuff here and there and took a few prisoners when small caches were found but by and large, this operation didn't pan out. Money Pit turned into a change purse. I guess you can't win them all, but what the hell. At least we cleared out another area and in the process learned a few new routes and provided that all-important presence to the good and bad citizens of Ramadi.

After we returned from the Operation, we grabbed a little evening chow and the truckers invited me over for some Texas Hold Em. I haven't played in a few days so I figured what the hell, it's a good way to unwind. As we played, a camera crew from NBC came in.

"Would you guys mind if we film you while playing and ask a few questions about the war?" they asked.

We all say we don't give a shit one way or the other but deep down I'd rather just play cards than have a camera in my face and answer stupid questions.

"How do your families feel about you being here? Do your families know how bad it is here?" he asked to lead off.

One of the Lance Corporals came back with the quote of the night. "I told them it wasn't that bad but

I guess once they see this they'll know I'm full of shit."

Then came the silliest question of the interview. "Is this kind of war more difficult to fight than the last time you were over here?"

Well no shit! Last time we toppled a government and had a pretty clear-cut enemy and objective. Now we're battling piece of shit insurgents supported by the very people we're supposedly here to help. Trust me on this one. The good citizens of Iraq, in this case, Ramadi, very much help the insurgency. They don't tell us shit or call the tip line to report terrorist movement. They don't stop terrorists from planting IEDs all over the fuckin' place. In fact, they don't do shit to help us or themselves. This whole city can go fuck themselves as far as I'm concerned. But we kept our mouths shut.

"Yeah it's a tougher fight and a harder and more dangerous mission."

The funny thing, most of us want to be here. The bottom line, there's a no-shit fight going on and Marines are right in the thick of it. Call it crazy; call it what you will, but one thing about Marines most people just don't understand is, we believe we belong and want to be where the fight is. We don't sit around and discuss the "Why are we here?" politics. We go where we're told by whoever is in charge and we whoop ass. That's what we do, that's why there's a Marine Corps.

The reporter actually tried to get us to disagree with being here. He tried to get us to say we disagree with the President.

"But do you think you should be here? Do you think there are weapons of mass destruction?"

We aren't about to give him or any other detractor

the satisfaction of griping about our current boss. In fact, for the most part, about 90% of the Marines I talk to actually like, fully support and plan on voting for President Bush in the upcoming election.

"What would the average American be most surprised to learn about you guys?"

"You can go to my company and ask any Marine if he wants a free ticket home right now and not one of them would take you up on it. NOT ONE, I guarantee it!"

Let's see if they use that quote on the news.

11 Oct. 2004

The great example of the frustrations of a Company Gunny. I am the "go-to" guy for practically everything aboard my side of camp. If there is any problem with any aspect of life, with the exception of administrative matters, then I'm your man. The enemy targeted the shitter truck and another shitter man was killed for working with the coalition forces. Who would have known a shitter man was such a high-risk profession? We built Viet Nam shitters in order to accommodate the daily necessity of nature. The old port-a-johns are now full and unusable so we have to use the Viet Nam era outhouses we built ourselves. This means that the lower ranking members of the platoons get acquainted with the ultimate shit detail, burning human shit. This comes with all manner of pain in the ass complications, especially if the boys are in the mood to be either lazy or retarded. In addition, there are other matters pissing me off and since I can't ever get my whole company together at one time for an ass chewing. I put my creative writing skills to use and send a nasty gram. This is an example of what I deal with:

## COMPANY GUNNY WORD

***VIETNAM SHITTERS** - The shitters will be labeled as 1st, 2nd, 3rd 4th, HQ, etc... You are responsible for burning and cleanup of your assigned shitter and the area surrounding your shitter. The shitters will be marked and that is who I expect to use them. For example, if a shitter is marked as 1st platoon, I don't expect anyone not in 1st platoon to be using it. I realize there are cases of emergency but these better be few and far between. If I have to inspect your assigned area and discover it unsat, then I will personally supervise your team leaders in shitter field day. The next time will be squad leaders and the next, guess who?*

* * *

***IN THE THINGS I DIDN'T EXPECT TO TALK ABOUT DEPARTMENT:***

***#1. PISS** - I am trying to get the backhoe to arrive and dig sizeable trenches for pissing. You've been around our S-4 long enough that it should not shock you to learn this will not happen soon. Therefore, pissing will occur in water bottles. Then the water bottles get properly sealed and thrown in the trash* *which gets taken to the dumpsters every day. Let me repeat, every day or when the trash cans are full whatever comes first. You can utilize one of the support vehicles to haul your trash, or you dig your own piss trenches. See the gunny if this is what you desire and he will show you where you may dig a trench.*

***#2. DO NOT PISS IN THE SHITTERS**. They are for SHIT. That is why they are called SHITTERS. Piss does not burn quickly or at all and the buckets fill too quickly to be filling them with piss. Whatever morons are filling piss bottles and leaving them in the shitters need to be dealt with. The same goes for ignorant retards who throw trash in the shitters. Let me explain to avoid confusion. Shitters get shit in, then you wipe your ass with toilet paper or baby wipes, or maybe even both for you hygienic fuckers. This is how to take a shit and clean your ass. Therefore, reasonable man theory assumes that only shit and the resultant cleaning aids should be in the shit buckets. Unless you wipe your ass with milk cartons, soda cans, MRE bags etc...*

**Shit detail**

* * *

***VEHICLES*** – *It was my displeasure to ride in several vehicles this week other than trusty #4. Here is what I learned; PMs are not happening. Vehicles are not being refilled with the fluids necessary to keep them running efficiently. Believe it or not, filling a vehicle with gas when it gets low does not constitute a proper PM cycle. Amazingly enough, there are other vital fluids, cleanings and maintenance procedures necessary for efficient and continued operation. The drivers should know this because they were taught this and told what was expected of them. However, due to lack of supervision, this has been gaffed off. Therefore, by close of business today, (meaning within 24 hours of reading this) you will turn in a roster of all drivers and an NCO driver buddy. The drivers and their NCO buddies will report to Cpl Buentello and Lcpl Carpenter for a PM class as a group. These drivers will be assigned a* ***specific*** *vehicle they are responsible for conducting a weekly PM on. Also, Plt Sergeants will identify the drivers of each vehicle for that day's mission on the vehicle tracking board. For example, today is the 12th of Oct. QRF A is 2nd Plt. QRF B is 3rd Plt. QRF C is whoever is not on OP. Post and relief of OP will be done with the Charlie vehicles when all Charlie vehicles are up. For now, post and relief will be done with the Bravo vehicles. This does not absolve QRF B drivers from responsibility for QRF B vehicles. A vehicle should not need another PM just because it went out for post and relief.*

* * *

***THIS LEADS TO THE NEXT POINT**, which seems to be on a level of difficulty equal to quantum physics: responsibilities of the platoon returning from OP. You just came back from OP. You just parked the **Bravo** vehicles back where they belong. Now what do you do? You assign a Charlie vehicle to each driver. You put his name on the board. The drivers go to their assigned **Charlie** vehicles and ensure they are mission ready (which they should be because the platoon that relieved you already prepped them.) However, if they did not, your drivers will get them ready and you can deal with the platoon who fucked you over later. Now that the drivers are employed, what else do you do? You clean up the mess on the Bravo vehicles. You clean up the bay the Bravo vehicles are parked in.*

* * *

***NOTE TO LEADERSHIP;** Collecting trash and consolidating it in one place does not constitute a completed cleanup. After organizing trash into cans, bags, piles or all of the above, you must move on to the next and most crucial phase of the cleanup. This is the part where you then take the trash cans and bags to the dumpster or burn pit and bring back the empty trash can. Next, you check **your** shitters and the surrounding area and you clean the head.*

***NOTE TO LEADERSHIP;** Cleaning the head consists of wiping down the sinks and mirrors and* *picking up and dumping all the trash. Strenuous work that takes 5 Marines 10 minutes to accomplish.*

* * *

***LIVING SPACES -*** *Get up off your asses, put the movie on pause, and check your platoon areas every day. And here's a though—make your NCOs do the same. High OP-tempo does not allow Marines to live like pigs. If they have time to sleep, they have time to clean their living space. Another daunting task that takes all of 10 minutes to accomplish.*

* * *

***SHAVES AND HYGIENE- WHAT THE FUCK? - ENOUGH SAID!***

* * *

***CIGARETTES*** *- I am almost to the point of making a single smoking area for the whole camp or, since I don't smoke and find it to be a disgusting habit anyway, I am about to go to a smokeless camp. Either field-strip your butts or find a butt can. If you throw your butts all over camp, especially the COC area, then don't complain when I secure smoking. Especially don't complain if you stand there with your lack of balls and watch others do it.*

* * *

***SIDE NOTE:*** *Marines are continuing to smoke*

*in the vehicles. In case you are the dumb-ass doing it, I can tell because it glows a very bright red at night. Also, putting your butts out on the deck of the vehicles and leaving them there are a dead give away. I'm beyond explaining the dangers of smoking and having open flame near explosives and fuel cans that leak. Let's just go with the old standby-"Because I said so!" You don't want to be the next asshole I catch because I really do need to make an example of someone.*

* * *

***FOR OUR LEADERS -*** *I think for the most part we are doing an outstanding job of operating in this environment, except for the continuing loss of bayonets and k-bars from all of our hand-to-hand knife fights with the Mujahadeen. However, it is the small things, what you refer to as Company Gunny bullshit, that make us who and what we are. Attention to detail and discipline in* ***all*** *aspects of our daily lives, not just operations, is what makes us the 911 force for America, the Army and Golf Company.*

* * *

***P. FUCKIN' S.——WEAR YOUR FUCKIN' COVERS TO THE CHOW HALL!***

* * *

This is the kind of bullshit I have to deal with in addition to all the other stuff that goes with running an infantry company in a combat zone. In fact, I spend more of my time, much, much more of my time, dealing with this kind of shit than I do with any other aspect of combat. In that, combat is not much different for me than training back at Camp Pendleton.

13 Oct. 2004

We responded to a QRF call and ended up with the mission of strong-pointing the worst intersection in all of Ramadi, #296 to be exact. This is the intersection we can't monitor from our rooftop OPs. We know it and Haji damn sure knows it. Every fuckin' day someone gets hit with IEDs right around this area, usually several times a day. In fact, just about every time a convoy goes past it they get hit with IEDs, RPGs, small arms fire or all of the above. Today, our job was to go on down there and keep the area secure until Golf and Whiskey swept an area to the south. We got to the intersection and because of the inherent danger at this particular unprotected place, we hurried to get our boys out of the vehicles and onto the nearby rooftops. Coming into and getting out of an area, is our most vulnerable time. Usually, we have eight Marines in the back of every 10-man Hummer and eighteen to twenty in the back of each 7-ton truck. The vehicles were way too close to one another and everyone dismounted at the same time.

About this time, I noticed a 155mm artillery shell right in the middle of the road. ***EVERY*** Marine in the company was within the effective casualty radius of that shell. There is no time to think of personal safety. The very last place on earth I wanted to be was right there. Talk about a puckered asshole. Bob fuckin' Villa couldn't have hammered a nail through either half of my ass. Unfortunately, my job was to get all of my boys and all of my vehicles out of the way. Sometimes it's good to be the Gunny. This was not one of those times!

I screamed and yelled and tried to get everyone back in the vehicles and get the vehicles out of there, but everyone just looked at me and no one moved. Meanwhile, I'm still right there praying this fucker is not still hooked up to its trigger device, or the trigger man is taking a shit or something. I couldn't run away or take cover and leave my boys unaware of the danger. I bellowed louder and finally they understood and hauled ass out of there with my Irish ass right behind them. Whiskey drove up and put a few rounds into the shell with a .50 cal machine gun. As it exploded, I couldn't help but breathe a sigh of relief because that thing packed a serious wallop and shit went flying.

As for the rest of the mission, we put a shit-load of rounds down our sectors of fire. At first, different Iraqis peeked out and observed us. Thanks to the, in my opinion, too tight Rules of Engagement (ROE), we can't just shoot every asshole that decides to be a fuckin' Lookey-Loo while a .50cal and MK-19 are pointed at him. Because of this, we were caught slightly off guard when suddenly an RPG was fired and impacted right next to our 7-ton truck. Luckily, the asshole was a bad shot and even more luckily, no one was hurt by this blast.

We declared an end to the bullshit and opened

up with the big guns. Amazingly enough, the peeking nonsense stopped for the day, when we let loose and sent a few bursts downrange. Word came down from battalion since we had the area locked down to stay there until the re-supply convoy went to the Combat Outpost and came back through on its way home. Even though this meant we would be out there for five or six more hours, it was hard to gripe since the boxcar brings us our supplies and gets fired at and blown up on a daily basis. Other than the occasional bursts from the big guns, the rest of the mission involved sitting in place and waiting for a fight.

The best part of the whole day was when Swartz went into the building behind us and reemerged with about fifty ice cold Pepsi's. Now, I could have asked him where in the hell he went and also where in the Blue Hell he found fifty ice cold Pepsi's in the middle of a firefight but I just kept my pie hole shut and grabbed me a cold soda. Swartz and I did a combat re-supply and got one out to each of my boys. Just seeing the looks on their faces as they grabbed a cold soda in this environment was worth the trip. Even us, before we came to this shit-hole. I often wonder if this place will change me permanently. I don't think it will in the sense that it will warp my mind or that I'll have PTSD or any other psychological problems. I think the only changes to me will be appreciating the shit out of all the small things in life that most people never even notice.

16 Oct 2004

Happy anniversary Janet! In October of 1989, Janet packed up all her belongings and her seven-year-old daughter, Sonia, and moved to America. People have done crazy things in the name of love since the beginning of time but moving from Scotland to America to marry Lance Corporal Tracy ranks right up there. I don't know what kind of life she expected and I'll never know what she saw in me to take such a chance but after sixteen years we're still together.

Life as a military wife is without doubt the toughest, loneliest and scariest existence I can imagine. Even when we're not deployed we have early mornings, late nights and constant training evolutions that keep us away from home.

Since 1989 we lived in Virginia, Pennsylvania, North Carolina, South Carolina, Hawaii, Colorado and now California. Granted, we're well traveled and have seen a lot of things and been to a lot of places most people never will, but the lack of a lasting home, friends and family make for a very hard and often lonely life.

It's so much harder for the families than it is for us Marines. We usually know someone where ever we go and Marines are Marines and the Infantry is the Infantry so for us the transitions are usually quick and painless. I know that's not the case with the family but even after all these years, I never get complaints.

Whenever I think of the great times we've had as a family, the trip to the Grand Canyon pushes itself to the front of the memory pack. When my tour as a Drill Instructor at Parris Island, South Carolina ended in 1996 and orders came through as Oahu, our next duty station, we decided to drive to California and fly to Hawaii from there. We packed up and headed cross country. Along the way, we stopped at a few places of interest and I really thought nothing could compare to the drive up and over the Rockies in Colorado.

We hit the Grand Canyon and Janet, Sonia, Dani and even Molly the dog piled out of the car. We walked around, checked out the views and had a picnic lunch on a cliff, overlooking the most unimaginable view I've ever seen before or since. I remember my wife and children laughing as Molly frolicked with all the sniffing opportunities and had the time of her life

Sometimes, when I'm really tired and about to drift off to sleep, I can hear their laughter and faintly picture the sun as it sets into the canyon. My family and me on a rock as we enjoy life and eat sandwiches. It seems so far away from here and sometimes I wonder if I'll ever have such simple joys in my life again. I'm not sure what keeps each Marine going but reliving that memory reminds me of what I fight for.

* * *

I wanted to get on the phone and let her know I was thinking of her but a soldier was killed yesterday. Anytime a death occurs, all communication with the outside world ceases for 24 hours. That way the family can be notified in person in the proper manner rather than finding out because someone says it over the phone or internet. Instead, we went out on Operation Back Door, aptly named because we went out the rear entrance to our compound to see what's out there.

Apparently, Echo 2/4 never patrolled back there, at least not in their last few months at the Outpost, and not knowing your neighborhood is just no way to live. We are literally surrounded by the enemy and we don't even know the roads or areas right outside the rear gate to our own compound.

A note to all you comedians: Ha Ha, very funny, believe me I've already heard all the ass jokes associated with the name of this mission so let's just get on with the story.

**Back Door of Outpost**

We rolled out with 1st platoon and that's always a good thing. The three squads foot-patrolled out first in order to gain overwatch positions, then the three gun trucks mapped out our routes while we simultaneously supported one another. We were pinned into a really tight alley with no maneuver to the right or left. But, if this is where the enemy hides, and thinks it's to his advantage, then we have to show him we're coming anyway and loaded for bear. A vehicle blocked the one road we needed to travel east. Very suspicious and more than a little scary, especially if the vehicle was rigged with explosives. We couldn't have the boys search it and I really didn't want to drive past it or move it with my vehicle.

Luckily, I decided to actually use my brain.

"Sir, why don't we pound on a few doors and see if this jackass lives around here?" I asked the lieutenant.

He took my suggestion and the interpreter asked if anyone knew the owner. Sure enough, we found the guy. He saw us coming, got scared, ran out of the vehicle and left it there.

"It's not so smart to leave your car parked in front of Marines." The interpreter explained to him. "Next time they will blow it up."

We face this kind of shit every day. A car is in no way just a car over here and an abandoned car is guilty of being a bomb until proven innocent. However, the judicial process is to blow it up with one of our own rockets and if the resulting explosion is really huge, it was a VBIED, if not, it wasn't. Either way, the owner is shit out of luck.

After our fun with the car, we carried on with the rest of the mission. Suddenly, mortar shells landed back near where we had to re-enter our compound. At the time, we were more than a safe distance away but the call came from the Combat Operations Center (COC), to bring us back in. When the call came, we were searching a house because the owner had a big ass, pimped-out Chevy Suburban with Jordanian plates and a Texas registration. It seemed weird and a little out of place so we decided to conduct a detailed search. We didn't find anything incriminating but we detained the guy and the vehicle for further questioning when we got back home. All things considered, it was a good mission. We put our footprint out the back gate and got a good look as far as the people, the roads, and the buildings. Hopefully, we threw the enemy off balance while we were at it.

When we got back from the mission, Fox 6 wanted to take a convoy out to inspect the Observation Posts (OPs). 1st Platoon was a bit worn out from the mission so I decided to get as many of my Goons together as possible to make up the 20 Marines needed for a 4-vehicle convoy. I even threw in a few drivers and my mechanic. I also saw this as a unique opportunity to head out by the lake and let the boys blow off a little steam.

We loaded up the vehicles with enough ammo and explosives for an entire platoon and off we went. When we got to the Graveyard OP, Fox 6 told us to go out to the lake and conduct weapons training. Another thing that might surprise most people is not all Marines, hell, not even all Infantry Marines, know how to fire all of the weapons that exist in an infantry battalion. First, I gave all those who never fired a SMAW the chance to shoot a few and then we shot AT4s, shoulder-fired rockets that pack quite the wallop, meaning they make a lot of noise and really blow up shit. I gave all the boys the opportunity to fire the .50cal and MK-19 grenade launcher. We also shot at some birds with our rifles, pistols, and M203 grenade launchers. This accomplished two things and I'm not exactly sure which was more beneficial. The Marines got valuable training on weapons heretofore they did not know how to operate, which was the purpose of the whole exercise. But the added benefit and perhaps equally rewarding aspect, the Marines felt great afterwards. They were all motivated as only Marines can be after shooting heavy caliber guns and blowing up shit with rockets. It's easy to forget that keeping up morale and letting the Marines have a little fun is a very important aspect of combat, which many of our leaders forget from time to time. Hell, I know this is combat and I also know how hard these guys work day in and day out. But if you don't find a way for your Marines to blow off steam and actually have fun you'll end up with a bunch of mental cases by the end of it all.

17 Oct. 2004

Tonight we have a QRFA mission to assist Golf Company by strong pointing a fairly dangerous and busy intersection known as 297. Along Route Michigan, recently named as the most dangerous four miles of road in the world, there are three major intersections, from east to west, 297, 296, and 295. All roads leading into or out of Ramadi can be accessed by entering any one of these intersections from the north, south, east or west. They are very busy, very dangerous and extremely deadly. Marines have died and many vehicles blown up at all three. We don't have enough manpower to keep Marines at all of these intersections around the clock, and whatever genius set up our OPs caused blind spots at these three intersections. The end result; IEDs can be set in place because the enemy knows where we live and thanks to cellular phone technology, observers report our movements whenever we leave our compound. Therefore, even though we do dismounted and vehicular patrols, the enemy need only wait and put his toys in place whenever the coast is clear. Another dangerous aspect of this mission is there are only so many clever ways to position ourselves at these intersections. Either we block the roads with our vehicles, dismount the troops to take over some houses and rooftops or a combination of both. We already know the enemy is reasonably smart and pretty resourceful. We also know every time we set a pattern in our operations it eventually ends up with bad results for us. The biggest challenge we face in our current operational status is, we can't help but set patterns because of the repetitiveness of the mission.

**Map Study**

At least, I'm with 1st platoon again so I'm not too worried about the tactical end of things. I've gotten into a pretty comfortable role with 1st Platoon. The lieutenant handles the plan, the SSgt gets the boys moving to where they need to be and I handle the placement of the vehicles and the heavy guns. This works pretty well with this platoon and the same can be said when I go out with 2nd Platoon, but 3rd and 4th Platoons continue to be my biggest challenges. 3rd because of the aforementioned reasons, and 4th because that platoon is really our Weapons Platoon. They had to become a no-shit rifle platoon on their first day in-country and any leader will tell you how difficult that is. It would be nice if I could choke out the platoon commanders and platoon sergeants and just tell them how it's gonna be but there is a delicate balance in the whole Corps where leadership is concerned. All the way down to the most junior team leader, everybody wants total control of their own people and they want to operate how they see fit to do so. Nobody likes to be told how to do business by someone else. Sometimes it's pride but often it's a respect thing. The good leaders recognize and respect a more experienced Marine and rely on his talents and experience to help them. They use this leader as another tool in the box and make themselves and their platoon better and more efficient.

The other side of this coin, the experienced leader has to remember where he came from and to respect the leadership that already exists within that unit. There is always the old standby, "Because I said so," but I find that it's usually the weak leaders with no people or social skills who rely on that one in order to work with others. Can I do that? Have I done it in my time here? Damn right! But what does that teach the people you try to lead and what kind of atmosphere do you create when you're the one-trick pony pulling that shit every time you open your mouth.

This was not the time when the smart enemy waited on us but I'd bet half my ass and both of my balls that pretty soon we'll be on the receiving end of some nasty shit, if we keep fucking around in the same goddamned area. Please God let me be wrong about this one!

19 Oct. 2004

Operation Trashcan was supposed to have

occurred about a week or so ago but it got canceled at the last minute because the Army left one of its soldiers in town after being hit by the enemy and all operations were suspended until this guy was found. It's a little comforting to know that should something like this occur, the entire brigade willingly ceases all operations and puts maximum energy and emphasis on finding even one lone man. Operation Trashcan II hoped to find more bad guys or weapons caches in our own AO. We haven't been on the ground there in quite a while. For this mission, I was attached to 4th platoon and once again I volunteered to take the vehicle portion of the movement.

Lately, both Bruce and the CO tell me I should scale back and not put myself out there all the time. There is a lot of merit and good common sense in this thought process, especially since they seem to think the company would be in a bad spot without me around to take care of all the little bullshit things I do in my normal duties as Company Gunnery Sergeant. For my own mindset, I can't even imagine not being out there when the company operates. I honestly believe anybody could fill in and handle my job if I were to go down. Maybe I am good at what I do and I know I'm a good man to have around, I always have been. But if my place in combat is not right out there in the middle of the action then maybe I don't have a clue where my place really is. I do know this: When the company is out there and I'm a part of it, it feels right. When I'm not, it just feels wrong.

As for Operation Trashcan II that turned out to be a good name, because that's exactly where that operation belongs; in the shitcan. We got nothing!

Either we hit big or we get nothing at all. At least we got a lot more familiar with yet another area of our sector. Pretty soon we will have the entire area completely mapped out and that's a big part of dominating an AO.

20 Oct. 2004

We did a recon of the area directly outside the front gate of our outpost, supposedly an Agricultural College. I'm making the assumption the students have long since hauled ass. My guess is the Muj use the area as an OP on our ass. There are many different ways the Muj get in unseen by our sentries and many different buildings with great observation sites of all that goes on within our compound. So much for OPSEC!

**College Patrol**

We took three platoons over to check it out and attached to us for this patrol was a photographer, Jim Macmillan from the Associated Press.

Now how's this for a small fuckin' world? Mac used to work for the Times Leader out of Wilkes-Barre Pennsylvania, the very same newspaper I delivered so I could have beer money in my youth. He even covered the Pittston Tomato Festival on more than one occasion. We swapped stories about the different dive bars, so frequent in that part of the world. How weird! Of all the conversations I never expected to have in the middle of a combat patrol, recalling the cultural juggernaut, the Pittston Tomato Festival, certainly ranks way up there on my list.

We found a window that overlooked our compound and under this window was a sketch of our base and fifty or so bullets. An incredibly easy shot for even an average marksman if they ever decided to chance it. Other than that, we mapped out yet another area and found out what was right across the street from where we operate. If you ask me, which the Colonel doesn't, we should seal off that whole college and shoot anybody we ever see anywhere near it. Or we should take over that area and operate out of there as well as the Outpost. It's obviously not being used as an institute of higher learning, unless one of their subjects is to learn about the Combat Outpost.

We finished the operation and now my XO and I have to go over and deal with Golf Company's XO and Gunny. Sometimes people rub you the wrong way. This guy rubs just about everyone the wrong way. Then again, it could be a Golf/Fox thing, where if he was my XO, I'd love him, but to be honest, I doubt it.

I've had all of the shit I can handle from Golf Company and the latest and greatest has to do with flashlights, of all stupid minutiae. The Battalion Gunner told me he ordered spotlights for the two companies. Today, four spotlights showed up but Golf Company claims all four belong to them. Why? Because they asked the worthless S-4 for spotlights on this ridiculous request form the S-4 had us fill out so we can order things they can't deliver. I assumed since the Gunner said he was going to get them for us, I would not need to ask the fabulous four for yet one more thing that they couldn't produce.

Every now and again I try to put common sense and rational thought and behavior into my repertoire. And damn if I don't get shit on every time I do it, but I can't seem to stop myself. I assumed since Golf got four and we have none their Gunny would do the right thing and just give me two. That's what I would do for him and what any Gunny would do for any other Gunny. Wrong answer on that one. Of course, this is the same teammate who secretly signed for all gear from the incoming attachments and ended up with three extra machine guns. When I asked for one of those guns, he played stupid and then did the unbelievable and to me unforgivable.

"It's not up to me. I can't make that decision. Your CO needs to talk to my CO," he said.

He got caught fucking me and now that I found out, instead of fessing up and making things right, he's gonna hide behind his CO.

"You know that's a crock of fuckin' shit," I replied.

This is some buddy fucking, piece of shit nonsense

I can't believe is coming out of the mouth of a fellow Gunny. But to me, what's even worse is, this guy is supposed to be my friend.

The argument goes from flashlights to the machine guns and then his XO started up with his nonsense.

"Golf Company has a harder mission and our AO is worse than yours. We go out the gate much more often than you do, our company deserves more machine guns," this guy actually had the fuckin' nerve to tell me.

If my lieutenant ever said some similar nonsense when I had a discussion with another Gunny, he'd get sent home with a boot up his ass.

Their Gunny just stood there.

"We're in the same fuckin' place, doing the same fuckin' thing! We go on joint OPs all the fuckin' time. You call for QRF's from us every fuckin time you get in some shit," I growled heatedly.

They seem to think since the supply convoy goes through their area, and since they go out to protect the convoy they are anointed as the King Shit of our battalion and therefore rate more than anyone else.

I walked away shaking my head in a state of bewilderment.

At least, now I know who and what I'm dealing with as far as Golf and especially their Gunny is concerned. I also know when he no longer has his CO and XO to hide behind he'll come around and try to convince me there was no malicious intent involved here. I've been around long enough to know when a so-called friend and fellow professional SNCO pisses on my back and tells me it's raining.

There used to be an unwritten code between the

Old Corps SNCOs, especially between the Gunnys. The bottom line, the Company Gunny runs the company. He's the beginning and end of everything that happens or fails to happen in his company. Every Company, or Battery, or Section or Squadron has this senior-most Gunny. This guy is a politician, thief, conspirator, dealmaker etcetera. We look out for one another. The saying goes, "as long as it's not cutting my own throat, it's yours." Along with, "you owe me one, motherfucker!"

Of course, I'm not talking about giving away crucial shit. Maybe your CO is obligated to keep because he signed for it. I'm talking about dealing in the "extra" shit we all have. In this case, we get attachments and my so-called friend and fellow Gunny horded their gear while knowing full good and well he's getting way plussed-up while I'm still in need. I'm not about to learn how to kiss ass or fuck over my friends and fellow SNCOs.

"Bruce, I'm so fuckin' pissed, I'm ready to call it quits at the end of this enlistment."

"That's why guys like you and me need to stay in the Corps, Pat."

Deep in my heart, I know he's right, but I'm just so frustrated and sick and tired of all the bullshit that goes on between firefights. I hate to give up on the Corps and I especially hate to turn it over to guys like this, but I always thought it got nothing but better as you got nearer the top. Turns out for me it doesn't work. I always said I'd get out when the Corps was no longer fun. Well assholes, you win! Having to be around people like those I described above, and see these kind of people succeed, has made me realize maybe it's time to move on. Of course, there is always the possibility it's me who's fucked up. Stranger things have happened.

21 Oct. 2004

Once again, we headed out on another strongpoint mission at 297 with my favorite, 3rd Platoon. When it's bad, it's bad, but by the same token, when it's good, it's good. 3rd Platoon either finally pulled its head out of its collective ass or the blind squirrel found his nut. Our emphasis was on Canal St. and we pulled in by the Al Haj Mosque, with those same few buildings to go in for overwatch, which continues to make me nervous as hell. We obtained overwatch, set our trigger lines and got ready for action.

When a taxi ran through our trigger line, the boys opened fire at point blank range with three different M-16's and the 240G machine gun. The guy jumped out of the taxi and the rounds impacted all around him. He did this dance out in the street like something out of a Western cowboy movie or even a cartoon. How, I don't know, but of the fifty or so rounds fired at this guy at point blank range, not one of them hit him. Allah definitely saved his ass, but the same can't be said for his car. We told him to haul ass so he pushed his taxi back down the road and probably went home to clean the shit out of his man-dress. An hour later, we packed up our shit, loaded the trucks and went home.

As luck would have it, my night was not meant

to be relaxing. 2nd Platoon got hit pretty hard with a combination IED and rocket attack and they ended up with a disabled vehicle right in the middle of the road on Michigan. They activated the QRF, 3rd Platoon, to reinforce while at the same time recover the downed vehicle and bring it back to the Outpost. We rolled out of the gate and for some reason the lieutenant dismounted the troops right across from the OP instead of near the downed vehicle, although the exact location of the downed vehicle was a bit unclear. I figured we would just head east until we located 2nd Platoon and the vehicles.

After the troops dismounted, I told Swartz to drive ahead and find my broken vehicle. Sure enough, it was right in the middle of Michigan so Swartz got the tow strap on while 2nd covered our asses. Then 3rd rolled up and cluster fucked around the area. We got everything together for our movement back to the Outpost.

**Mission Accomplished**

This was a fairly typical and easy recovery mission but when your ass is in the middle of Route Michigan at night, with the adrenaline pumping and the dark pressing in, it damn sure doesn't put you at ease.

23 Oct. 2004

The Gauntlet is the run from Combat Outpost to Hurricane Point along Route Michigan. It's the same run the Boxcar does every day, but they have much more protection and support than when we have to go it alone as a company operation. But, the battalion commander wanted to see all the heavy hitters in our company to pass some top secret, hush-hush shit. I felt somewhat at ease about the run because 2nd Platoon ran the convoy and we brought all the heavy guns. Half of me hoped these motherless bastards tried some shit so we could hand them their ass. The smarter half of me knew they wouldn't and the real danger lie in the IEDs we would encounter either going there or coming back. However, any way you slice it, we go whether we like it or not. We all know the big secret because the simple truth is there are no secrets in an infantry battalion.

We're moving out of the Combat Outpost and the Army is moving in. We're going to divide this AO into an east/west split with the Army on the east and the Corps on the west. Living in the East (Combat Outpost) is definitely the shitty end of the stick, but as it stands now, it's a less intense area from which to operate and run OPs. Moving to the west and consolidating our battalion will make our living much better, but now we divide up the western area into three parts and it's bound to get even more intense than we're accustomed to. This is due in large part because Boxcar will no longer need to run the Gauntlet and we will no longer spend half of our time either securing the route or reacting to attacks on the log train. We can devote our time to conduct operations in our sector. The Muj will undoubtedly react to this by becoming even more active with his bullshit IEDs and sniper tactics. Oh well, that's why we get the big bucks.

**Gunner's View down Michigan**

At the meeting, we decide who moves where and how to divide up the new AO. We had three choices: Number one; we can move to HP with Golf, and all the pogues from HP can move to Junction City, the Army HQ, just south of HP. Number two; Fox and Golf can each have two platoons living at HP and two platoons living at JC. Number three; Fox moves to JC, Golf moves to HP or vice versa. The Colonel voted number one out. He refused to live and work from JC. This is either because he is King at HP and would only be a prince at JC with all the Army and Marine brass there or he doesn't want to be away from the fight. Even though JC is literally just across the bridge, it seems like it's away from the action. Number two voted a big no-go for all involved, because to split your company makes absolutely no sense and it's a logistical nightmare. Number three won out! We are away from pain in the ass, self-proclaimed main effort Golf Company. And

I'm nowhere near a good enough writer to express how fuckin' happy that makes me. Fox moves to JC and we have ten days from today to make this happen. Good luck! We'll get the western 1/3 of the new AO and we're not sure what the exact breakdown or how much better or worse the area, but we'll wait until we get there to figure that out.

We ran the Gauntlet back to the Outpost to tell the boys about the big news. We didn't encounter the enemy on the way, but that didn't make it a worry-free ride. Every second of the drive, your body is completely wired. It's a rush like no other. It's this combination of adrenaline, energy, anticipation, and yes, fear. Every alley can hold an RPG shooter. Every piece of garbage and debris can be a bomb. Every car can be a vehicle IED or suicide driver. It's a wild, wild ride and it's a trip!

28 Oct. 2004

Ten days is barely enough time to move an entire infantry company from one camp to another in peacetime. In fact, it's damn near impossible. Now I'm expected to do it while still conducting operations, turning over the camp to the Army and getting my new living arrangements squared away. Add to this our S-4 is overall in charge of the logistics and the major movement of the gear, personnel and ammunition, and it's no fuckin' wonder I am officially stressed the fuck out! Every day the S-4 finds some new way to screw me. The best part of it all, they're fuckin' me from both ends.

They have to help me move from the Outpost while at the same time set up my living arrangements at JC. Needless to say, they can't even do one simple thing, let alone, two difficult ones. Every day it's something new. One day they don't have my shipping containers, the next, they don't have my new buildings set up. Anyway you slice it, we have to be out of there by Nov. 2nd and every day they have one more excuse of why nothing is set up and why it's everyone's fault but theirs. Worst of all, I have been so busy with the move, I haven't been able to go out on any QRFs. For some people this may seem like a small vacation, but for me, torture. I can't wait to get this all over with so I can get back to my normal way of doing business. At least I was able to get a little stress relief because we had a company operation, Rocky Road II, in what will be our new AO.

The whole purpose of the Operation was to raid a few suspect houses and then sweep through the surrounding area to see what was up in this part of town. Operating in a completely new area made us all a little edgy. It's hard enough when you know the routes, the attitudes of the locals and the basic lay of the land but when you don't know jack or shit even routine missions become much more difficult. I traveled with 3rd Platoon, but by now, I figured a way to keep them from irritating the shit out of me. We had a few good arrests with a couple of decent sized weapons caches. One guy had a shit load of match grade sniper rifle ammunition, a few had way too many weapons for honest folk and one guy had a shit load of cash.

The rules of the road: Each male living in a house can have one weapon with a maximum of three weapons total. Each weapon can only have 30 rounds. Sniper rifles, machine guns and such, do not qualify as a personal protection weapon. They can have no more than $7000 of American cash or the Dinar equivalent, which is some ridiculous amount like $10,000,000. The whole process is a giant pain in the ass but we have to do it by the numbers and dot all the Is and cross all the Ts or they can't send these assholes to prison. The money is the biggest headache. It's turned over to the senior man on scene and the count verified then turned over to me and I re-verify the count. When we get back from a mission it gets recounted yet again and then sent up the chain. Needless to say, money being money and Marines being Marines, that's a lot of people touching sometimes large amounts of cash and sooner or later someone will get sticky fingers and then some legal asshole will come around to sniff my underwear. But, I'm The Gunny and it's my job to deal with anything that is bullshit or has the potential to be bullshit.

The money guy had $7800 U.S. and a couple million Iraqi and I can't even begin to tell you what a pain in the ass it is to sit there, counting fuckin' money while a mission is in progress.

"What Muj operations do you finance with all this cash." I asked the interpreter to ask this asshole,

"Gunny, he's a money exchanger. He's licensed to operate from his house."

He produced all the documents to account for his money, so we had no choice but to let him go. Sorry pal, didn't mean to cuff you and blindfold you and tear your house apart and drag you down to my vehicle. No hard feelings, huh? Oh well, I'm probably off his Christmas card list!

Pretty soon after that fiasco, the operation came to a halt and time to retrograde back to the Outpost. We made it all the way back to 297 without incident, but 200 yards from home BOOM! An IED hit right at the side of my vehicle, my side, no less. Smoke and debris and this horrid stench spread through the vehicle. Standard Operating Procedure (SOP) is to continue to push through so we rolled into the Outpost. The real kick in the ass, we really can't stop the terrorists from planting IEDs right under our noses because there just aren't enough Marines between the two companies to cover our entire area. Pretty soon, we will have Marines hurt real bad or killed right where they should be safe.

I'm so fuckin' frustrated that the Corps, or the Army, or whoever the fuck, can only provide one fuckin' battalion for this whole fuckin' town. I realize there is a siege of sorts going on in Fallujah, but how about another company or so down here to fight until they get ready to roll through Fallujah? While I'm at it, I might as well ask Santa fuckin' Claus for a new goddamn ten speed. Fuck It!

Once we got inside the camp and out of the vehicle to assess the damage we discovered serious shrapnel pieces lodged in my door and the driver's door. Thank God for these armored Humvees. The vehicle was still operational and all the Marines were uninjured but some disgusting, smelly chunks of shit spattered all over the truck. Of all the no-good, lousy, disgusting, piece of shit tactics, this takes the cake. A goddamn dead dog had an IED slipped under it. What in the blue hell will they think of next?

29 Oct. 2004

Every criminal from the biggest of the big time to the smallest back-alley sneak thief knows you do not return to the scene of the fuckin' crime. I knew if we kept getting these bullshit strongpoint missions, sooner or later the enemy would catch on and hand us our ass. Everyone knew this would happen, from the lowest PFC to the Brigade Commander, but we keep on doing the same, pattern-setting, and repetitive shit over and over and fuckin' over again.

Fox Company 4th Platoon went to strongpoint intersection 296 and what did Haji do? He waited until my boys dismounted their vehicles and hit them with two IEDs. Then, as they tried to regroup and evac the wounded, he opened up with a small arms ambush to ice his cake. He knew where we would pull up, dismount and what buildings we would try to enter. Let's face it, he knew our moves.

Thirteen Marines lay wounded on the scene, four urgent medevacs, four more evac'd after they got back and five were treated and returned to duty. Even Kabi, the interpreter, was slightly injured. The injuries included the Platoon Commander, Platoon Guide, all three Squad Leaders, and a few Team Leaders. The entire platoon had to remount the vehicles and return to the Outpost with their casualties and another platoon had to go out and fill in for them.

Where was I during all this? At fuckin' JC, trying to un-fuck the living arrangements for our big move. Why did we spend all day at JC? Because the incompetent S fuckin' 4 could fuck up a one-car funeral and if I didn't go down there and find out about all the fucked up shit, which I will complain to the Battalion Commander about, then my company would get fucked over when we finished our move three days hence.

To return to my company, I hitched a ride on the Boxcar convoy when it came to JC to pick up chow and supplies. By the time the convoy was ready to leave, there was a huge fight with several medevacs called in. Since the route was anything but secure, we were told to hold in place until further orders. It sounded like one massive fight and bad enough I couldn't be with my company but the real kick in the balls, I had to spend the fight, sitting on the sidelines with all the fuckin' pogues. I know I complained about pogues before, but I really do believe all Marines are Marines and I know it takes every one of us to have an effective Marine Corps. But deep in my heart, I'm a grunt. I love being a grunt and I only want to be around my fellow grunts. That's just the way it is with me and if a pogue ever reads this I hope he (or she) knows even though I love them as Marines, I don't want to be hanging out with them when a firefight is going down. I was with some of my best goons, Swartz driving, Hobbs on the gun and Sgt D and Crazy Mike as wingmen and I told the Convoy Commander, "Sir, when we get near Fox, I'll peel off and join up with my company if there still out there when the convoy rolls through."

"I wouldn't expect anything else, Gunny."

Unfortunately, the convoy never got clearance to leave JC and I spent the whole night there. I finally got to a radio and found out the actual injuries and damages. The Platoon Guide, shot through the leg, was the worst of the injuries. The Platoon Commander caught shrapnel to the face and upper body. One Marine had a severe concussion and the rest shrapnel injuries that required different levels of care. At the end of the day, eight Marines required evacuation to TQ (a larger Army base nearby), Baghdad, or Germany. We don't think four of them will rejoin us for this war. That's a pretty high price to pay for one mission. The worst part of it all; we will continue to get these bullshit, casualty-waiting-to-happen missions until we get out of the Outpost and over to JC. There are still plenty more IEDs but, at least, the enemy won't know where we will be and exactly when to set the timer.

31 Oct. 2004

Lieutenant L, a Platoon Commander from Weapons Company died today, right in the same mother fuckin' goddamn spot where I was hit the other fuckin' day. Only this time, they packed enough shit to kill some Marines. MOTHERFUCKER! MOTHER FUCKING COCKSUCKER! GODDAMN IT! I watched about five of our corpsmen try to do everything they could to save him. To make matters worse, he didn't even need to be here. He got sent over here with 2/4 when they needed casualty replacements. He volunteered to stay here and serve another tour with us. By all accounts, he was the best goddamn young lieutenant in the battalion.

1st Platoon strong-pointed intersection 297 so Weapons Company could sweep the road for IEDs. I was still in the firm base when I heard the explosion, the loudest by far. About one minute later, the call came in we have four urgent surgical medevacs at 297. I was dumbfounded for a minute because my boys were out there. Then Lieutenant J. came on and said it was not Fox Company Marines. I feel shitty about saying this, but I felt so relieved.

We mounted up in our vehicles and went out to pick up the injured. Fox 1 rolled through with Lt. L. as we headed out. When we got there, two Marines lay on the ground by the vehicle. Both of them had legs shattered, blood, guts and bone all over the place. Although in severe pain, there was nothing we could do but load them into our ambulance and get them to the surgeon at the BAS. I went in because I helped carry the stretcher and I should have walked right back out. The two wounded Marines screamed with pain but it was obvious they would live. Most of the corpsmen and the Doc worked on Lt. L. They tried to pump air into his lungs with that breather thing you squeeze but it kept filling up with blood. A chunk of shrapnel flew across and tore most of his throat out. I think he was DOA but goddamn if those corpsmen weren't trying their asses off to bring him back. I walked over and stood next to Capt. Rap, the Weapons Company Commander. There is nothing you can say to another Marine at a time like this. I gave him a grab on the shoulder and stood next to him as we both watched the corpsmen work. A feeling of utter sadness and complete rage came over me. I don't know any other way to explain it. I'm sure the only people who can relate are those who lost loved ones due to a crime. When they finally pronounced the lieutenant as a KIA, I had to walk out and get some air. I stood for ten minutes crying for a Marine I never even met and feeling about as shitty as I've ever felt. Then we had to go back out and recover the vehicle.

I was in absolute shock to see this armored Humvee, tires completely thrashed and driver's side rear door shredded like a piece of paper shot at close range with a shotgun. I could not believe something was set up that could cause that much damage. IEDs called platter charges are the same nasty shit we always deal with but with the ability to place all of their charge and payload in a specific, concentrated direction, in this case, the driver's side rear door. Only the pictures I took can tell that story. The vehicle was also filled with so much blood and shrapnel it's a true miracle anyone survived that blast. As my vehicle dragged that vehicle into the Outpost, the Marines who saw it stared with mouth's agape. We've all been hit with IEDs and by now we've grown accustomed to it. I think we all believed we were pretty impervious to any real damage because of how well our vehicles always protect us.

**Platter Charge on Hummer**

This was a wake up call for all of us. Our enemy is not willing to maintain the status quo. He will keep adapting to us and change his tactics to inflict as much harm as possible. He knows he cannot defeat us, but history has proven he does not have to defeat us in battle. His goal is to weaken our resolve and especially the resolve of the American people. He does not care if any Iraqis get hurt or killed along with us. He figures sooner or later the American people will say "enough is enough" and just give the country over to these fuckers and let them deal with their own shit. His ultimate goal; to work on turning this place into the kind of Iraq where he can grab power and return to the good old days of human rights violations, tyranny and torture chambers.

Do we give these fuckers what they want? How can we when so many have already died? Then again, is it worth any more lives? I guess what we have here is a conundrum; kind of damned if you do and damned if you don't. I don't really have the answer. I do know this shit is personal and if we leave right now, then what did anyone give their life for? My honest opinion and one I feel is shared by many Marines is; we were right to come here and hand that no good bastard his ass. A threat to our country and our families, Saddam got what he had coming. It's about time we have a President with balls. It's also about time we put the world on notice. The bottom line; we are ready, willing and able to kick your ass so if you want to be a piece of shit dictator or tyrant you better not try to involve us in your bullshit or we will come over, kick your ass and run your little shit hole country our way until we're damn good and ready to leave. Now, how do you do that and leave? That's the big question and one I'm glad I don't have to answer. But I do know this shit hole is not worth the life of one more American.

The Army is on deck and anxious to get started, but maybe too anxious. They want to go out on foot patrols but they don't have any gun trucks to back them up. I tried to explain to one of their First Sergeants' that a foot patrol is more than likely to find an IED the hard way.

"Look boss, it's best if the vehicles take the brunt of the hit. Or you at least need some there to run medevacs," I said.

If I'm lying I'm dying, he replied, "We'll carry our wounded back."

The Army wants to do things their own way so who are we to tell them how to operate? They have only been here two days and the wildest two days in a long time.

Constant mortar attacks and the shit going down out in the Ville is at an all time crazy. As if to punctuate the whole damn changeover, a mortar round just crashed through the middle of the roof in what used to be our gym. Thankfully, we just moved all the equipment out of there and onto a truck. Any other fuckin' day and a lot of people would have been hurt or killed. I hate to turn over a camp to another unit in the manner we changed over with the Army but we did all we could to make it as good as we could in the short time we were there. Tonight is the last time I will sleep and wake up at the Combat Outpost. I can't say I'll miss the place!

01 Nov. 2004

Another month has gone by and now I have four more to go. The brief stay at Combat Outpost lasted a pretty wild two months and ten days. It's hard to believe that much time has actually gone by. That's almost exactly 1/3 of our deployment.

We made our final move early this morning, packed up all our shit, said goodbye and good luck to the Army and drove a huge convoy right down the Gauntlet. The Muj must have taken the morning off because we didn't even get a sniff of action or any explosions on the way to our new home. The boys seemed pretty happy, largely because their living arrangements are no worse than Combat Outpost, in fact, the living is almost too good but our buildings do not have overhead cover. Our hooches, as we call them, are wooden structures built out of plywood. They are big enough to fit six bunk beds in each but it's very close quarters. Large HESCO barriers on the sides protect them, but if a mortar came through the roof then everyone in the hooch is pretty much fucked. I guess we just count on the fact we won't get any direct hits. Security by luck, percentages or even prayer is how we will live out our days here.

**The Goon's Hooch**

Let's compare a few differences: At COP (Combat Outpost) we had 10 shitters and had to burn our own shit. At JC we have 20 port-a-johns and they get emptied and cleaned daily. At COP we walked across a mortar impact area to use a shower with three working nozzles and a pump that broke almost daily. At JC we have a shower trailer with 12 working showers located within our compound. At COP we got two hot meals a day delivered by our fellow Marines who ran the Gauntlet in order to feed us. We ate in a dirty building that often got hit with mortars. At JC we get three hot meals a day, four, if you include midnight rations (mid-rats) and in a modern cafeteria with a main line, fast food line and huge salad and dessert bar. Oh, and huge TVs with satellite TV and ESPN. At COP we had a small, shitty gym that got blown up right before we left. At JC there is an ultra modern $1,000,000 facility, a computer room and a lounge with TV's, pool tables and a snack bar. With a PX here, we no longer have to hope the truck will show up once a month. All of these things make this a much better place to live. It's not even close when it comes to all of the above, which are largely morale issues.

Maybe I'm crazy but I would rather be back at the Outpost. All things being equal, we had a rhythm going and lived right in the middle of the action. It seems like we went from front line warriors to rear echelon pogues overnight. I hope it doesn't really turn out that way. Maybe it just seems like we're out of the action. But in reality, we're a bit away from the fight. At COP we could load up and be in the fight in less than ten minutes. Here, it takes ten minutes just to get to the main gate. But, I'm sure once we get into a battle rhythm we'll feel better about our new camp and our new AO. For now, I'll just tough it out and figure out where I can find the time to eat four meals a day.

02 Nov. 2004

What a difference a day makes. Just when I started to feel out of the fight, I go out with Gun Slinging

2nd Platoon and now I'm right back in the action on one of those crazy missions that barely make sense even for those doing it. Our mission was to go down Route Michigan, recon an area for a possible new OP and check out this furniture store to see if its rooftop had any possibilities. We wanted to get a look at our new area and get the layout of the terrain. Near dark, we pulled up and got into overwatch and strongpoint positions. With no good spot to tuck in our vehicles, we just pulled them off the road as best we could and oriented our guns toward oncoming traffic.

There are a few ways to keep yourself safe and the best among these are clearly marked trigger lines, a couple of traffic cones and a spike strip or use a sign, wire, wood and such, anything that blocks the goddamn road and if anyone drives past them they get shot; hence the name, trigger line. If, for some reason you find yourself in a situation where you don't have any of those handy items or it's dark as hell, you could use the old standby… Chemlites, spike strips and warning shots. One would think Chemlites strung across the road, spike strips busting the tires and a Marine firing a tracer into the grill or ground in front of an oncoming car would make the driver stop and find a new route. We stacked up three cars along Michigan that did not get the hint.

Once again, we are placed in a tough position. What do you do when a car runs your trigger line? My answer is to shoot that fucker full of holes. When suicide car bombs blow up Marines and soldiers regularly, what are we supposed to do? Let the car through and hope for the best? My biggest problem with this is that some people probably don't have to die, for they may not be suicide bombers. But I'm not going to be the one who errs on the wrong side of this one. No Marine that's out with me is going to be blown up because I have a crisis of conscience at the wrong time. The Iraqis must know what goes on in their own city. They see this shit, day in and day out. When will they learn driving right up on Marine positions, or worse, trying to drive through, is bad for their health? I wish I could go on Al Fuckin' Jazeera TV and do a public service announcement.

"Hey retards! The Marines are here to help your stupid asses but you may notice the bad guys all look the same as you do. You won't defend yourselves and you won't point them out so we can't tell the fuckin' difference. Maybe, just fuckin' maybe, you might not want to drive around or walk around during firefights. Oh, and if you see shit in the road and a Marine points his rifle at you and shoots at you, stop the car or turn your stupid ass around!"

This may seem a bit cold and callous but even amid the killing and stress of combat, funny shit happens. I was in Fox 6's vehicle. Beeker was his driver and it would not be a stretch to say old Beeks is not all there. In fact, I believe he's about half there, one of those California surfer types who's probably a closet genius but more often than not off in his own little world. As the third vehicle of the evening gets fired up and ignites into a giant fireball on the street, Beeker looked back at me.

"Hey, Gunny, what's the purpose of this Op? Just to sit here and shoot up cars as they drive by?" he asked seriously.

The CO and I belly laughed for about five minutes.

Beeker might have called it right, we damn sure didn't do shit else and it sure as fuck didn't stop him from joining me in shooting some of the moving targets. In proper Goon fashion, he fired right next to my head and helped contribute to my future deafness.

At one point, Mikey came over to my position. "Gunny, if we don't get the fuck out of here, we'll be stacking cars up all night."

If a few Iraqis have to lose their cars in order to ensure parts of me and my Marines are not scattered all over this street, then I ain't gonna lose any sleep over it. That's the truth on that one. I'm beginning to wonder if Echo Company ever set or enforced trigger lines. Or maybe they let the inmates run the asylum. But I'll tell you this: the people in this area are gonna learn one way or the other The Blackhearts are now in charge. We haven't shown weakness or given any of these suicidal assholes a ticket to see Allah on our watch and I'll be damned if any civilian vehicle ever rolls up on my position. I'm not sure how the Army or any other Marine units in this country operate, but if you hear about a suicide bomber killing a bunch of Marines or soldiers by driving right up on their position then someone needs to take a hard look at our current ROEs.

04 Nov. 2004

I have officially divorced myself from 3rd fucking Platoon. I told the CO after today's mission I was finished with that retard fuckin' platoon, once and for all. On a personal level, I like those Marines most of all the platoons. But I promised a few people back home I wouldn't do anything stupid and get myself killed. Going anywhere and doing anything with that platoon qualifies as stupid. I used to believe the lieutenant was to blame. Now, I'm beginning to think the Platoon Sergeant or maybe even the whole damn platoon is to blame. Or, they just have this weird dynamic that makes them the Wild Card in any situation.

This all began before we even stepped off. I told all the platoons that Swartz is my driver and that he and I travel in gun truck #4, period, end of fuckin' story. I also went so far as to write it on the wall of the COC where vehicle manifests are turned in. Not only that, but I already jumped in this particular Platoon Sgt's shit once before over this. With this platoon and only this platoon, I need to double-check they had their shit straight. Sure enough, Swartz and I wake up, go out to the vehicles to load our gear, and the idiot Platoon Guide and some boot PFC driver are in vehicle #4.

"What The Fuck, I thought we went over this shit?" I said to Flann.

"The guide has to navigate because the Platoon Commander doesn't know the route."

I'm so mad I'm about to embarrass him in front of God and everyone and then he has the nerve to show the vehicle assigned to me. It's the biggest piece of shit we have in the company right now and it's the only one with L-shaped doors, designed by a moron who figured being able to see out of the door was more important than keeping your head from being blown off by shrapnel.

"Are you fuckin' kiddin' me? Have you lost your entire fuckin' mind?"

"But Gunny, it's the only vehicle left."

I have been taking every L-shaped door to the Navy Seabee's to weld the openings shut with steel sheets. This is the only one I have yet to fix and it wouldn't even be going except we need the extra vehicle. I'm so fuckin' bewildered that I don't even cause a scene.

"Get the fuck away from me and I'll deal with you and your retard platoon later."

"Fuck them. This is fuckin' bullshit, Gunny. I'll go up there and pull those mother fuckers out of our vehicle," Swartz freaked out, all kinds of pissed off.

It's bad enough he thought he'd be in his own gun truck and even worse he went to all the trouble to get his truck prepped and mission ready and ended up with this dirty, unstocked, and low on gas piece of shit. For the coup de grace and final kick in the balls, the doors won't stay shut.

I don't think I'm better or more deserving of anything over any other Marine in this company. I also don't ask them to go places and do things that I'm not willing to do myself. I would think the leadership of a platoon would think enough of the Company Gunny to try to provide him with as safe a ride as possible. Whereas the company could go on pretty much without a misstep if any platoon were to lose any one Marine, it would be a major upheaval if the Company Gunny got hurt or killed. Mine is not a billet a company could just do without. If I go down, the next senior Marine has to take my spot. A good Gunny gets a lot done and makes life a lot better for the Marines. A not so good Gunny can destroy a company and its morale. Any SNCO worth his stripes knows this. Every other operation with every other platoon, this is never an issue. With this platoon, everything is an issue because of rampant, unbridled buffoonery running wild. If the Platoon Sgt did this on purpose, then he is fucked up and a worthless piece of shit. If he's so stupid he doesn't know better, then the previous assessment remains the same. The most frustrating thing about the whole situation is this is one of my best SNCOs. If I could only pick a few guys to watch my back in any situation, this is one of my go-to guys.

We got lucky and arrived at the dismount point without getting killed. I took my leave from these idiots and attached this piece of shit truck to 4th Platoon's convoy for the remainder of the mission.

A battalion mission, Operation Tiger, called for another movement to contact/sweep and clear or whatever they wanted to call it. We got on line and moved a certain direction for a certain amount of time to see if the enemy wanted to come out and play. The Gunslingers (2nd Platoon) had the day's first bit of action with some guy up on his roof at 0400 doing who knows what. A Lance Corporal saw him peek over the roof from several different locations, acting pretty suspicious, and they thought he was armed. If he was not an insurgent, or working for the insurgents, he was at least guilty of being a stupid idiot. They yelled at him to get down, fired a warning shot and still he did not listen. The next peek earned him a bullet and he went down for the count. By the time they got up to the roof, his brother came out to tell them he was only fixing the satellite dish. Okay, in the dark, no light, no tools. Sure, we'll buy that for a fuckin' dollar. At least, Fox 6 was compassionate enough to let the guy take his brother to the hospital. That's another reason why I will never be an officer. I guess this will once again sound very evil, but fuck that guy. My guess is he spotted our positions for his Muj buddies and didn't count on alert Marines with great instincts and night vision capabilities.

We moved through our sector without any contact and only found a few suspicious items: a few sniper-type rifles, ammunition, and things of that nature. Halfway down the last street, about 100 meters from our limit of advance, this guy popped out with an RPG and took a shot and ran like hell around the corner. It hit a garbage heap and wall right in front of Cpl. Siv from 2nd Platoon and hurt him pretty badly. Doc rushed to the scene as 2nd let loose with some rounds down range.

The real kick in the ass, the shooter got away. He probably sat back down in his living room and waited to lie to us when we showed up at his house. It's very, very fucking frustrating when this shit happens. Siv had a bunch of shrapnel wounds, but Mikey said you could tell right off he'd be okay and the worst of his injuries, his left index finger, pretty much no longer attached. As they prepared to have him medevac'd, he asked Mikey to get a picture of him and his injuries for his scrapbook. Now that's a tough guy!

Luckily, no other injuries occurred and soon after we retrograded back to JC. Luckily again, I didn't get a face full of shrapnel for my trouble. When we returned, I went right to the CO to tell him my time with 3rd Platoon was at its end. I told him I have no problem with dying in combat, but I have a big problem with getting killed because of the idiocracy of the leadership or lack thereof in that platoon.

"Sir, I can't handle being around that fuckin' platoon. I won't make it through this war as the Gunny if you send me out with them anymore."

Hopefully, he will respect my request if he thinks I'm valuable enough to keep around. Now that the mission is over, I will talk to that Platoon Sgt When I no longer feel like killing him, I will teach him a lesson about biting the hand that feeds him.

06 Nov. 2004

Yesterday, we had another precious day off. We got word Siv was medevac'd to Germany and Doc said there was a slight chance of saving his finger. After a long run with Bruce, I signed on to messenger and my oldest daughter, Sonia was waiting for me. Most people feel isolated and very much separated from their families but I've actually grown closer to Sonia. We always stay in touch but in typical college-age daughter fashion, I usually get 15 or so minutes on the phone every weekend. Since I've been here, I get 15 minutes nearly every day. She knows more about the war, politics and Iraq than I do. She's extremely worried about me and her catharsis is to learn every bit of information she can off the internet. I try to reassure her everything is fine and even tell little lies such as "it's not really that bad," but she's nobody's fool.

"Dad, how come Route Michigan was just classified as the most dangerous road in the world if it's not so bad there?"

"Where did you hear that nonsense, Baby?"

"I 'Googled' Route Michigan and a whole bunch of horrible stories came up and that was one of them," she answered hysterically.

"It's not that bad, really. I'm usually in an armored Humvee."

"Dad, I've seen pictures of what's left of some of those Humvee's."

"Sonia, I'm okay. I'm not getting hurt over here, I promise."

I thought, thanks, Google. Thanks a fuckin' lot.

After assuring her I'm still alive and unharmed, she wanted to discuss my mental state. She thinks I might have a hard time readjusting and will suffer from Post Traumatic Stress Disorder (PTSD). I assure her I'm fine and I believe I'm one of those people who will be no worse for wear when I return to my "normal" life. I have nothing but respect for anyone who's done their time over here and I can definitely see why some would have lasting, negative memories from this war but I just don't think I'll be one of them.

Our talk finally left the war and settled in on Seattle, where she lives with friends. I caught up on all the gossip about Willy, Aaron, Bobby, Melissa and many others who I'll probably never meet in person but who would be shocked to know how well I know them. Then we talked about her current boyfriend, Jason. My wife sent me a web-cam so Sonia could actually see me as I was typing messages. Why waste an opportunity to meet her new boyfriend? I convinced her to sit the boy down so he could have a look at me and then I showed him my fighting knife, pistol, rifle, AK-47, and my grenades. You never get a second chance to make a first impression right? Sonia came back on to let me know I could stop with the psycho act but what else is a dad supposed to do?

I laugh when I think of my time with Sonia before I became her father. One day Janet asked me to baby-sit while she walked to the store. At the time, they lived in what the Scottish people called "high flats." Translation: tall apartment buildings. Sonia, age 5 at the time, had a bag of balloons and the temptation was far too great for a ball buster like me. As soon as Janet was out of sight, I introduced Sonia to a great American past-time; water balloon bombs.

We filled a few of them and snuck out onto the balcony.

"Watch this." I whispered and let one drop on a group of kids 15 stories below.

Sonia laughed with delight as the bomb landed with a splash. Naturally, she wanted her turn but I had to explain, dropping too many would result in our capture. She caught on quite well for such a youngster when she pointed out we could do it again from another window on the opposite side of the flat. Then and there, I knew I had a friend for life.

We've never had a problem with the stepfather thing, probably because I never considered myself as anything but her real father and she's such a great kid.

I love my girls beyond all things imaginable and if any boyfriends believe I'm a true nut job with a deadly arsenal of weapons and the skills and training to use them effectively, Hey, what can I say?

**My girls**

Sonia used to get pissed off in high school because whenever she would introduce a new boyfriend I would look him in the eye as I crushed his hand in our initial handshake. I wonder if my latest greeting was as effective as the old handshake.

I said goodbye to my girl and assured her I'd sign on again in a few days to do some more gossiping. Now it's time to turn the switch and get back into combat mode. OOH- RAH!

08 Nov. 2004

Operation Tiger II was supposed to kick off early this morning. I guess we're running out of creative names for these Operations because every one has a part II these days. Oh well, who gives a shit what they're called. Tiger got cancelled because Echo got into heavy shit and we activated a battalion-size QRF, which activated 1st, 3rd, and 4th Platoons. I traveled with 1st Platoon as we mounted up in a hurry and headed out. We often don't know what we'll face until we get there and today was a real treat.

One of Whiskey's Platoons held an intersection at our dismount point, were already in contact just before we got there, took sporadic sniper fire and just lit up and roasted a vehicle packed with explosives.

We quickly dismounted and Fox 6 called the Platoon Commanders together for a quick frag order. As soon as he finished, each platoon got set in their lanes and headed out. We weren't even in any houses yet when all hell broke loose. We took sniper fire before I moved two steps then rockets impacted all around us. The Platoon Commander, Platoon Sgt and Radioman from 4th all got hit. SSgt Kesl had a bunch of shrapnel injuries and both he and the Radioman were urgent surgical medevacs. Lt S. was only routine, but he also had to be evac'd. In fact, this was his first time out since getting blown up on his last operation.

This QRF was a tough one because the movement was restricted to these small, narrow alleyways, which made mutual support difficult at best. The premise is vehicles, with their heavy guns, support the movement of the troops. The troops gain overwatch positions on the rooftops and then support the movement of vehicles. Lt. J moved his boys in his area of responsibility, but we lost sight of each other. He took heavy sniper fire and we couldn't suppress any buildings for him. He moved closer, shrunk his sector of search and we continued with our movement. Enemy snipers took potshots to slow us down as we got close to a sensitive house or area. His tactic is to put one man up to take a semi well-aimed shot.

**Vehicle Patrol in small, narrow alleyways**

We stopped our movement and laid down a shit load of fire at the buildings it came from, but our Muj buddies slipped out the back door.

As we progressed east, two cars came down our alley at a high rate of speed. We didn't have trigger lines set, so SOP is for one of the front riflemen to shoot a warning shot. The vehicles should stop, back up and find another route. At least that's what *we* think they should do. The rear vehicle did exactly what we wanted, put his shit in reverse and got out of Dodge. To our surprise, three men jumped out of the front vehicle and ran down the alley toward us while the vehicle stepped on the gas and kept right on coming. With about 200 meters between them and us, the heavy guns opened up. They stopped it within seconds; a .50 cal and MK-19 tend to have that effect.

The riflemen, me included, concentrated on the assholes running toward us. These weren't typical scared Iraqis running aimlessly, they ran straight at us, moving from one piece of cover to another. I was about 100% convinced they had grenades or were strapped with suicide vests. Two of them went down in a hurry but one of them was smart enough to abandon his attack and run down a side alley. We couldn't pursue because we were ahead of the troops and the vehicle sat there looking very ominous. Suspected VBIEDs tend to do that. There was nothing we could really do about it except check it out once we got up there and even that was a very scary proposition.

For some reason, we held in place for a few hours. It seems on every movement we get to a point where we just sit there in place for God knows what reason. This time, it was nearly two hours and day bled into night. I grabbed Swartz and SSgt D and the three of us moved up to check out the vehicle. There was a dead body directly in front of the vehicle and a dead body in the back seat. SSgt D looked over at me.

"Holy shit, Gunny, there's a little girl in there."

My heart sank right out of my body. Never in my life have I felt shittier. SSGT D frantically tried to get the door open. I thought he lost his mind.

"What the fuck are you doin? Get the fuck away from there," I yelled.

"I gotta get her out of there," he replied and smashed the window.

I finally realized he meant the little girl was still alive. If you don't believe in God, maybe now's the time to start, I thought, there ain't no way anyone or anything should be alive in that vehicle. The .50 cal must have shot 100 rounds and the MK-19 fired a whole can, 32 grenades, on that car. The car should have exploded, or at least caught on fire.

SSGT D reached in and pulled out a little, tiny girl with just a small scratch on her arm. I still felt pretty shitty. She sat in the car on top of a dead body for about three hours without a sound. She must have only been about two years old. Maybe it's wishful thinking, but hopefully she was too young to know better or be traumatized for life over it. I'm mad as shit at the people who were in the car. What the fuck were they thinking? Why would they charge a Marine position with a baby in the car? Why did they get out and charge on foot? I guess I'll never know because stupid dead people can't tell you what they were thinking when they forced you to kill them. I didn't want to kill anyone in a car nor did I plan it. Their actions forced my reaction and the result is they got killed because of it. That may sound like an escape mechanism for my conscience but the truth of the statement is fairly obvious.

I had to call this shit in to Fox 6. Then he had to call it in to battalion. I wish I could've been a fly on the wall when that one came over the net. At the end of the mission, we were ordered to drop the girl off at the Women's and Children's Hospital. Seems as good a place as any if you ask me. We were able to get the wallets and ID's off the dead guys so hopefully they can locate someone in her family to take custody of her.

This will haunt me for a long, long time. We came here to help these people, and in this case, I wonder if I just ruined this little girl's life. I have two daughters of my own who I love beyond words or description. I would never want something terrible to happen to either of them. I thank God every day I live in a country where they can grow up to have every chance at a great life. It's hard for all of us who have families of our own when something like this happens.

We have this job where we fight and kill people nearly every day but we are as "normal" as any other "normal" person. We all have the same hopes, dreams, feelings, fears, you name it. It's just when the time comes, we can put everything aside and do things so beyond the realm of normal I can't explain it and even if I could, no one who has not been there would understand.

When the lieutenant and SSgt went down and got evacuated, the next senior man in the platoon, Corporal Ox, took charge. In order to apprise the Captain of the situation, he crossed about 100 yards of open terrain under heavy fire. The Captain gave him his marching orders and he ran back and briefed the platoon. As soon as they moved out, a well-aimed sniper round hit him right inside of his helmet. The impact was hard enough to knock him on his ass and everyone thought he was killed.

He got up, laughed and dusted himself off. "Well, I guess I'm not dead," and proceeded to lead an attack on the insurgents' house.

In a matter of a few minutes, they killed eight insurgents and continued moving with the rest of the company. This was a crazy day and the first time all platoons were engaged at the same time with different elements of the enemy. Each platoon fought hard and well and each took care of its sector and the insurgents within that sector.

Whether fighting together or separately we can still bring the fight to the enemy. Perhaps the best indicator of a well-disciplined, well-trained unit and once again I am very proud of every man in this company. No one backed down, no one stopped and no one quit. Not even when they get shot in the head!

10 Nov. 2004

Happy Birthday Marine Corps! All Marines around the world will pause and celebrate the 229th birthday of our Corps. Most will be able to dress up in their Blues and take their wives and girlfriends to a Marine Corps Ball ceremony. Others, especially those deployed, will at least have a big dinner, cake cutting ceremony with the reading of the messages and all the trimmings and maybe, even a couple of cold beers and a cigar. We were told we could piggyback with 2/11, an artillery unit, and get in on a big meal with a couple beers of our own. What we got was jack and shit. It seems whoever was in charge of getting all that shit, most importantly, beer, couldn't deliver as promised.

We've had a birthday on this same fuckin' date for 229 goddamn years. It's not like this day just snuck up on us. There is not one Marine in the entire world either active, reserve, retired or just plain out who doesn't know the date of 10 November. If you ever meet a former Marine and ask him the birthday of the Corps, if he doesn't say 10 November, I'll eat my fuckin' hat. Because of the incompetence of some pogue, we will delay the birthday celebration until the 15th. Apparently, they need five more days to get their shit together.

We tried to celebrate by getting in a fight with the enemy when we responded to a QRF call from battalion but that didn't work either because by the time we showed up on the scene, the small battle had pretty much ended. I got no cake, no beers, no kills, no nothing. Some birthday this turned out to be. But the Corps and me are another year older and despite my complaints, another year better. Happy Birthday to my Corps and my brothers in the Corps. I hope the world, or at least, the country takes the time to notice!

* * *

I had time to reflect on some past birthdays. Whenever 10 November rolls around, I remember where I was on my very first Marine Birthday. It's not that hard to remember because I was in Boot Camp. We were only one month into training and not yet thoroughly indoctrinated in love of Corps and country, as the speech goes.

Our Drill Instructors marched our platoon, along with every other swingin' dick on the Depot, to the parade deck for the big ceremony. I didn't really know what was going on, but they said we were going to the birthday celebration. In the cartoon land that made up my brain at the time, I had visions of songs, presents, cakes and all the other fun shit associated with a birthday party.

We were put into a formation and we stood at attention while the band played, speeches made and Commandant's messages were read. It was supposed to wrap up with the playing and singing of the Marines Hymn.

Why, oh why, did a platoon of sand fleas decide to have a formation of their own inside my ear at that particular time? And why, oh why, did I decide to scratch my ear right as our meanest DI looked at me. From the way they acted afterward, I might as well have unbuttoned my trousers and took a piss on the parade deck. I was called everything from a communist infiltrator to a dope smoking hippie. Every DI in the company came down and took turns chewing my ass and taking me to the sand pit.

As I lay in bed that night, sure I would be expelled from the island the following morning, I thought, these guys sure don't know how to throw a fuckin' party. There was a whole lot I didn't yet know about the Marine Corps and why these guys took their birthday so seriously.

**Home at Marine Corps Birthday Ball**

12 Nov. 2004

Operation Destroyer, with the entire brigade, had a little bit of everything out there; tanks, air, mounted and dismounted troops, the whole ball of wax. I traveled with 4th Platoon and paired with none other than Lt. S, the Shrapnel Magnet. He's the most low-key Platoon Commander of the bunch but he has good control and doesn't try to do too much. He allows his NCOs to run their show and he has a pretty cool head. He's come a long way since I first met him when I checked into the unit. Back then I thought he was indifferent and way too timid. Maybe he was but he's got his shit together now. He's a little spazzed about the IED thing but who wouldn't be?

Marines have this funny way of busting balls about everything. Nothing is safe, nothing is sacred, especially if you have the bad habit of getting blown up on every operation.

Before we stepped off, Lt. J yelled to Lt. S, "Hey Sipes, I'll come visit you at Charlie Med when the mission is over."

Charlie Med is the Army triage clinic where casualties are treated and they know Lt S on a first-name basis.

The route we drove today was no picnic and chances were better than 50-50 someone would end up there. Route Nova is at the extreme northern end of our sector and probably the preferred avenue of approach for all Muj vehicles. It's supposed to be pretty IED intensive so all we can do is be vigilant and hope we spot them before they spot us.

The mission proceeded along nicely and soon 2nd platoon had a righteous bust going. They bagged six assholes who had weapons, ammunition, pro-Saddam propaganda and an absolute shit-load of high speed surveillance equipment. Suddenly, a call came in that 3rd Platoon got the 7-ton stuck in a mud hole. I went back to check it out and the vehicle was buried up to the undercarriage and canted at a 45-degree angle. It was bad, real bad. We tried to pull it out but it wasn't going anywhere so I called Fox 6 and asked him to call battalion and request a tank recovery vehicle, an M-88 tank retriever if I'm correct. That's the only vehicle with enough ass to pull this thing out of the hole.

**7-Ton Sideways**

Of course, it had to be 3rd Platoon that got it stuck, it just fuckin' had to be them. Three hours later and we were ready to move again. Luckily, we didn't cock up the entire brigade movement because we tried to stay somewhat on line and the units to our south, Golf and Echo, moved a lot slower than us. As we prepared to drive forward and secure our final street, Swartz noticed a funny looking rock pile on the corner. He swore that it just didn't look right and that it might be an IED.

"Gunny, those rocks and shit look different than they did earlier."

"Well, we gotta keep moving, drive wide around that corner."

The vehicle behind us didn't pay attention and cut the corner a lot tighter and an IED exploded right near their vehicle.

Now how's this for luck? The other day I was mad as hell when 3rd Platoon tried to kill me with that piece of shit vehicle. When the mission ended, I sent Smalls, one of my HQ Goons, straight to the Seabee's to get it armored up. It came back late last night with welded up doors and higher sides with thicker armor. The doors and high armor on the side took the brunt of the hit and I'm happy as hell to say that not a single Marine got so much as a scratch. Looks like I owe the Navy boys a bottle of booze when I can get my hands on one.

We had too many people, so the Muj didn't come out to play, as usual, but it's still a scary place to live or hang out. We chase insurgents around and find a lot of shit but it seems we only scratch the surface.

In Fallujah, the Marines know where the enemy is and are only waiting for the go ahead to get in there and kick his ass. Here, a bunch of them come and go and hide among the citizens. How are we supposed to tell the difference between them and anyone else? I honestly think after two months of blood, sweat, and tears, this place is no safer or secure than when we got here. If we continue to operate as we do now, it will be no better when we leave and someone else takes over.

13 Nov. 2004

Operation Tiger II…again. I gotta believe whoever makes up the names for these missions failed creative writing. This is the third Operation Tiger, or maybe it's the fourth, but we really need a new name…or at least a new goddamn animal. I rode with 1st Platoon, which was fine by me. This time we did a hard hit on a house and then cleared through the neighborhood. Sort of the same old thing but at least we combined our sweep with a raid.

The other day our aerial surveillance plane spotted the enemy running away from the fight and into some of the houses we hit today. Our mission was to detain all males from age 16 through 60 so the Intel weenies could get a crack at them.

We hit the first group of houses without contact then we got a call from the second house over the radio from the squad leader on the scene. He had a suspicious male in the house, claiming to be an Iraqi Police Officer. Last week, we were briefed that real IPs do not have beards. It's against the dress code. The squad leader remembered and reported this guy had a nice Santa Claus. We decided to bag him up and drag him along. As luck would have it, we ran into a police Captain in another house. We asked him to come out and see if this guy was legit or not. Guess what? The guy was an imposter with a fake ID. Score one for the quick thinking squad leader.

The people in this neighborhood were pretty friendly and the kids were out saying pro-American things like, "Yes Bush, No Saddam!" I had a big bag of toys and trinkets in my trunk and it's been a while since I passed any out to the kids. I gave some away and pretty soon every kid on the street came over. It felt good to be able to be nice for a change and to see the little kids smile and get their little gifts. We didn't hang around for any particular or tactical reason for

10 or 12 more hours and we called it a day and went back to base.

That made four missions in five days. My vehicles need a lot of work and my old ass needs a day off. Of course, a day off around here only means no mission. There is still plenty of shit to do and I'm sure we'll be right back out there for extended operations in no time. I really, really need a full day of laying on my big comfortable couch and plenty of cold beers. Four more months. Three have gone by fast so let's hope the next four hurry the hell up, too.

* * *

Although there are many hardships and sacrifices with my chosen profession, there are also many benefits. One of the great ones of my career was being stationed on the island of Oahu from 1996 to 2000. Janet's Mother, nephew, sister and Sonia's friend, Melanie, flew from Belfast for a visit one summer. We did the entire tourist stops required when your family flies 10,000 miles to visit but when you have local knowledge you learn how to avoid the crowds and go to the best places at the optimum times.

We spent one day snorkeling at Hanauma Bay and I took turns going out with the girls and Janet. Hawaii is such an amazing place but when you can enjoy it with your children, it's 100 times more special and spectacular. We chased after dozens of species of bright and beautiful fish and even fed them from our hands. While Danielle and I explored in the shallow water, a sea turtle floated past and she pointed, laughed and squealed with delight. Afterwards, we all went out to eat and we ended the evening on the balcony of our hotel looking at the moon over the Pacific Ocean.

I suppose every family has memories like mine but what I realized during this tour of hell is I never sit back and simply remember the great times of my life. I will gladly leave a lot of this place behind me but I hope I remember to put my hectic life on pause from time to time and relive memories of having fun with the people I love.

14 Nov. 2004

I was supposed to rest today but 1st and 2nd were tasked with a mission so I jumped in the command vehicle with the CO. We went up north to recon another site for a possible OP. While we were there, we searched a bunch of buildings so the Muj don't catch on to what we're up to. If they see us using an area more than once they will wire it with explosives. Therefore, we had to make this look like any other mission. The site we originally went to see was, for lack of a better word - shit, but we came up with a great replacement. This new spot will enable us to lock down the North Bridge into Ramadi and give us vision about 1000 meters down Route Nova.

We made a very hasty search and reconnaissance of the place and then headed back into camp. All in all it was a two-hour mission. I could definitely get used to that. When we got back into camp we got word that

H&S Company had a convoy attacked with a SVBIED right outside of the base. These pricks are getting very ballsy, very desperate or both. Luckily, it was set off far enough away from the vehicle and no one was seriously injured. Sgt Boros, our motor pool mechanic, got the worst of it with hand and arm injuries. I heard he was in the turret, behind the gun, when the blast occurred. Why our best mechanic was behind a turret gun I'll never know. A few days ago, I was pretty pissed at 3rd for hanging me out to dry and the same argument holds here. If a mechanic, and a good one at that, has to go on a convoy then he should be very protected.

Vehicles go down at the cyclic rate and we *absolutely* cannot afford to lose any mechanics. We have Intel of a very elevated SVBIED threat. I think this is because they no longer have the Boxcar to attack and we're keeping them off balance with our AO shift. Desperate times call for desperate measures so our enemy willingly uses this attack with more regularity. I also think he's getting frustrated with our armored vehicles holding up so well to his IEDs. I guess we'll have to wait and see and then adapt, once again, against our ever-changing enemy.

15 Nov. 2004

The worst goddamn day of this deployment. Captain Rapicault, Whiskey 6, was killed by an SVBIED as his company was coming home from a mission. They were almost back inside of friendly lines when the bomber drove his vehicle right up alongside the Capt.'s vehicle and detonated his payload with a massive explosion. We were in the gym on JC, at least a mile away, and we felt the whole building shake. We thought we received incoming mortar rounds.

When we finished working out, we went back to our hooches and Doc Chavez told us what happened. At first, he said three Marines from Whiskey were killed in the vehicle. Then he found out one of them was Capt. Rap. I don't know why, but you just never expect to hear one of the COs was killed. They're usually right there with us, and Capt Rap was ***always*** with his Marines, and in no less danger, but it just doesn't seem likely.

Initially, I was stunned and in a state of disbelief. I talked to Capt. Rap a few days ago. He came over to me at HP. "How you doing, Gunny. You all right?"

We were together when we watched Lt. L die in the operating room as the corpsmen tried to save him. He was devastated at losing one of his lieutenants.

"I'm okay, Sir. How's the boys?"

"They're good. We'll be okay."

If I knew that would be my last conversation with a man I had tremendous respect for, I would have told him I thought he was a great Marine. But you never fuckin' know over here! He never worried about himself, just his Marines. That's the way it was with him and why I liked him. He only had command for a few months and already his boys would follow him anywhere. The SNCOs thought the world of him and that's good enough for me.

The sadness and disbelief were quickly followed

by anger when I thought of how Capt. Rap became the Whiskey Company Commander. The previous Capt. took the coward's way out. That guy couldn't command because he worried about himself and his own safety. He kept thinking about his wife and kids every time he left the safety of the base and couldn't concentrate on the job.

Well no fuckin' shit! Not one, not fuckin' one married Marine or sailor with a wife, kids or both doesn't think about that. We all think about being killed and how it will affect our families. That's why we get extra life insurance and do our wills before we deploy. We all know the risks and accept them, especially those of us in leadership billets.

I'm sorry it had to be this way Capt. Rap, and I salute you! You were a man's man and a Marine's Marine. If I make it out of here, I'll drink my first beer in your honor and I'll think about all of your Marines 'cause that's the way you'd want it.

This day started so well and ended like this. We had the Colonel and Sgt Major over this morning to do yet another Purple Heart ceremony. We pinned 10 more on our guys today, mostly from the IED attack a few weeks ago. That makes 25 purple hearts so far, and just think, we're not even halfway finished.

16 Nov. 2004

I had a rough night last night and therefore, due to lack of sleep, I was very irritated when the Captain came in and said we had to go out on a mission to clean the rest of the debris from the SVBIED off the street. Even though the street is in our sector, it just pissed me off to go out on such a bullshit mission. Plus, I didn't want to clean up chunks of the bombers body and parts of his car. But, orders are orders so I got my shit together and off we went.

To get to our sector, we have to cross over a narrow bridge. Usually, we scare all traffic off the bridge and secure the route to get us rolling into town. Because of the VBIED threat, we absolutely do not want to sit in any traffic or drive alongside any other vehicles. Our two lead vehicles turned out of the gate and headed up toward the bridge when a vehicle pulled off to the side of the road to let us all pass. As the other vehicles pushed across, this car stepped on the gas and tried to jump right in our convoy. This is exactly how Whiskey 6 was killed yesterday.

The army sentry on post at the top of the bridge opened fire and Beeker slammed on the brakes. Sgt D and I quickly jumped out and put several rounds through the rear windshield. This was effective enough to stop him and between Sgt D, myself and the Army sentry, we probably killed him. There was an extremely intense couple of seconds as the vehicle came to a stop right at the beginning of the bridge and my heart stopped as two of our vehicles had no choice but to push right past him.

Fox 6 yelled at me, "Gunny, put some 203 rounds into that fuckin' car!"

You don't have to tell me twice, I thought, and sighted in. About to let fly, he screamed, "Gunny, hold your fire. Hold your fire!"

The car stopped right under the army post at the top of the bridge. If the car was packed with explosives, it would be real dangerous for the Army sentries. We were in a really tight spot, cut off from the rest of the convoy, army sentries trapped above us, and what could be a SVBIED sitting on the bridge.

Fox 6 yelled at me, "Go see if that guy is fucking dead. "If you see a gun or any type of explosives or a trigger device, shoot that fucker in the head."

I worked my way into position and sighted in with my rifle but the guy was clearly dead.

As we sat there, an Army convoy rolled up and helped us secure the area. Lucky for us, because we were alone, exposed and unable to cover all directions. The only thing to do at a time like that was call battalion and let them figure out the next step. They sent some Iraqi Police (IP) down to inspect the car and deal with the body. The IPs showed up, got the body out, loaded it into their car and drove away. They said the only thing in the car were dead sheep, in the trunk, no less. I was blown up a few weeks ago with an IED in the form of a dead dog so I was pretty suspicious of dead sheep in the trunk.

Battalion called the Explosive Ordnance Disposal Team (EOD) to deal with the car. They were worried about blowing it up and causing damage to the bridge so the Master Sergeant decided to use some sort of water bomb.

"I never heard of a water bomb. What the hell is that?" I asked.

"Gunny, it's a great bomb," he said. "It'll only destroy the vehicle and nothing else."

"Well, shit buddy, you're the bomb expert. I don't

really care what you do, I just want to cross the fuckin' bridge."

"Trust me, in two minutes that won't look like a car and it'll be safe to cross."

A robot dragged this little cart with two plastic trashcans full of water and parked it next to the car and came back. Ten seconds later, the bomb went off and a massive explosion completely disintegrated the car. It turned into a shell of metal and four flat tires that barely looked like a car anymore. We went up to the wreck, hooked a tow strap to the frame and dragged that hunk of metal off the bridge.

Meanwhile, some numb-nuts in a white Mercedes with tinted windows drove past the HP gate and opened fire with an AK-47, the preferred weapon of our enemy, which makes a distinct sound when fired. He drove off to make his escape but he never left sight of the sentry at HP. He went into hiding in a house and we were ordered to go snatch the asshole.

Quick as shit, we rolled into the neighborhood and took down a complex where the moron parked the Mercedes. The sentries at HP guided us to the house, we went through the door like shit through a goose and had four males on their faces in about ten seconds. We confiscated a bunch of weapons, bomb making material, other contraband and the prisoners.

**Not bad for a half hour of work.**

We took the assholes back to HP, debriefed the colonel and rolled back to JC. I told Fox 6, "If this is street cleaning, you can sign me up for as many of these missions as you want."

17 Nov. 2004

What began as a 2nd Platoon mission quickly escalated into a battalion-sized operation. 2nd Platoon had a simple mission of mapping out some routes in our AO. One thing we learned back at the Outpost, we have to know the neighborhoods inside and out, especially the roads. We have to be able to move around without setting patterns and we can't get lost or stuck on a mission.

We heard Echo Company, off to our east, heavily engaged and the Government Center was also under attack. Was either of the positions being overrun? Was a company taking casualties and in need of assistance or resupply? No, to both. But every time a platoon fires a round, their whole company gets involved. If a company is engaged, against a squad-sized element of the enemy, we activate the whole damn battalion.

I'm not the Battalion Commander, and respect the hell out of our Battalion Commander, but even the Lcpls and Cpls make jokes about how we respond to every firefight by getting the battalion on line.

The two fights occurred north of Route Michigan and the fighting sounded intense. Of course, I've seen Golf Company pump about 4,000 rounds into a building in response to sniper fire and we're no slouches when it comes to expending ammunition either. All of the fighting happened in the north, and we were sent to Buckeye and Sunset, way down south. We stayed out there all goddamn day and did absolutely no fighting and didn't even get a sniff of action. Then we sat at our Limit of Advance (LOA) for a few hours and waited for the call to come home.

Oh well, I'm not the Battalion CO and I'm not trying to be. Maybe we're doing what we need to do in order to keep as many Marines as we can from being hurt or killed. I know that as a battalion, we don't seem to be as aggressive as what I think we should be. We're Marines, let's locate, close in and destroy the enemy, goddammit!

18 Nov. 2004

We conducted a company operation in the very far northeastern sector of our AO, near where Echo was in the shit yesterday. This was not so much of a search as a movement to contact. The difference between the two is movement to contact means we just move through and see if we can pick a fight.

The reporter who interviewed us at the Combat Outpost recently aired his special report. He had an interesting viewpoint and reported on the NBC news our technique is to use ourselves as bait in order to get in a fight. I guess you can look at it that way but how else are we gonna' find and kill these pricks? It's not like they wear Muj uniforms or fly Muj flags over their houses. Moms were not happy when they watched that special. Thanks for comforting our families, dickhead.

I traveled with 4th Platoon and we patrolled the same sector we went through for Operation Destroyer. I knew the route like the back of my hand. I especially remembered not to get my 7-ton stuck in shit creek. We found a few things along the way and grabbed a few detainees. The most notable; one house had bricks stacked up along the wall and a Marine noticed a plastic bag barely sticking out behind the brick. We unstacked a few bricks, pulled out the bag and dumped it out. Inside was the favorite headwear of the Mujahadeen; black ski masks. We pulled this asshole out of his house, "What's up with the little hidey-hole, buddy?" I asked.

"I didn't know it was there. I don't know anything about masks. They are not mine." He responded, in typical liar fashion.

"Why are these masks hidden in the wall of your house?' the interpreter asked.

"I don't know. It's not mine. I didn't know a hole was there. I didn't see anyone put those there."

Now there's a shocker. Here I thought, we found a homeowner who actually knew what went on in and around his house. Maybe getting detained and thrown in jail will jog his memory. We put the asshole in the truck and continued moving.

We made it to Tower Road and as we prepared to cross, a sniper shot rang out. Cpl. P from 1st Platoon was hit in the lower back. 1st Platoon responded Golf Company style and pumped a shit-load of rounds into the building. They also pumped a few SMAW rounds into it just for good measure.

Doc Chavez got over to Cpl. P and luckily the round deflected a little and didn't penetrate all the way through his back. We found out later his flak jacket took some of the punch away. Since we were already at the LOA and wanted to get Cpl. P back to medical, we called it a day and headed back to JC. My vehicle took the lead because we were most familiar with the route back.

**Cpl P shot by sniper**

As we turned the first corner, a guy came flying down on a motorcycle, jumped off and ran. Me and Boot Garcia, 4th Plt. Radioman, ran up to the roof of the nearest house and saw this guy running like hell. I tried to draw on bead on him but he turned the corner and I lost sight of him. I told the lieutenant the guy was gone and we decided right there this must be an IED.

"Sir, why would anyone park a motorcycle in our path and run off?"

"I don't know Gunny, but we can't stop here. Take it out."

Orders like that are sweet, sweet music to my ears. I took a shot at the gas tank with a tracer round and it caught on fire. Why stop there when you have a grenade launcher? I fired a 203 round at it for shits and giggles and it made a nice explosion but not as big as if an IED was strapped to it. God only knows why this moron rode down and decided to park his bike in the path of a Marine convoy but the result is one less asshole driving around Ramadi tonight.

20 Nov. 2004

The army had to finally do a mission in their sector of town and they wanted us to secure the bridges to ensure no one could drive into town during their operation. We used two platoons and the Mobile QRF and secured the North Bridge, South Bridge and Route Michigan. It took all of ten minutes to set our roadblocks and trigger lines and the Command Vehicle, with me in it, sat behind the safety of a large HESCO barrier for the next five hours. No cars were stupid or crazy enough to approach our positions. This was without doubt the most pointless and boring mission since arriving in Iraq.

When we have company missions, the CO, 1stSgt and myself each ride or move with a different platoon for obvious reasons. Usually, unless I'm with 3rd Platoon, I will get a gun truck, with Swartz as my driver and Crazy Mike the gunner. The CO and 1st Sgt have their own permanent gun truck with Beeker their driver, Sgt Hobbs their gunner and PFC Barb their radio operator.

Now that we've moved to JC, the vehicles and missions are manned a bit differently. We have a platoon out on OP for 24 hours at a time and are supported by their own Mobile QRF, which consists of four vehicles. We also have a Mission Platoon, a QRFA Platoon and a QRFB Platoon. The Mission Platoon is tasked with going out in our AO and conducting one or two platoon-sized missions per day. They have the Mobile QRF and the QRFA in support, if needed. The MQRF is already out there, very close in proximity and response time and the QRFA is pre-staged at HP on a five minute alert.

The QRFB has a day off because they have no vehicles left to get them off base and into the fight. If we are having a normal day of operations, the only attachment to the QRFA is the Command Vehicle. Since the QRFA goes out every day, whether to pre-stage or in actual response, the 1stSgt would be out all day, every day. If he did this, he would never get any work done on the 1stSgt level, which does not stop just because of combat.

Therefore, we decided to alternate days of riding in the Command Vehicle. One day on and one day off, not counting company missions, which we have every third day or so. That way we do missions one day and concentrate on our no-shit jobs and responsibilities the next. This is where the Goons come into play because I heavily rely on these guys to help keep my head above water. Crazy Mike and Beeker take care of all vehicle issues from assignments, cleaning, maintenance, mechanic issues, stocking, arming and so forth. Smalls has come into play with the vehicles for armor upgrades with the Navy Seabees. Reyno and Smalls take care of all issues with the Armory and all company weapons and serialized gear. Reyno drives the ambulance with Doc on all company missions. Ski and Barb take care of all comm. and radio issues. Swartz, the Police Sgt, is responsible for all gear, supplies and everything else around camp in addition to driving for me on all missions. Sgt D rounds out the crew of Goons and he's my go-to guy for everything else I have or have not mentioned.

These guys are a great crew, get along well and have great personalities. I wish I could tote them around with me for the rest of my career. The key to having a great company is to build a great HQ unit to run all the little things that go unnoticed and unappreciated. Most other Marines think the Goons get over because they're not out on post and doing all the little things the platoons have to do. I'm sorry to say even the NCOs and some SNCOs don't see the role these guys play in running the company.

I'm here to tell you, we have a great HQ unit, which in turn, leads to an awesome company. Of course, I never tell the Goons these things. I constantly tell them the only crew worse than them is the bunch of retards who work for Tony Soprano. And, at least, Soprano's goons pay the proper tributes!

21 Nov 2004

Operation South Side at Buckeye and Sunset was once again a battalion-sized operation. Lt. J asked the CO if I could be attached to his platoon because SSgt Flammang got evac'd back to the States. He went to the BAS with a lump in his abdominal area, a possible tumor on his pancreas, and was immediately flown to Baghdad, then to Germany and off to a stateside hospital. Of all the ways to get injured and evac'd over here, he gets sent off with a tumor.

The Lt. wanted me to show SSgt D how to run the tactical side of a vehicle movement and to keep an eye on him until he got his feet wet as the new Platoon Sergeant. Not a big deal because this is what a company has a Gunny for anyway. Long before we took over the logistical bullshit for our companies, Gunny's were primarily the duty experts on all things weapons and for training the NCOs and junior SNCOs.

We arrived at Sunset and a car slowly creeped toward our position with a lone, young, male driver. I thought, suicide bomber. I took a warning shot and put out one of his tires. Did the idiot stop? No, of course not. If I were driving and an armed soldier pointed a gun at me and shot out my tires, I would drive right on up to him and ask him "What the fuck's happenin' man?" He kept creeping closer so I shot another tire. Now he's down to two rims so did he stop? We all know the answer.

He continued to come and waved a white flag out the window. Like this isn't a popular trick with these fuckers.

"Sir, I'm about to put one between this guy's

running lights and I don't mean the fuckin' vehicle," I said to the lieutenant.

Luckily for this moron, the interpreter came and shouted in Iraqi to stop, get out and slowly walk toward us with his hands up.

"What is so fuckin' important that you kept driving toward us while we were shooting at you," I had the interpreter ask.

"I didn't know what you wanted me to do so I was driving closer to find out," the dipshit replied.

"How about this you retarded bastard? If someone shoots at you and shouts at you as you get closer to them, that's the international signal for go the fuck away. Now get the fuck out of here and tell your friends."

22 Nov. 2004

Today we had a two-in-one mission. We wanted to check out a building on Nova for a possible new OP site. We brought along some engineers and other experts to see if what we wanted was plausible. Civil Affairs Group (CAG) wanted to come along and make nice-nice at this big water treatment plant, part of their ongoing effort to help with matters of infrastructure. We decided letting CAG do their thing would be good cover while we did ours. Plus, we could take a look around the grounds of the facility because it's well known, our piece of shit enemy has infiltrated all aspects of this new bullshit government.

We went into the water treatment plant and right away I had a bad feeling. About thirty or so employees hung around and only two or three looked like they actually worked there. Six of them were IPs or claimed to be, and another three were on-site security guards. Maybe you need a lot of security at a water plant, who knows?

We started our search while CAG went with the chief engineer to see if the place was up to snuff. We checked all the buildings and initially didn't turn up anything suspicious. We came to the last building and planned to leave as soon as we cleared it. The security guard with the keys acted suspicious because he claimed not to have the key for this building. It was locked with a big chain and padlock and we could see inside the windows. No other buildings were locked and there didn't seem to be anything in this one in need of a lock. Finally, one of the Marines grabbed the keys, tried them all and sure enough, one of them opened the fuckin' door.

Sgt Dom. went in while one of the PFC's held onto this guy by the scruff while they searched the joint. They lifted one of the steel grates on the floor,

*"Holy shit, what is this? What, the fuck, is this Pvt. Pyle?"*

It was definitely not a jelly fucking donut but the biggest weapons cache we have found yet in this fucked up city. On initial inspection, just sitting under the steel floor grates was a machine gun, loaded, with a box of ammo attached, 7 RPGs, a few AK-47s, a few RPKs, bags of ammo and magazines. The green light flashed to tear the place apart.

I went in, lifted a floor grate and found another loaded machine gun and spare barrels. There were several cylindrical canisters on a shelf and as I looked in these, found pretty sophisticated trigger devices for IEDs and a gas mask. Let me tell you, when you find gas masks, the pucker factor goes way, way up.

We started a detailed search of the grounds and shit turned up all over the place. Rockets, bags of TNT, fuses, more rockets, 21 artillery shells, more guns, ammo, and explosive type shit. This was a big fuckin' cache and time to turn up the heat on these fuckers.

I grabbed the interpreter and the so-called head of security and we took him off to the side.

"You have exactly two fuckin' seconds to tell me what's going on here or you're going to Abu Ghraib," I said.

What those piece of shit army fuckers did was wrong, but mentioning Abu Ghraib scares the living shit out of these fuckers.

"There are two, big, very important Mujahadeen pretending to be security guards. You have the one who had the keys. The other is Mahmoud. He's sitting with the rest of the employees," my new best pal replied.

He wouldn't finger the guy because, "They'll kill my family if they know I told you."

I went to the head engineer, the boss of this place, and told him to divide the group up into who no-shit works there and gets paid by him and who does not.

"If I find out you're lying to me or helping these fuckers, I'm gonna stomp your fuckin' head in," I diplomatically explained.

There were nine legitimate employees, nine were IPs or security guards and four high-ranking government employees with credentials from the Governor. I had eight more assholes to detain and Mahmoud the terrorist. They were all getting detained, but I wanted to separate this Mahmoud bastard from the rest of the group.

I walked over to the nine of them and this one small, squirrelly looking punk gave me the stink eye. I grabbed the little bastard by the head, jerked him to his feet and introduced myself, "Hello, Mahmoud."

**Muj and cache at water treatment plant**

I got the asshole on the first try. He was so shocked I knew his name he didn't even deny it or resist. I spent the next hour reading these fuckers the riot act while 1st platoon tore the place apart. We concluded with our biggest cache to date and took nine of those fuckers to jail for further interrogation by the experts. Sometimes the biggest finds come when you least expect them.

25 Nov. 2004

Happy Thanksgiving. Everywhere in America, families are getting together to celebrate with a huge meal, maybe many beers, and definitely some football watching. If you're lucky, you get to do all three.

I remember a particular Thanksgiving at home when the Tracy family flew East for my sister's wedding. Going home is always a special occasion and being there for a holiday like Thanksgiving made it really special. Everyone had an amazing time at her great wedding. My sister went off on her honeymoon but everyone else stayed long enough for the big turkey dinner.

All my life we had Thanksgiving dinners at my Mom and Dad's house and my Mom's sisters and their families always joined us. This year, all the kids showed up with kids of their own and we had a full house.

The family tradition at my mother's house, the men watch football until the meal is ready and then we say grace, eat until we can't move and roll back to the couch to watch more football. After the recovery nap, we bust out the cards and play poker while downing ice cold beers. I love Thanksgiving at home, for the obvious reasons, but when I'm in my Mom's house with my own family intact, I think I'm one of the very few who really understand the true meaning of giving thanks.

* * *

In Ramadi, we celebrated by going on Operation Turkey Hunt. Today, we went across the street from the water plant in a large area made up mostly of open farmland that continues to the banks of the historic Euphrates River.

Most people, including me, think of Iraq as this vast, Arabian-type desert with sand, camels and all that bullshit. Parts of Iraq may be exactly that but Ramadi is mostly a huge, urban city like any other city, except dirtier and full of scumbags trying to kill me.

The parts not urban are farmlands and marshy areas just like any other area near any other huge river in any other part of the world. As soon as you cross Route Nova, the city stops. There are a few ramshackle farmer's huts and one or two places of business, but it's mostly palm trees, farmland and thick vegetation, more like the rice paddies of Viet Nam.

Our mission was to start in the east, past Tower Road and move west to Ice Street; a dismounted foot movement of about 2000 meters. We asked Whiskey Company to come along and secure Route Nova so we would only have to worry, fight and move in one direction; west. Whiskey screened our left flank, the Euphrates protected our right, and we began our movement west.

The pain in the ass aspect to this operation was the ever changing time of departure. The Army put together a huge Thanksgiving feast and we sure as shit didn't want to miss out. They were having the meal from 1230 to 1530, so for the third and final time, we decided on a 0630 departure and a 1200 finish. Something else unusual about Ramadi, it's Fuckin'-A cold at 0630 on November 25th. I'm talking see your breath, wear your scarf and gloves cold.

The purpose of the mission was to search for

weapons caches. We're always ready for contact but because of the lack of houses and such, we really didn't expect any. Suddenly, bullets whizzed and cracked over our heads. Mikey's platoon took the fire and his boys responded quickly and accurately. Within seconds, they charged a small complex. A few of the boys threw stun grenades into a few of the trailers and within two minutes they had four enemies down and cuffed with one bleeding nicely from a gunshot wound.

As I arrived on the scene, they ripped apart the offices of the Al Jihad Trucking Company. It would seem the Jihad boys tried to live up to the company name. Naturally, they played the innocent Iraqis, but they were a little stupider than the average idiot. There were no other buildings or people in the whole damn area. Just to be sure, I busted out the gunpowder test kit and sure enough, two positive hits.

We conducted a thorough search of the area and uncovered several AK-47s, an SKS rifle, another automatic weapon and a shit-load of magazines and ammunition.

"Time to go to jail, boys," I said while admiring the nice bullet hole through one guy's arm.

We brought along the military working dog, an expert at sniffing out explosives, and he had a good old time. He went to a safe in the office and sat his ass right down which means explosives are in or were in the safe. I grabbed the engineers and told them to get the thing open. The first try was unsuccessful so we doubled our C-4 and put it under the safe. Bad move! This thing *Blew The Fuck Up*. When the smoke cleared, there was no more safe. Oh well, at least we got it open, in a manner of speaking.

When we finished with the complex and loaded up the prisoners, we continued west. The area 1st Platoon traveled was completely open and without cover so they mounted up and headed down the road about 300 meters. 2nd Platoon had cover so they continued west, mostly along the riverbank.

As 2nd Platoon neared a farmer's house, he waved them over and said there were weapons and such being brought across the river from the north and buried all along the riverbank behind his house. He claimed he waited for someone to come around someday so he could point it out. The skeptic in me said, he's full of shit. He saw us coming and knew we'd find it so he played it off to keep from going to jail. However, he gave us info and was extremely cooperative and informative.

2nd platoon dug up the largest weapons cache found in Ramadi since 2/5 has been here and quite probably the largest cache found at one site by one platoon since the war began.

There was so much explosives damaged or unstable, along with many of the mortars, rockets and fuses, we decided to detonate a whole shit load right there. Luckily, we had a squad of engineers and the Battalion Gunner along so I let the experts fuck with that shit. After they rigged it all up, they popped smoke and ran as far as two minutes of time fuse allows. That explosion was even better than the day with the water bomb. It even made a nice mushroom cloud that could be seen from miles around. I thought blowing up the safe would be my demolitions highlight of the mission but that was baby shit compared to this.

**Euphrates Cache**
**So big, it wouldn't fit in one picture**

It took so long to dig everything up and sort it all out we missed the Thanksgiving meal but they had a repeat meal for evening chow. In the end, we really didn't miss a thing and got all that shit off the streets and out of the enemy's hands. What a great way to spend Thanksgiving.

To cap it all off, Gordon England, the Secretary of the Navy, paid us a visit. He came over to meet and shake hands with the Marines and was pretty impressed with our work for the day. He seemed down to earth and straightforward for a politician. He said he viewed us defending our country in one of two ways. We could make a goal line stand on our own five-yard line and try to keep the enemy from scoring or we could be on the enemy five-yard line and let him try to keep us from scoring; The old 'a good offense is the best defense' theory. I, for one, agree with him!

26 Nov. 2004

With nothing to do but sit around fat and happy after our big day and huge feast, I decided to spend the day catching up with my family on the messenger and all my friends by both e-mail and regular mail. My friends keep sending all sorts of encouraging messages and well wishes over e-mail. Mostly, it's just a few lines to say hello but a few words from home are immeasurable. I'm not sure if all those who contact us will ever know how much we appreciate every little thought, prayer and letter.

Although contact with our families is easily the best and most favored correspondence, I am absolutely overwhelmed by the kindness of strangers. We get so many letters and care packages the stuff is filling up our hooches and even our shipping containers. I am certain the troops are supported to a degree unprecedented in history. Literally, if all packages stopped today, there would still be stuff left over for a couple of years. And we haven't even begun to receive the Christmas packages yet.

My undisputed favorite mail is from the schoolchildren around America. If I had no other reason to defend everything our country is about and stands for in this world, all I would have to do is read any random letter from any random child. My father recently retired but out of boredom took a part-time job as a janitor at a local school. To say one of the classes and their teacher has adopted me would be a gross understatement. I receive cards, letters, drawings, pictures and packages almost monthly. All the kids tell me I'm their hero and they pray for me and hope I come home safe. Then they get into the serious stuff like "Who's your favorite Sponge Bob character, mine's Squidward" and "What's your favorite food, mine's pizza" And believe it or not… "How many bad guys did you kill?"

I told my father I had a flag signed by every man in the company and would personally deliver it when I came home. I don't think the response could have been any better if I told them I was taking them all to Disneyland. No matter what happens in this war, I'll always remember who I am, where I'm from and that thousands upon thousands of people are in my corner.

29 Nov. 2004

We're well rested after a four day vacation of sorts without battalion missions and QRFs for the past few days. This gave everyone the chance to unwind a bit. There's not much to do for entertainment, but Marines find ways to relax and unwind even in combat. Mostly, they stay inside their hooches and play cards, watch dvd's, play Nintendo, write letters and do laundry. We have to wash our clothes by hand and hang them out to dry, which pretty much sucks. Surprisingly, morale is good. Grunts don't ask for much, don't get much and rarely complain in combat.

One of my favorite sayings is; "Marines are not trained to be miserable, they are trained to endure misery." Amen, brother!

We still feel pretty good about the big cache we found on the 25th but it's time to get back out and either find more weapons or the people stashing them. Tonight we conducted Operation Shocker, a double raid on two separate targets. 2nd Platoon raided a house up on the north end of our sector near Route Nova while 1st Platoon hit a house right off Route Michigan.

2nd Platoon's target was an IP Major who apparently supplies the Muj with weapons. 1st Platoon's target was a house where the Muj holds meetings. 2nd looked for one specific person while 1st took down everyone in the house.

I went with 1st Platoon once again. It seems I've been with them on every mission since SSgt Flammang got evac'd. I don't mind, but I'm worried the lieutenant keeps asking for me because he doesn't trust his young Staff Sergeant. I'll talk to him about it later.

1st is a great platoon but if the lieutenant doesn't trust his SSgt, the troops will pick up on it and quickly become a bunch of disrespectful shitheads. There is a delicate balance of leadership in an infantry platoon. The good platoons have balance and the bad ones do not. It's that simple. The SSgt is the senior enlisted Marine in the platoon and responsible for discipline, development of the NCOs, training, administration, accountability, and pretty much everything else. He also has daunting responsibility of training and mentoring his lieutenant. If a platoon sucks and the lieutenant is all fucked up, the blame lies squarely with the SSgt

Occasionally, you run into *that guy* who apparently learned everything he ever needed to know at college and MOS school, but that moron really is quite rare.

Mostly, the problem lieutenants are those who were formally enlisted personnel. They want to be officers but can't forget how to be NCOs. They try to do too much and think since they have as much experience as their SNCOs and NCOs, they can use their people for the minor details while they run the whole show in their own way. This causes major problems and leads to a platoon that can function as necessary but never puts their heart and soul into what they do and who they are. In other words, they become the army.

I'm not saying 1st Platoon is like this, but if the lieutenant is not careful they can become like this in a hurry. It's a tough situation for a young officer. It's not like Camp Pendleton where the Marine can be safely evaluated and fired if found incompetent. Over here, incompetence can get Marines hurt or killed. Still, I think if the lieutenant gives him a chance, the SSgt will prove himself.

We pulled out at 2330 and got to our target house within five minutes, rolled up slowly and dismounted the troops. The gate was a little hard to get into but the squad busted through and quickly moved to the front door. They blew the lock off with the shotgun, using our recently acquired lock-buster slugs. A flashbang, or stun grenade, was thrown inside the house and the Marines poured in right after the blast. They stacked furniture against all the doors and we knew right away that these guys were dirty.

**Weapons at ready**

Two suspects got taken down right after entry and we did a quick search. We found a blasting cap and wiring and there is only one purpose for a rig like that. A nice little question and answer period ensued. Let's just say although we did not physically abuse anyone, and despite the language barrier, we got the point across. We did not appreciate finding bomb making material.

We stayed on scene for less than twenty minutes because this was a classic raid in the sense you hit the target, do your job, and get out of Dodge before anyone knows what hit them. 2nd didn't have any luck on their raid because the asshole wasn't home. Oh well, maybe we can go pay him a visit some other time.

In retrospect, this was not a very intense mission but you have to be ready for whatever comes at you. We used speed, violence and surprise and those techniques took away the enemy's home field advantage.

It felt good to get back out there. I think we become adrenaline junkies of a sort in this environment and all the Marines were ready to get back in action. You get to the point where you feel lazy and inactive when you sit around with no missions. I know this sounds ridiculous and most normal people would never be in a hurry to go right back out into harm's way. Then again, no one ever accused me or any Marine in this company of being normal.

30 Nov. 2004

For our final mission in the month of November, we went to pay a visit to two local schools: once again, a mission within a mission. Part one, we needed to see if the schools were staging points for weapons, bomb making materials or the enemy. Part two, the CAG once again joined us to assess the situation in the schools. We searched the buildings and grounds while CAG checked if they needed any materials, books, supplies or help with maintenance issues. We are sure that our cowardly enemy uses the schools in the same way he uses mosques, hospitals, Red Crescent buildings, and any other public service facilities.

They know we visit their houses with regularity. If we find anything in their house, they go straight to jail and they know it. Therefore, they hide it in public places because first of all, they don't think we'll search there and secondly, they don't get caught along with their stash.

I didn't go on this one and I feel pretty shitty about it. I woke with the most agonizing neck pain of my life and by the time we were ready to step off, I couldn't even turn my head either left or right. Bruce saw me agonizing with my gear and told me to stay home and he would go in my place. Although I'm stubborn as well as stupid, I agreed with him.

Doc gave me a muscle relaxer and I sat down and prayed for relief. An hour later, the company came back. Bruce said they locked down Michigan and rolled into the schools but both just reopened after being closed since the beginning of the month. Apparently, the siege on Fallujah knocked out most of the power in all the public facilities here. There was nothing suspicious at either place and after passing out a few supplies and some soccer balls, the boys came home.

We didn't really foresee any action because lately the Muj aren't willing to come out and play. The weird thing is most of us are disappointed with this development. Like I've said before, we ain't normal!

01 Dec. 2004

In keeping with the creativity battalion has displayed in naming operations, we conducted Operation Wolverine III today. Once again, there must have been two other wolverines, unless we're completely deranged or adopting a new strategy to confuse the enemy.

"How come the training and what we do is so confusing?" a PFC in our battalion (H&S Company) once asked his CO.

In other words, it was a cluster fuck and a disorganized goat rodeo.

"Hey, if we're confused then the enemy will be even more confused," the CO replied in all seriousness.

Now how can you argue with that logic?

Today's operation brought us back to the site of the huge cache we found on Thanksgiving. This time, we sweep and clear south of Route Nova while the Army swept the riverbank for cache sites. The 44th Engineer Battalion would do the honors. I guess they figured if we could find that much shit with three mine sweeps and a dog, they could find even more with an entire engineer battalion. I hope they do but I'm thinking we cleaned it out. We've been in this area several times now and that's both good and bad. Good, we know the area and the routes. Bad, Haji knows we've been here and he may have wired some buildings or put out some IEDs. Worse, there's a sniper working from somewhere around here and he already shot one of us last time. Beyond worse, Fox 6 asked me to go with 3rd Platoon and I swore I wouldn't hang out with those guys. If my calculus is correct, that's three bads and only one good.

I'm not too pleased with the hand I was dealt on this one but just like in Texas Hold Em, you don't have to have a good hand, or even the best hand to win the pot.

We reached the drop off point with no drama and about to go into the first house, one of the SAW gunners had a negligent discharge and shot a burst right into the wall we were stacked against and I about shit myself. When a burst goes off two feet away from you and you weren't expecting it, it literally scares the shit out of you. SSgt Flann and the idiot's squad leader were right there and jumped knee deep in his shit but this is combat and we really didn't have time for a proper ass chewing. We still had to get in the house and do our thing.

That was the only firing of a weapon by 3rd Platoon for the whole mission other than the few warning shots here and there. 4th Platoon, moving adjacent and north of us, had a few sniper shots crack overhead but they couldn't draw a bead on the shooter and therefore never returned fire. Just up the road from where we stopped, Whiskey Company found three rigged IEDs. These consisted of 155mm artillery shells, the IED of choice for these assholes. A little further from there, they found a pile of nine shells that looked as if they were being stacked for emplacement but I guess we showed up on the scene and scared off the set-up man.

No insurgents came out to get killed but we know they're still here. The boys, they're not showing signs of complacency yet and that's good. I still think the Muj regrouped after Fallujah and he'll be back with a vengeance. When he does, we'll be ready for his ass. That's what he doesn't seem to understand and why he'll never win.

02 Dec. 2004

Operation Goodwill Hunting, renamed the Great Haji Handout by my smart-ass Lance Corporals, was our first 100% humanitarian mission.

**The Good Guys**

We went to the ghetto, one of the poorest neighborhoods, and passed out toys, soccer balls, shoes and school supplies to the kids. None of the Marines had any experience with this type of operation except myself. When I was with 2/3 out of Hawaii in 1997, we went to an orphanage in Thailand with a bunch of toys. The kids were kind of scared until we opened the bags and then the shit hit the fan. The kids went absolutely ape-shit and it got so bad ten kids had to be treated by the corpsmen after getting trampled.

I had a feeling we would have a repeat trampling on this mission. We did our best to put them in a line and maintain some order but it seems Iraqis do not understand the concept of getting in line. We had a translator yelling at them to listen and wait their turn but they weren't having any of that shit. The kids wanted soccer balls and went nuts to get near enough to get one. We did our best, but eventually we jumped back in the 7-ton and handed out stuff over the sides. Even the adults joined in and in most cases they were worse than the children. We also brought out one of the battalion surgeons, some corpsmen and set up a First Aid Station.

The Marines had a lot of fun passing out the toys and stuff and it felt pretty good to go into a neighborhood and do something nice for these people. A news crew from ABC came out to do a follow-on story about Fox 2/5 and we brought them along. Marines have never been slouches where propaganda and self-promotion is concerned.

During the war, now known as OIF 1, Mike Cerre was the "embedded" reporter attached to Fox 2/5. He did a Nightline special and won an Emmy Award. He has kept in touch and he's back to do another piece for ABC. Who knows what kind of spin he'll put on it, but he's well liked within our battalion. He was a Marine with Fox 2/5 in Viet Nam and he did us justice in the first go-round so we think he'll do us right again

My only worry about the media is they shoot all this footage and they decide how to relate our story to the people back home. They can show everything we do and tell a fair story of what it's like for us or they can do some creative editing and make us look really bad. I'm not too worried because we aren't committing atrocities or being unnecessarily cruel. We don't do the Abu Ghraib bullshit so let them show what they want and I hope everyone sees what it's like and what we really do over here.

**Haji handout**

03 Dec. 2004

Somewhere, someone came up with the bright idea of rebuilding a neighborhood in the middle of our sector and making a "perfect" neighborhood, sort of Ramadi's answer to Baghdad's Green Zone. I haven't been to Baghdad and seen the Green Zone nor do I know how it was established but I can use the reasonable man theory and venture some guesses.

I'll bet it was established prior to the heavy fighting with the insurgency. I'll bet there is a shit-load of troops there to operate and protect it and they did not randomly select an area right in the middle of a residential neighborhood. I'll bet they are able to control access in and out.

Operation West Side, a movement to contact through our area, was one of those missions where you just say, "Aye, Aye, Sir," do your job, and get it over with. We brought along some pogues whose job was to assess possibilities of a potential "Green Zone" from an engineering and infrastructure standpoint.

1st Platoon raided one house of suspected terrorists, bagged and tagged four upstanding citizens and joined us as we moved through the area. I think the bottom line is some high level people want this to work so we have to figure out how to make it happen. In my opinion, the wheels of bureaucracy and logistics spin slowly enough and this will become a huge problem for whoever relieves us in March.

I don't see how we can designate a certain section as safe and set up a little paradise surrounded by the rest of this shit-hole town. It will be a major, major undertaking and become the focal point of all Muj attacks from there on out. I think the "perfect neighborhood" will become worse than the Combat Outpost and will not be as safe or secure as the Outpost because there is no way to control access, no standoff, no QRF force, no guard posts and especially there will not be two Marine companies living there.

If it's up to us to do all this work, all we're doing is making a military compound within the city but without the security we have on our compounds now. We'll have to use who-knows-how-many Marines to work all these access points, patrol the neighborhood, provide security for anyone building anything and fix all the shit they blow up. If not us, these people will need the neighborhood watch from hell. Oh, by the way, while we decide on this perfect neighborhood, we will not move out everyone who already lives there.

Essentially, we're not letting out but keeping

the fox in the hen house and making it easier for him to live there. There is no way we have any idea who these people are or where their loyalties lie. The only possible way to make any kind of perfect neighborhood is to make it on one of our already secure military compounds and we decide who gets to live there and who does not.

The CO calls this Operation Pipe Dream, the 1stSgt calls it Operation You Gotta Be Kiddin' Me and I don't even have a name for it. I realize we need to protect the Governor, Mayor, Police Chief and all other government officials and all these people need a safe place to work and do business. Cordoning off a section of town and thinking it's going to work just because you want it to work is not the answer, period.

I've heard all kinds of estimates on how long it will take before U.S. troops can completely pull out of Iraq. I have my own opinions and they are definitely not politically correct. I compare this situation to the problems the British Military has with Belfast, Northern Ireland. Unlike many of our so-called "experts," I have been to Belfast on many occasions because my wife happens to be from there. The British Military has done a lot of hard work in order to try to control their own "insurgency." Many brave men have died in the line of duty. They continue to provide a presence and have reaction forces available in case of major rioting, violence or conflicts.

However, the British Military is not the reason most neighborhoods are peaceful and safe. The residents of these neighborhoods took it upon themselves to make their areas peaceful. I'm not condoning everything that goes on over there and I think the Catholics have legitimate grievances. When they decided to settle their grievances with bombs, guns and terrorist tactics they crossed the line. The Protestants realized you fight fire with fire and knew the military and police couldn't keep everyone safe at all times. Their answer was to take matters in their own hands. This has led to all manner of violence and "troubles" but when's the last time any Americans were threatened or died because of that country's problems.

In some respects, the people of Ramadi who want to live in peace need to step up. They need to be man enough to stand up to those criminals who come into their neighborhoods and engage in terrorist activities. It shouldn't be up to us to find and kill all these insurgents because there is no way for us to know who they are or what they're planning. If the Iraqis never step up and our plan is to stay here until we kill all the insurgents, I'll give my own estimate of when we could pull out. How about fucking NEVER!

04 Dec. 2004

We returned to the scene of two previous missions for Operation Hood Rat, a return attempt to capture the IP Major we tried to get a few nights ago and another walk-through of the water treatment facility. We wanted to finally take this guy to jail and hoped to find another cache at the treatment plant. Fortunately, he lived right next to the treatment plant and no big deal to hit both targets. Most of us believe the weapons at the plant belonged to him.

Mike Cerre and the boys from ABC came along to film us in action. I wish they were here when we found the huge caches or when the enemy heavily engaged us. We want America and the rest of the world to see what it's like not only for us but also for all Marine units in every city over here and to know what we really go through on a daily basis.

After our first search, I felt sure the major went into hiding and I think the days of using the water plant as a cache site are over. It's still important to return to these places because we learned from Echo 2/4 the insurgents believe we never hit the same place twice. Echo 2/4 rarely hit the same places twice because of manpower. The insurgents caught on to this and as soon as the Marines left, they would move right back in.

The major wasn't home, but we snagged a terrorist we detained last time at the treatment plant ironically named Mohammed Daham. He's the third most wanted terrorist in our AO. The name might just be the Iraqi version of John Smith but there he was, smiling at me like we were two old pals. We detained him again on principle but we know they won't hold him.

The decision of whether or not to hold a detainee we bring in is not up to us. The pogues whose job it is to squeeze these guys for information and intelligence make these determinations. I guess it makes sense to someone. Let's get people who aren't out on the streets every day to make the decisions of who is or is not a terrorist. They usually make these judgments from available intelligence or from their interrogations. If we don't have hard evidence of wrongdoing, these guys walk.

The best insurgents are expert liars. It's a part of who they are and what they do. It also doesn't help that every person we have ever met or asked a question lied to us. I hate to classify and stereotype, but if anyone disagrees with me, I guarantee they have never been here or did the grunt's job. Now I know how cops feel when they make a righteous bust and the criminals get right back out on the street. It's very frustrating and it pisses me off! How can this guy be at two places within two weeks where we find weapons and at the house of a known terrorist or terrorist supporter? Because he's a no good, cock-sucking, scumbag terrorist who needs to go to jail, that's why. Why else does he keep turning up in these places?

"Why did you let this fucker walk in the first place," I asked the Human Exploitation Team (HET).

"We couldn't prove he had anything to do with the weapons being stored there," was their brilliant answer.

*Here's a news flash jackass!*

"That's why they store their shit at public places. Jesus Christ, am I the only moron who can figure that out?" I asked.

"Nothing we can do about it, Gunny."

When we catch them, they deny any knowledge of anything as usual. How could 12 so-called security guards who are off duty police officers not notice multiple machine guns, mortar rounds, artillery shells, rockets, boosters, ammo, IED timers, explosives and other such things being stored at a facility where they work, especially since there are only five or six buildings in the whole damn compound? Because they work with, support or protect the Muj. According to President Bush, that's reason for an ass kicking from us. But what the fuck do we know? Asshole gets to walk again.

At least the crew from ABC got it all on tape. I'll say this for those guys, they got balls! They ran in right behind us and didn't know what was behind the door. It turned out to be an easy hit but we wouldn't know that until it was over. Mike and the guys got one more look at what we're up against and I can only hope they tell it like it is.

05 Dec. 2004

Happy Birthday Mom! Like most Marines, I will argue I have the best Mom in the world. When I dropped out of college to join the Corps, she was not a happy camper. I'm sure most Moms are not too thrilled when junior walks in with that announcement. Over the years and all the ups and downs, Mom has always been there when I needed her. She completely accepted Janet and Sonia into our family and even puts up with me, which can't be easy. Like any miscreant, I put Mom through the ringer from time to time and like any great Mom, she never stopped loving me or supporting me. I call her once a month or so to let her know I'm OK. Although worried, she tries not to let me know.

I look back on the basic rule of my youth; you played outside all day in order to avoid irritating your mother. When it was time to come in for supper, Mom came on the porch and yelled your name. If you were too far away to hear, you didn't eat and got your ass beat when you finally came home. Like many other Irish-American households, Mom handed out the discipline. Mom had a belt and was not afraid to use it.

I think in early 1970s, the word discipline changed to something else, mainly child abuse, but whenever I think of what a little, snot-nosed bastard I was back then, I thank God for my Mom and her belt.

When I first got promoted to Corporal, a senior Gunny, whom I respected greatly, told me leadership was simple.

"Start out being a mean, unforgiving, hard-ass, son of a bitch and then get nicer as the situation dictates," he said with a smile.

"How do you know my mother?"

When I was young and stupid, I sometimes wished I had a different Mom. Now that I'm older and slightly less stupid I wish everybody had Peggy Tracy for a Mom.

I got on the phone and called her this morning and that's about the best I could do by way of a present. She assured me Dad and her were doing fine and gave me an update on my Redskins and life in general in Pittston PA. I told her I was sorry I couldn't be there, again, and she told me not to worry about that, just come home safe. Roger that Ma!

* * *

I hung up and celebrated her birthday by driving around Ramadi on the Mobile QRF. We're trying a few new tactics while the Muj are in hibernation. Our latest is to go gun truck heavy and drive around in separate teams in the same area. The idea is we can cover more space and cover each other's movement with satellite vehicle patrols. If one team of vehicles sees anything suspicious, we call it in, converge on the target and take care of the situation. This is not something a unit should try right off the bat. In order for this to work, you really have to know your AO and every street and alley in it, especially how to get from point A to point B in a big fuckin' hurry.

We brought the ABC crew with us for the last time and we did some quick hit and search raids whenever we saw a group of men near any particular house, shop or whatever. We didn't turn up anything but we gained experience with this type of vehicle patrol and, more importantly, we covered every street from every direction many times over. The residents, and hopefully any insurgents among them, must wonder what the hell is going on and how in the world we got so many vehicles in their shit.

After we dropped off the film crew, we went back out for another tour in a different area. We have reports of foreign fighters coming into Ramadi after the Marines in Fallujah handed them their asses and sent them packing. Of particular note; Afghanis with long beards and traditional dress hang around and cause trouble.

We drove up Smash St. and saw this huge, and I mean big motherfucker, standing on a corner talking to a few local hoodlums. He had a long beard and one of those little, chef looking hats. If you looked up Afghani terrorist in the dictionary, this guy's picture would be looking back at you. Therefore, we introduced ourselves and decided to bring him in for questioning.

I know, I know, the liberal, Michael Moore groupies are up in arms because now we're arresting people because we don't like the way they look. I know this may sound like Nazi, Gestapo shit, but we're the ones on the streets every day and if something doesn't look and feel right we take action. So Michael Moore can kiss my ass. How does that sound you fat, lying piece of shit?

We snatched Osama, would you fuckin' believe that was his name, and brought him back for the HET to talk. Maybe they can get decent intelligence during their interrogation. As for the satellite vehicle patrols, I think it's a good tactic and a good way to show our Muj pals a new look.

06 Dec. 2004

Another swarming vehicle patrol. I like to think of us like a pack of angry bees just looking for someone to sting. 3rd Platoon moved on the ground from Smash to Nova and we hit every street, alley, nook and path in between the two with seven gun trucks and a ten pack truck. 4th Platoon was MQRF and we broke down into three teams and literally covered every inch of that part of town. Every now and again, we'd cut through the sector, but mostly we kept 3rd in the middle and floated around their edges.

Once again, we had absolutely no contact. I have a feeling like I did a long time ago at the Outpost. I can feel them watching, waiting and planning. Personally, I'd enjoy killing a whole shit load more of them and I think most of the Blackhearts feel the same but more than a few are counting the days.

We now receive packages and everyone feels more than a little down and out when deployed over the Christmas holidays. As for me, I miss my family and my close friends more than I could ever explain, but I wouldn't leave if I had a free ticket home. I'll go when everyone else goes and not a minute sooner. We have a job to do and as Marines, we know what that means.

We also know every birthday, holiday and Christmas will be all the better when we no longer have to spend them away from home. We're not the first generation of Marines to spend time away from our families and we damn sure won't be the last, not as long as there are assholes that hate us and want to kill us and there's no shortage of assholes around the world. That's OK with me, because for every 100 of them willing to kill one of us, there's at least one of us willing, and more able, to kill 100 of them. It all kind of balances out in the end.

07 Dec. 2004

Mike Cerre's last day with Fox 2/5 and for the last hurrah, he interviewed me and then Bruce. I hoped he wouldn't get too political with the questions. Mike strikes me as being very liberal and probably a bit anti-republican, anti-war and therefore anti-Bush. I could be wrong but I doubt it. I don't hold that against him or any other American. Hell, I could say the same thing about my father and I love him to death. There are probably more Americans who want us out of here and this war over than the other way around.

"How can Marines be like any other American college kid of the same age one minute and then these complete professional warriors the next?" he asked.

"They've seen who and what we're up against. They know every time they leave the base, someone is trying to kill them. There's not a single Marine in our company who hasn't experienced an IED attack, up close and personal nor been in a firefight and on operations where Marines or soldiers have been hurt and killed."

"Do the Marines ever get into the politics of the whole thing. The whole "should we or shouldn't we be here" argument?"

"You know what, Mike? Most of the younger guys knew what they were getting into when they joined. They knew they'd be in a combat zone as soon as they got out of MOS school. Right now, they're getting exactly what was promised and exactly what they asked for. The problem will be in retention in a couple years. If all these guys do for their initial enlistment of four years is go to war in Iraq, train for war in Iraq, and then come back to war in Iraq, the Corps is going to have a big problem."

"Let me ask you this, Gunny. Is this personal now?'

"Of course, it's personal. PFC Folmar was killed. Twenty five others from Fox wear a Purple Heart. Plus, the KIAs and WIAs in the other companies. Goddamn right it's personal. We don't want to leave here and have to come back or make other Marines keep coming back."

Mike wasn't about to let me off the hook without a fight.

"Is this thing was winnable on a military level?" he asked and waited for me to wiggle out of that one.

"Let me tell you something, Mike. We go where we want, when we want and stay there for however long we want in the town of Ramadi. Every time the enemy is man enough to show up, we hand him his ass."

**ABC returns**

What I didn't say is; what would define a win? I don't think the policy-makers have figured that one out yet. Will there always be terrorists and insurgents? Yes. Will Iraq ever be on any American's list as a vacation destination? Does anyone really give a shit about the average Iraqi and his so-called freedom?

They had a piece of shit dictator running the show. History will show he ranks right up there on the all-time list of evil tyrants. His big mistake was fucking with the wrong country at the wrong time. He's not the first to do it and won't be the last. He got what he had coming and we did what we had to do to protect ourselves. At the same time, every other piece of shit dictator and anti-American government in the world was put on notice. Is it our responsibility to stay over here until every little detail of the reconstruction of this country is worked out? I hope not or we're never leaving. I realize we have to at least get this place somewhat stabilized but pretty soon, enough will certainly be enough. I think if we're still here for the next reelection of a U.S. President, we'll be back to the bad old days of the Democrats running the show. Mark my words on that one!

So much for my five minutes of fame. I just hope the story comes out the way I said it. Time to concentrate on today's mission: aptly named Operation Sleeping Giant. Mikey was in charge of naming this one and since he and I alone seemed to remember today is Pearl Harbor Day, maybe because we're old Hawaii Marines, we were the only ones who understood the significance of the name.

We decided to do a night patrol through an area of our sector. We've done a few day patrols near Tower and Nova, but we wanted switch it up and see if we could catch them with their pants down. 2nd Platoon moved dismounted through the area from west to east and I joined the MQRF on a swarming, satellite, eight-vehicle, gun truck patrol.

If ever there was a night to put a world of hurt on someone, this was it. Unfortunately, the enemy decided not to take us on yet again. The word from on high is the Muj are in a plan and rebuild phase. This couldn't have come at a better time for us. While he plans how to hurt us based on what he thinks he knows about our tactics, we adopt new tactics and really get to know his neighborhood. If any of these ass clowns are foreigners, we have the advantage of local knowledge of terrain over them. Plus, and a big plus it is, we're more ready for them than they are for us. We're slowly taking away his advantages and turn them into our advantages. I'm not talking or thinking in an over-confident, cocky manner. The truth is, we've learned this new AO the easy way when it could have been much harder and much deadlier. I'm sure the enemy is too disorganized and lacks the intelligence gathering tools to realize while we were most vulnerable; he was asleep at the switch. But you know what? Fuck Him! When he thinks he's ready to come back out and start trouble, the Blackhearts will be waiting! And more ready than ever!

08 Dec. 2004

Our first company QRFA mission since leaving

the Combat Outpost. QRFA was a way of life at the Outpost but lately not used or needed for its intended purpose. At the Outpost, 90% of our QRF missions were in some way related to supporting the Boxcar.

OP Ghetto was attacked with RPG and small arms fire. MQRF responded quickly and thought they had a good fix and called for a QRF and ten minutes later, we were on vehicles and out the gate. I was several vehicles back and as I rolled out, this guy stumbled around and held his forehead while a small trickle of blood leaked through his fingers and onto his shirt. His car was all shot up, which was pretty wild, considering I didn't even hear gunfire.

Once again, some stupid moron tried to drive his vehicle through our convoy as we exited the gate. Sgt Hobbs, turret gunner for the Command Vehicle, fired a few shots to stop him and when that failed, sent a few bursts of 7.62 through the windshield. I've seen some amazing unintentional, non-lethal bursts of machine gun fire since we've been here but this one ranks right up there. The windshield was stitched up and the groups centered where Dumbasses' head resided. He should have died but there he was, stumbling around the street bigger than shit. After rolling past him, we stormed into the ghetto and linked up with Mikey's platoon.

They were in the process of clearing some houses while 1st Platoon dismounted and did the same. Shortly thereafter, Lt. B came over the radio, "We got a house with a remote controlled launcher with a fresh RPG ready to fire."

That got the boys running out of the house like their asses were on fire. We did the smart thing and called for EOD back-up while we secured the rest of the area. Shit, those guys get paid extra money to deal with explosive bullshit and we were in no particular hurry so we hunkered down and strong-pointed at a few intersections.

A short while later, I saw Fox 6 aiming in on a rooftop about 500 yards away. A couple of assholes observed the road and surrounding area. One Rule of Engagement (ROE) says in order to shoot, you have to have positive ID of the target and confirmation they are a danger to you or others. Another says, we do not fire warning shots. Once again, bullshit rules made up by politicians who never endure the fighting or ever have their ass in harm's way.

Fox 6 went with the lesser of two evils and fired a warning shot to let them know hanging out on a rooftop is bad for their health; especially when some asshole uses a rooftop to fire rockets at one of our positions. Did this deter them? It was my turn to fire a warning shot and I steadied my weapon on the hood of our vehicle and aimed for the ledge right next to these two lookey-loos.

Hobbs and Doc talked some smack about my abilities to shoot at this distance. To tell the truth, I'm a pretty good shot, always have been: expert at boot camp and expert every time since. With the Advanced Combat Optical Gunsight (ACOG), that just about every one of us has, thanks ultimately to Pres. Bush who actually gets us the gear we need to fight, this shot was a cakewalk.

I sighted in and gently squeezed the trigger. I put the round about six inches from the one guy's head and deep in the caveman part of the brain, the reaction to this is universal and instantaneous. Hobbs cracked up laughing at how quickly those guys hit the deck.

We didn't want groups of people to congregate around our position and this always happens if we sit in one place for too long. Both Bruce and I fired smoke grenades from our 203's to clear off big groups of cars and people on two different occasions. These grenades are *money*. I don't know what the Iraqi people think are in these things, but when the smoke pops, they clear the fuck out. I carry at least six smoke grenades on every operation and they're worth their weight in gold.

EOD eventually arrived and sent in their little robot to check out the explosive device and discovered a remote control detonator rigged to a homemade launcher. I don't know if they planned to shoot it, but had to light out in a hurry or if they intended to blow us up as we entered the building. The robot set a charge next to it and in a few minutes the rocket, along with a major portion of the house, went Boom! So much for winning the hearts and minds, huh? Fuck Them! Maybe if they kept the Muj out of their fuckin' houses, we wouldn't have to blow shit up in them. Either way, I'd rather have a family angry with me than have any of my boys hurt or killed. Period! End of fuckin' story!

After the explosion, we gathered our boys and went back to the base in time for evening chow. Not a bad days work at all.

09 Dec. 2004

Holy shit, I actually had a day off of sorts. Back home, a day off means exactly that, a day off. Over here, a day off means I don't go out on a mission.

For the Marines, a day off might mean an entire day where they can do as they please. For me, it means I run around and take care of a hundred different things. For example, some of the heaters in the huts are not working so I have to find the S-4 and get them to take care of it, visit the Seabees to see if they can put a little more armor on a few more vehicles and convince the mechanics to fix a whole bunch of little things on my vehicles. I have 23 trucks in my company and these things take a beating on a rental car scale. In addition, I had ammo to order, supplies to order or check up on, and, if all that ain't enough, I began the next gear inventory, known in the business as a CMR, which is a nightmare that defies explanation.

To make a long story short, we have a few million dollars worth of shit, i.e. weapons, optics, gear, etcetera. I am responsible for the maintaining and accounting of all of it. The Platoon Sergeants are supposed to make my life easy in this regard, but with the exception of Mikey, I think some of them work for Al Qaeda. When SSgt Flammang was evac'd to the States, he personally carried the following: M16A-4 rifle, ACOG, Surefire combat flashlight (attaches to M16A-4s), PEQ-2A Infrared illuminator, ANPVS-14 night vision optics, 3X magnifier, GPS, compass, binoculars, and a bayonet. According to my paperwork, he owns these items and is responsible for all of them. When he got evac'd, the new Platoon Sergeant redistributed his gear amongst the platoon members, and my armorer, who I want to kill, did not record any of the changes.

So far, we have sent seven Marines back to Camp Pendleton. The average Marine has five or six pieces of gear which amounts to nearly forty items unaccounted for. I have to chew on the Platoon Sergeants for not documenting any of these changes and especially my armorer, for not being proactive or having any initiative whatsoever. I've said before my Goons make my job easy and the key to running a tight ship lies in a great HQ section. Unfortunately, the converse is true in spades. But that's the life of an Infantry Company Gunny. Anyone out there want to trade jobs? So much for a fuckin' day off, huh?

10 Dec. 2004

My Father-in-Law's birthday. Happy Birthday, John. While I'm over here fighting the Muj, John is in Northern Ireland fighting brain cancer. How's that for some perspective? My own personal opinion is he's too damn tough and stubborn to die so I try not to worry too much but I know it hurts my wife. That's life in the Corps for you: All the same problems and tragedies of life as any other person but usually dealt with amongst little things like training, deployments and combat.

Janet is very close to her father and I can't imagine how she deals with the stress of me being over here and him being very sick in Belfast. She has a great family that is very supportive and I'm sure they'll help one another to get through this very tough time but once again Janet is more or less alone in California while events she has no control over affect the important people in her life. One more reason to love and admire the poster woman for military marriage.

It's also my big, fat, lazy and crazy dog's birthday. Happy Birthday, Molly. I love my dog and miss her big, brown face as much as the rest of my family. Some people don't understand how others can be so crazy about their pets but Molly truly is my best pal in life. She's eleven years old today and she's done her share of traveling and deployments, too.

I bought Molly as a birthday present for my daughter, Sonia when we still lived in North Carolina in 1993. She's not just a part of the family; she's more or less taken over the family and at this point simply allows us to live with her. I'm fairly certain she's the most spoiled dog in the world but she's also the gentlest and friendliest dog I've ever seen.

**Molly and me**

In order to celebrate this special day, I went out with the company to see if I could shoot off some celebratory gunfire. The only difference is I wouldn't be aiming at the sky. The Mission and Mobile Platoons went to screen on Nova while a small boat company from Camp Lejeune checked out the riverbank on both sides and all the little bullshit islands in between. This has been the site of some huge caches found by both the army and Fox and we hoped to find even more shit today.

I staged with the QRFA platoon, Mikey's platoon, and our mission was to sit at HP and wait to come out in case of trouble. 3rd Platoon was hit with a small IED as they drove down the road but fortunately no injuries to personnel or vehicles. Whiskey was further east and also hit by IEDs. It seems the Muj are back in town and up to their old tricks.

We were called out when the company hit another IED and took small arms fire. The CO reported he thought they fled north of Nova so we drove up, dismounted, got on line and swept through the area. We ran into the Egyptian farmer who pointed us to the last cache. There were two other guys with him and my Muj meter was going off. Through our translator, Kabi, we discovered four armed, masked men showed up, delivered a beatdown with their rifles and ran off. The Egyptian was fucked up bad. He had bandages wrapped around his head, bruises and welts all over his torso and a possible broken arm. We thought the other two men with him played a part in this so we took them all in for questioning.

We got the snitch medical treatment and then the interrogators went to work on the other two. This beatdown really angered our new best pal and he gave up all kinds of info. When he gets out of the hospital in a week or two we're going to stake out his house and see what turns up.

In my opinion, they would have killed him if they thought he was an informant and did it purely on principal and to send a message. I guess this guy is in a "damned if you do, and damned if you don't" situation. Hell, almost all these Iraqis are in the same boat.

But, no one ever said that gaining freedom, liberty and democracy was an easy, painless struggle. Sometimes you have to be willing to go through these things in the course of change and liberation. At least this guy has balls. It's more than I can say for just about every other Iraqi man I've met so far. Then again, this guy is an Egyptian!

11 Dec. 2004

We went back near OP Ghetto and conducted a more detailed sweep of the entire sector. If a building had the ability to see any part of our OP, we paid them a house call. Instead of bringing a cake, we paid our neighbors a visit and introduced ourselves by letting them see our weapons, gun trucks and a bunch of hard-looking, angry Marines. Hopefully, we are at least, if not more, scary than the Muj.

**Sweep the sector**

We didn't turn up any information or detain any suspects on the mission and didn't really expect to because Ghetto has never been an insurgent hotbed. As I entered the living room of one house, I saw a decorated Christmas Tree, of all things, and on the mantel, a bunch of Christmas cards all written in English, straight up Hallmark cards. I called him in and asked, "Are you a Christian?"

I figured maybe if he were, he'd be inclined to be a little friendlier and more forthcoming than the average, hear no evil, see no evil, and speak no evil Iraqis we deal with every day.

"Many members of my family are Christians and they are the ones who sent the cards. I am not a Christian, but we celebrate Christmas anyway."

"That's like having the best of all possible worlds. Just pick what holidays you like from each religion and have parties all year round," I replied, in my usual smart-ass fashion.

He kind of smiled and shrugged like "Hey buddy, quit breakin' my balls."

The guy spoke English well so at least I could communicate without an interpreter.

"Look, our post was attacked with rockets from this area. You must have seen something," I said.

"Two days ago, four men drove around the neighborhood and threatened people with guns. They were in a red Opel. They rode around threatening everyone. They put on masks, broke into a house and fired at the Americans."

Now we know how they operate and what kind of car they drive, at least, these four assholes anyway.

We gathered decent intelligence that will help us identify and hopefully kill those fuckers next time they show up. Most importantly, any mission is successful when you come back with no injuries to Marines or damage to vehicles and equipment.

13 Dec. 2004

We decided to try something new by locking down both the North and South Bridges and setting up vehicle checkpoints and Operation Drag Net would be an appropriate name for this most basic of police work. The mission allowed so many cars across and stopped them at a point of our choosing to search the vehicles and passengers. The part about this that sucked was twofold. One, we don't speak Iraqi and it's always difficult to make them follow instructions. Two, it's the perfect opportunity for a suicide bomber to easily kill a few or many Marines.

Because we are experts at improvising, adapting and overcoming, we brought along two Showani squads to communicate and search. I'm not a big fan of these guys, because I've seen them in action and to put it nicely, they suck, but we work with and train them, hopefully to turn the country over to them so let them do some of the dirty work.

Today was the coldest day since we got here. All anyone talked about prior to coming over was the heat. It's Pennsylvania fuckin' cold over here in December and they say January gets even colder. Oh well, the song does say in every clime and place.

Motivated to do this mission, the Showanis really do want to do their part. I also think they want us to see them as fellow professional soldiers. To be fair, they were all business and even looked like a well-trained unit. Their Colonel must have trained them pretty hard because even if his unit is not there tactically, they have discipline. If you can instill discipline and a warrior spirit, you have a foundation to build upon. The Showanis have a long way to go but it looks like they are on the way.

Aside from the entertainment of watching the Showanis roughhouse a few citizens that gave them lip, we really didn't do anything but provide security. But, unlike the movies, combat is a whole lot more about boring missions than blazing gun battles.

14 Dec 2004

We had three significant events worth mentioning. The Commandant of the Marine Corps came to visit, Lt. Jones got promoted and Corporal Lundy was awarded the Navy and Marine Corps Commendation Medal.

The Commandant visiting the troops is always a big deal, especially since we've had such a tough battle here. Our battalion has more casualties and KIAs than any unit in Ramadi, largely because we are the only unit in the actual downtown district. An artillery battery got here when we did, but they weren't put right into the meat grinder. I'm told they're a squared away unit and are doing a great job but even those guys will tell you that 2/5 has taken the brunt of the battle. There are also all the associated admin pogues and division staff weenies running the operations center and such at a base called Blue Diamond but they are locked into that base and 95% of them never dream about going outside the wire.

So who does the Commandant and Sergeant Major of the Marine Corps come to visit? Believe it or not, not 2/5. This is the biggest slap in the face I can imagine. We took a ride and at least tried to hear what he had to say, but the 2/11 arty guys told us to get lost. Apparently, the Commandant was there to see only them and we didn't rate to hang around. I know the Commandant's time is valuable and he's a very busy man. He can't visit every unit, but he was right here on our base not half a mile from us and we would have gone to him if he couldn't come to us. At the very least, the Sergeant Major could have popped in.

I can't explain to the average civilian how the Commandant is revered. A few words of encouragement or even some recognition would have motivated our Marines and brought their spirits to a new level. It's a sad, sad, fuckin' day when the Secretary of the Navy has time to stop by and our own Commandant and Sergeant Major can't.

His schedule was probably made up by the same pogues who hung out with him at Blue Diamond. You know what? Fuck it. I'm here for the Marines from Fox and 2/5, so I'll quit worrying about why the pogues seem to always stick it to us infantry grunts.

Lt. J was promoted to 1st Lt. and it's always a good thing to see a young officer climb up the rank structure, especially when he's a good man and a good Marine. The real highlight was when Cpl. Lundy got his medal. Not too many corporals wear a Navy and Marine Corps Commendation Medal and this one has the "Combat V" device, which signifies heroism in combat. This is a big deal for any Marine and Lundy deserved it.

I'm sure by the end of this tour we'll have quite a few more awards to hand out but for me, seeing the young, motivated, hard core Marines getting well deserved awards makes all the hard work and training worth all the time and effort we put into it.

Here's some poetic justice to end the day. As we came out of the chow hall, it was darker than three feet up a bear's ass and this Marine came up to me in the parking lot.

"Where's the chow hall?" he asked.

"How about over there." I pointed over my shoulder.

As I walked away, the Goons laughed hysterically.

"I think that was the Commandant," Hobbs said.

I looked back and sure as shit, it was the Commandant. And here I was all pissed off 'cause he didn't talk to me today.

16 Dec. 2004

Any Marinc Gunny worth his salt has a million sea stories. No matter the subject, or how unique someone thinks their story may be, most Gunny's have one to top it. Most of mine begin or end with the phrase, "That's why I don't drink______ anymore." Today is my sixteenth wedding anniversary. Most people think about how they met their wife, or their wedding day or any number of romantic memories when their anniversary comes around. I think about why I don't drink Bushmill's Irish Whiskey.

In 1989, Janet Potter was silly enough to say, "I do" when I asked her to marry me. We were married on December 16th in my hometown of Pittston, PA. and only her Aunt, who lived in Virginia, attended the ceremony. As a wedding gift to ourselves, we flew to Belfast, Northern Ireland for Christmas.

When I was stationed in Scotland, I met her mother and father but only for one brief weekend. Her sister, Karen, lived with her and we were good friends, but other than the one weekend with her Mom and Dad, I never met any other relatives. This visit would take care of that and I felt sure they would accept me into the family after getting to know me.

We arrived on Christmas Eve and for our first night, her sister and brother arranged to take us out for a while before we all return home to a big party with the rest of the family. When we got to the bar, Janet pulled me aside and informed me her brother, Desi, was between jobs at the moment and it was my duty to not allow him to keep buying rounds.

"How am I supposed to do that?" I asked.

"If you see him about to finish his drink, finish yours first and then buy two more and give him one," she explained, as if giving instructions to a simpleton.

What could have gone wrong with a plan like that? She could have informed me only one or two people in the world could down a pint of beer as quickly as her brother. Who those people were was not nearly as important as the fact that I was not one of them. But, I was only married for one week, wanted to make a good impression and especially wanted to make my wife happy.

Desi would just about finish his pint, I quickly downed more than half a glass, and ran to the bar to order two more. This continued for a few hours and later we all went to her parent's house for the big party.

Everything would have turned out okay if not for Bushmill's Irish fuckin' Whiskey. Naturally, there was a bottle handy and since I was too drunk to not be a complete fuckin' retard, I proceeded to drink shot after shot with her brother and dad.

The rest of the night escaped my memory but I

pretty much knew I was fucked when I awoke early the next morning with the worst hangover in the history of Ireland. If the hangover, coupled with no recollection of going to bed weren't enough to clue me in, I received confirmation of my predicament when my wife entered the room and looked at me with disgust.

"Don't ever fuckin' talk to me again," was not the loving "Good morning, dear." I prayed for.

Considering I never heard her curse in the two years of our relationship, I could only surmise I did something really stupid. Although she apparently did not want to talk to me *ever again*, I figured I was married for only a week, had a really bad hangover and was in a whole 'nother Goddamn country. It couldn't be that bad, could it?

"Janet, wait, what happened? I don't remember anything since coming home from the bar."

"You attacked my dad."

"What! What do you mean? When? Why?"

"You tackled him into the fireplace in front of my whole family, and you ruined everybody's Christmas."

And the jackass award goes to! Did I mention that her dad is a former winner of the Mr. Northern Ireland bodybuilding competition? Why, I don't know, but he didn't appreciate me tackling him. Luckily, there were enough people there to keep him from killing me and my wife was able to drag me up to bed.

"Were we fighting? Did he provoke me? Was it an accident?" Please God let it be one of three.

"No, you were sitting in a chair and as he walked by, you jumped out of the chair and tackled him into the fireplace."

Jesus Christ on a Christmas Eve. Who does that? What kind of idiot tackles their father-in-law into a fire for no earthly reason? Just when I thought it couldn't get any worse.

"And you ruined my mom's bathroom," she continued.

"Whatta' ya' mean I ruined the bathroom?"

"You fell down against the wall and broke all the shelves, and the mirror and you ripped the towel bar off the wall."

"Please tell me this is a bad dream," I moaned.

"And my mom just redecorated that bathroom. And if that's not bad enough, you came in here and puked all over her new bed! You're an asshole! Why did you have to drink so much?"

There's a saying, "You really don't want to get her Irish up." I never quite knew what that meant but I was getting a clue.

There are many categories of low, but even whale-shit-on-the-bottom-of-the- ocean-low didn't come close to how I felt. I got myself together, profusely apologized to everyone in her family, especially Dad, and suffered through the worst Christmas day hangover of all time. And that's why I don't drink Irish whiskey anymore!

**The happy couple**

* * *

Happy Anniversary to me, we decided to give Tower, Nova, and Give Me another try. Every now and again there's trouble up there but we never seem to find it. We were not going to search every building but conduct a straight up movement to contact.

The name for this one was Operation Angry Pirate. No earthly idea what the name signifies but the XO made it up and occasionally we humor him. We started off well when 2nd Platoon rolled up on some suspicious looking vehicles. Right away this guy took off with what looked like a gun in his hand. That's a bad idea with 2nd Platoon and a young Marine with a split second decision whether or not to shoot.

They checked the body and the gun turned out to be a video camera. I felt bad for Mikey because his platoon seems to get most of these situations. All you can think is there will be an investigation and those who judge are never the ones who have to make the hard choice under those circumstances.

Luckily, Mikey checked out the video tape and guess what he found? It seems this asshole peddled films, starring himself, engaged in such leisure activities as bomb making, rigging suicide vehicles for explosions, wearing his Muhajadeen mask and attacking coalition forces. That's why the dickhead ran away.

The shooter goes from looking at a possible investigation to being a hero. Once again, the old ROE reared its ugly head. The criteria is positive ID and imminent threat and we had a hard sell for either one. I talked to Mikey and his boys but it's hard to criticize now that we know this guy made a living killing Marines.

The rest of the mission consisted of a combination of mounted and dismounted movement and we moved through the zone rather quickly. When we got to the LOA, we strongpointed the area and waited until the whole company consolidated at our position.

There was a shit-load of kids in this neighborhood and we passed out candy. Soon, the shit-load turned into a shit-ton and kids everywhere. At one point, I was mobbed by about fifty of them screaming for candy. It was so bad some of the corporals yelled at them and tried to chase them away. I laughed my ass off and encouraged the kids while the corporals shooed them away. Eventually, we got cleaned out because these little kids wouldn't take no for an answer.

The Marines called me "Gunny Clause" again. It doesn't help to get rid of a nickname you don't want when fifty kids mob you for candy at Christmas time. Oh well, fuck it. I'm Gunny Clause!

17 Dec. 2004

Another joint operation with the Army known as Operation Discovery. We had a platoon of Army engineers attached and we went to the canal that separates Ramadi on the north side from Tamin, the Army's area, to the south. Our area of Ramadi is located between the Euphrates River to the north and the Habinniyah Canal on the south. Since we found such huge caches along the Euphrates in the north of our sector, we figured we might as well search the banks of the canal on the south.

This is not some small bullshit canal. It's almost as wide as the Euphrates. The 9th Infantry Division set their people in place to search their side, while we did the same on ours. We had an engineer platoon from the Army to do the actual searching and digging while we provided security with both mounted and dismounted troops.

Today was also the debut of my almost brand new gun truck, the one blown up at the Combat Outpost, with a new engine, transmission, brakes, tires and front end. It's powerful as hell and it's all fuckin' mine. Now, when we go out, I take my hand picked crew of Goons and I don't have to rely on finding space with one of the platoons. I have Swartz behind the wheel, Sgt.

Davidson as my wingman and crazy "Mike" Buentello in the turret.

We attached the Goonmobile to the MQRF. We weren't into the mission for ten minutes when our boys found two artillery shells buried in the dirt by an abandoned house, rigged with a blasting cap and the other not yet primed. The engineers made a call and said we could transport them both back to the rear but never in a million years would you travel around in a training environment with a blasting cap inside an explosive. I know this is combat but it's still the same concept. Besides, we carried enough of our own explosives with us and it wouldn't be a big deal to prime a charge and blow the shit up. Luckily, the Battalion Gunner made the same call I would have. As the Gunner, he has the final say-so when it comes to shit like this.

We went down by the canal and dug a hole while Gunner and Reyno prepped the demo. Then, we primed the charge, ran up the bank and took cover. The explosion was awesome. Two 155mm artillery shells primed with a pound of C-4 packs quite a wallop. We waited for thirty seconds and got up to go look at the hole and no shit, suddenly,a piece of shrapnel fell to the ground about ten feet away from me, thirty seconds after the blast. I'm sure some math or physics genius could tell you how high that piece must have flown but I'll just say it in grunt terms, pretty fuckin' high! The hole we dug was about a foot deep and about a foot wide. After the blast, it was about four feet deep and six feet wide.

One of our Be-On-The-Lookouts (BOLOs) was a gray, '80s model, left-side driver, Toyota Corolla. Intel said it was a verified SVBIED. After making a few laps of the area, we turned into an alley, headed north and the lead vehicle turned quickly west. The next three vehicles followed the lead vehicle but Mike yelled he saw a gray car just up the road to the north. The driver and passenger saw us, jumped in and sped off. I called Lt. Jones over the radio.

"Sir, swing back around, I think we got a line on that gray VBIED."

We still had the rear vehicle behind us and we took off up the road. We pulled up behind the Corolla with the tension and pucker factor at an all time high. How's this for a thought? Great, we just found a vehicle with a suicide driver and his goal is to blow up our vehicle by getting close enough for his explosives to be effective. We drove up to him but how the fuck can we stop this car without getting blown up in the process? I couldn't ram him with my vehicle, block him off, get out and pull him out and I couldn't let him get away. I could shoot him and blow up his fuckin' car but how could I do that without positive proof?

All this ran through my head in about twenty seconds so I did the only thing I thought might possibly work. I got out of the truck and ran a little forward of my vehicle and yelled at this asshole to stop which he did. I was out of my truck, Sgt D beside me. I couldn't get too close 'cause I surely didn't want to get blown the fuck up in this dirty fuckin' alley in Iraq.

I yelled at the guy to get out, he stepped on the gas and like the dumb-asses we are, we gave chase on foot. I yelled for him to stop again and once again he did. I told my boys if he didn't get out this time I was going to take a shot at his tires. As we cautiously approached, he gunned it again. I took two shots at the tires, the passenger turned around,

"He's got a gun," Sgt D yelled!

"Mike, light that fucker up," I shouted.

Before the words were out of my mouth, Mike lit up the whole back window with the machine gun while Sgt D and I fired from the street. The car sped down the alley and turned the corner while Mike sprayed the machine gun. We ran like hell down the alley and my vehicle passed us just as we turned the corner. This corner spilled out into a big traffic circle and the vehicle was there with the driver's door flung open, two sandals lying by the door and the passenger in the final stages of dying while he lay across the front seat.

All of this happened in about twenty seconds but it was like slow motion for me. I didn't have time to dwell on it because the guy with the gun got away. He sure as hell didn't get far but there were a bunch of possible places to hide, not enough Marines to cover everything and most importantly, I was separated from the other vehicles.

I told the only Team Leader there, Lcpl. Ottman, to get on the roof of the nearest tall building and get me some eyes on the area. I tried to report the car leaked gas, the passenger still kind of alive, but dying and a shooter somewhere close but my radio didn't work. As the senior man on scene, I had to handle the entire situation. We got into the best positions we could and pretty soon the rest of the gang showed up. We searched a few of the buildings but this no-good son of a bitch with the rifle got away.

When the other guy finally died, we approached

the car and searched it for explosives or whatever. Nothing, not a goddamn thing and it was a Toyota CORONA not Corolla, not even the right fuckin' car. They did have a gun and fired back so they must have been up to no good.

I can't begin to describe how weird it was to be in a situation like that. All of it unreal, from the bullets, the excitement, the adrenaline rush and especially the aftermath; looking into the dead eyes of a guy you just killed or helped kill. I felt kind of numb.

I was in a courtyard outside a mosque in Iraq, searching a car and the dead body of a young guy who just died for nothing. Really, what's his legacy? What the fuck did he die for? Did anything he did help anybody or anything? I don't know the answers and I'm sure I wouldn't understand even if he could answer me. I'll bet at this point, pure hate, pure cowardice and not much else is the motivation behind everything these guys do. Even when they all have the same religion and we're not here to focus their hate on, they would still be killing one another instead of trying to kill us.

I'm glad that I have a great team of Marines that I can depend on. Swartz never hesitated when he drove up on that car even though he knew what it might contain. Sgt D got out of the vehicle instantly, without being told and covered my ass even though he would have died right there with me if it were a car bomb. When Mike saw the guy turn around with the gun, he fired before that fucker could pull the trigger. That's what I fight for, what keeps me going and what my boys fight for. That's our legacy. Goddamn right it is!

**Goon Mobile**

20 Dec. 2004

Echo Company was ambushed twice over the past few days and had five Marines medevac'd with gunshot wounds. I talked to Gunny Jaime, Echo's Company Gunny, and he said all five injuries happened during the initial bursts of fire from the enemy. For better or for worse, Echo does a lot of dismounted foot patrols. I'm not sure if this is good or bad. I do know there is an easy or hard way to find and trigger ambushes and IEDs.

Given the choice, I'd prefer to be in a vehicle for the initial bursts and explosions with my Marines in the vehicles. I think since we have the assets, we should use them. We also do dismounted patrols, but we usually dismount at the start point, wherever that may be, and move on from there. Meanwhile, the vehicles either satellite the movement or in most cases precede it just a little. I think this is the smart way to travel in this environment. Then again, I'm no Rommel, like some people like to think they are, so maybe I'm wrong. It has happened once or twice before.

* * *

Operation Treasure Hunt. Somebody must have watched Pirates Of The Caribbean and gotten onto some sort of pirate kick. We considered doing this mission for some time. A major target for an air strike in the first go-round was a Saddam Fedayeen training barracks. The bombs hit the target and the building turned to a big pile of rubble. Recently, there have been reports of suspicious activity around the building and foot patrols have noticed footprints leading into the basement where they possibly stored ammunition and weapons.

I was once again attached to the MQRF. We got to the building, secured all roads, and sent the Marines in to conduct the search and came up empty handed.

On the way home, we ran satellite routes in the vehicles as 4th Platoon did a sweep through the area in order to emplace a sniper team in a hide. We thought they might be able to gather intelligence and maybe catch the enemy with his pants down.

I do not like the concept of emplacing snipers and leaving them in this environment. In order to get a good look at the area, they have to use the roof. As much as we like to believe differently, the enemy has night vision capability. Ours! A four-man sniper team from Echo 2/4 got compromised in a hide and all four were killed. The enemy helped themselves to all of their gear, which contained a sniper rifle, regular rifles, pistols and all kinds of scopes and night optics. Maybe the gear is still in town and maybe not, but why take the chance?

Snipers cannot expect to function in the manner they were trained in an urban environment with no friendlies in town. If anyone sees them at any time it's a safe bet they're compromised. I love having the snipers attached and they're good, smart, tough Marines. I'd rather have them on missions where they cover our movement and come home when we do. The only other alternative would be to emplace them in a position where they don't have to be exposed like they are when hanging over a rooftop.

Once again, I'm not the guy charged with making the plans. I get my say-so and I'm usually listened to, but we keep trying to find a role for our snipers when I just think there isn't one.

22&23 Dec. 2004

Since our own intel weenies pretty much suck, we decided to conduct a night raid based on information of a new Showani. I knew this would be a goat rope before we finished with the order but when the Battalion S-2 and S-3 shops generate the missions, you play ball. A fuckin' night raid on a suspected insurgent leader because a Showani convinced someone he had knowledge of this guy's illegal activities. To say I was skeptical is a bit of an understatement.

The last time we gave any information to the Showani's about an operation, we were hit with the worst and best-planned IED attack of the war. Now they get told what's going on just before we depart and amazingly enough, we haven't gotten blown up with them since.

Another sure sign I was in for a wild night; 3rd Platoon was the raid force. Maybe we should recruit Bozo the fuckin' Clown to run our intel and get the Keystone fuckin' Cops to do the raid.

We got off without any problems and that was a major feat with the Showanis involved and took Michigan to Nova and moved at a fast rate of speed. The lieutenant was in the lead vehicle and overshot the street of the target house but not a big deal and easily corrected. We drove right up to the house and dismounted vehicles and hit not only the target house but also the houses on either side of it. They usually are asleep at 0330 and tonight was no different.

All we had to do was get the ID cards from the assholes in our target house and bring in the Showani to ID the guy. I called for the interpreter,

"Get one of the younger detainees to round up the IDs of everyone in the house," I ordered.

This guy had what looked like a legitimate ID and it did not match the name of the guy we were looking for. But, he did have a briefcase with 10,000,000 dinars in it.

"Why so much cash, pal? Financing the Muj, are you?" I asked.

"I own a grocery store, I have to keep all the money with me or it will be stolen," he replied.

Whereas 10,000,000 in U.S. dollars would be very suspicious, that much in dinars isn't really all that much.

We brought in the Showani, let him get a good look at the guy, and asked him yes or no. The interpreter and the Showani had a five-minute conversation. I told the interpreter to shut this guy up.

"Look, we need to know if this is the insurgent and don't have time for a discussion. What is the Iraqi word for yes and the Iraqi word for no?" I asked the interpreter.

"You tell this fucker the next word out of his pie hole will either be "yes" or "no" and not one other fuckin' syllable," I said the interpreter.

I pointed at the suspect,

"Yes… No… I don't know," the Showani said.

I was about to apprehend the fuckin' Showani.

"We're in the wrong house, I could take us to the right house but we have to go to the Government Center and drive from there," he stammered to the interpreter.

"Yeah, right, that's gonna happen. Tell this asshole if he says one more word I'm kicking his ass," I forcefully told the interpreter so my new best pal would see I was not happy.

I wonder how many IEDs we would have hit on that fuckin' trip. Fox 6 decided we might as well take the guy with all the cash in for questioning and call it a night.

Rather than all vehicles getting some distance in between them and then driving others through to where they needed to go, the drivers tried to do three-point turns in the fuckin' alley. Literally, you would need to do a twenty-point turn to get a vehicle turned around in that small of a space. Eventually, we got it fixed after I got out of my vehicle and had a mental breakdown. I stood out in the middle of the street, screamed at the drivers to get their heads out of their asses and pretty much made a spectacle of myself.

That should have ended the drama but just as we hit Michigan, my vehicle blew a transmission hose and fluid sprayed all over our windshield. I didn't want to chance getting my brand new truck deadlined so we hitched it up to the rear vehicle and they dragged us back to JC. A poetic and fitting end to a cluster fuck, if ever there was one!

25 Dec. 2004

In our sixteen years of marriage, Janet and I have missed the Christmas holidays for the fifth time. Deployment over any holiday sucks, but Christmas hurts the most. The sad truth is when you make a career out of the military, you'll miss out on just about every holiday or significant moment in your family's life. It never gets easy but you do get used to it. I think it's harder on the families than it is on us.

My favorite family memories center on Christmastime because we often spend it with my family in Pennsylvania or Janet's family in Belfast.

Even on those occasions when we don't travel and celebrate by ourselves, we still have my whole family together and often have close friends over for a feast.

Like most parents, my greatest joy at Christmas comes when the kids get up way too early and attack the presents, particularly when the kids still believed in Santa Claus, but even now we still have a lot of fun. Janet fervently believes in not letting the kids have any idea what their presents are and wraps everything in secret. Then all the presents are put under the tree and sit there for weeks to torture and taunt the kids. By Christmas morning they have themselves worked into a frenzy and wrapping paper and boxes start flying through the air.

Even Molly the dog gets into the act because several packages of dog treats and toys get wrapped and put under the tree. We let Molly get up close to the tree and she knows exactly which presents are hers. I guess she can smell them through the wrappers but it never ceases to amaze me when she delicately picks one up and brings it to me to open.

To add insult to injury, we found out we'll be deployed next year and miss Christmas twice in a row. I'm pretty sure my family will not take kindly to that bit of good news. I could feel sorry for myself but the truth is I have a great family, great kids and a pretty good life. There will be many more Christmas holidays and I'll be right there in the middle of everyone. The funniest part of all is you appreciate and love your family much more when you are separated from them. Many people never realize how much they have and damn sure never appreciate how lucky they are. Marines don't have that problem.

**Front rt, Dani**
**Lt to rt, Sonia, Me, and Janet**

Christmas in Iraq. We were going to go out on a raid, believe it or not. Operation Bad Santa. However, battalion couldn't put the package together in time so we called it off. In its place, we conducted the single most important logistical movement of the Iraqi campaign. My mission was travel to Hurricane Point and return with 14 cases of beer and 175 mini bottles of rum.

A tactical beer run in a combat environment. If ever there was an operation to warm my Irish heart, this was it. We didn't expect trouble, but if the Muj ever wanted a company of crazed maniacs to come and kill their ass, let them blow up the truck with the beer in it. The boys were all smiles as we took off. They would only get two beers and a mini bottle of rum each but they couldn't have been happier if I brought back the Hooter's girls. The Sergeant Major kept the beer under lock and key in an Iso container and after exchanging a few pleasantries, we loaded up and headed back to base.

We unloaded the beer into my room and then the hyenas circled. It would have been a good practical joke to tell them they weren't getting any but I was in no mood to be killed in my own hooch, so we distributed the rations and everyone commenced to drink.

**Santa and Beers**

As luck would have it, there seemed to be an extra 12 pack when it was all said and done. Since there was no fair way to distribute it, and since it's good to be the Gunny, let's just say I got good and toasty.

I love Marines. I'm not just saying that because I am one and because I'm drunk. These guys have gone through some real tough times and been deprived of just about every creature comfort you can imagine. They have done nothing but bust their ass since the day workups for this deployment began and now they all thank me and get ready to elect me as the next President 'cause I went and got them a few beers. It never even entered their minds they deserve so much more and so much better than this.

These Marines are a cut above every unit and have the little bit extra that separates good Marines from great ones. Every now and again, I feel sorry for myself, like when I'm away from my family and in this shit-hole country for Christmas. Then I realize I'm with the best possible crew of men I could ever hope to hang around with. When it's all said and done, I'll look back on Christmas of 2004 as one of the great memories of my life.

**And a Merry Christmas it will be**

28 Dec. 2004

Today's mission was a raid of four houses we thought had potential bad guys followed by a presence patrol through the area. We had reporters from the Marine Corps Times along for the ride but by now having extra people around is no longer unusual. 2nd Platoon discovered the remains of an enemy mortar position. They found tracks, imprints and most telling of all, leftover mortar increments, the explosive charges that determine how high and how far a mortar will go. This is the first time Omar has left that much behind. Normally, he's real good at cleaning up all his evidence; including shell casings. Either he's getting sloppy or we have a new breed of amateur running around. If he is an amateur, he's probably stupid enough to come back to the same spot. If so, we have a little surprise for him.

Tomorrow, we have plans for a company-sized operation and we'll just have to wait and see what turns up when we roll through every house in this area.

29 Dec. 2004

There's a saying, "If you're going to be a bear, be a Grizzly." Today we conducted Operation Grizzly. We did a bunch of different things at the same time that may not seem like a big deal now, but as a measuring stick, we've come a long way since our arrival in August. We did a company operation with two dismounted platoons, one satellite MQRF unit, a sniper drop to cover the whole shebang, and a platoon leave-behind in an overnight OP.

This was a lot of moving parts and takes a combination of being very good at what you do and knowing your AO real well. The Marines don't see this as anything out of the ordinary, which is yet another sign of our evolution as urban fighters. As for Operation Grizzly, we did a few vehicle stop and checks, patrolled around the area and generally pissed off a portion of the city that didn't seem fond of us anyway. The highlight of the mission, a vehicle didn't stop at a check point and one of my favorite 1st Platoon Marines, the Brooklyn Brawler, pumped a burst of machine gun rounds into the engine block of the car to show he really wanted them to stop. Needless to say, they were not too happy as they pushed their car to their intended destination.

We left two squads from 3rd Platoon in their OP and drove off into the sunset.

**Off into the sunset**

The downside to this mission is we were all pretty confident there was going to be action today. It just really had that feel to it. We know these no good sons-a-bitches are by no means dead and gone. Unfortunately for them, when they think they're ready, we'll still be here.

31 Dec. 2004

At 0130 this morning we did Operation Black Vaquero. We're really hurting for cool mission names and right now our creative naming department needs to be fired. Our mission was to capture some asshole with the very annoying hobby of making car bombs. Recent intelligence says this guy made thirty or more such devices and he plans to use them for the January 30th celebrations as a deterrent to voter turnout. We expect something big on Election Day so I hoped the intel panned out.

Considering it came from battalion and knowing they've done the near impossible and defied the Blind Squirrel Theory, I put out 10 to 1 odds on us finding Jack and Shit. I went as part of the MQRF with 4th Platoon. Normally, I'm part of the raid team, but glad to go with the mobile because we didn't expect to find anything like caches or incriminating evidence and any males in the target house were detained on GP anyway.

As the Company Gunny, I try to go on operations and interact with all of the platoons as equally as possible. I feel it's important for the Marines to see me out there with them and to take the same risks as everyone else. When a company feels everyone is a part of the team and will be there if the shit hits the fan, the morale stays high and the company stays tight. As the months roll past, this becomes an important part to stay focused and fight complacency.

After having some slight problems with navigation, we got back on track and rolled near the raid sight just as 1st Platoon hit the target house. Our goal was to get in and out as quickly as possible. While 1st Platoon took down the house, we roved around the area in the gun trucks and looked, and hoped for trouble.

Although 1st got three detainees, they didn't get the target asshole nor find weapons or bomb making material. We roved all around that block and a few others in the immediate vicinity and didn't see so much as a cat or rodent creeping around. As soon as 1st got those guys bagged and tagged we packed up and around 0200 went back to camp. Another successful mission and if we're lucky the interrogators can get some info from these clowns. To be honest, none of us hold out much hope along those lines.

01 Jan. 2005

A new year and we're still in Iraq. It's not like I didn't know I'd be here during the changing of the years but it's still pretty depressing. Everyone at home is right now still partying, sleeping it off or recovering from the first hangover of the year. Last night, I drank my last Coors Light 24 ouncer, the last of my Christmas present from Big Ed, Mikey's dad. The rules are; we are not supposed to drink any alcohol but Ed got three through the mail and anyone out there who thinks I would throw away three perfectly good cans of beer obviously doesn't know me very well. I drank one so I wouldn't be a total loser on New Year's Eve. There were no missions requiring any action on my part so I sort of had the day off.

Bruce and I went for a run, I did thirty minutes on the stationary bike and another ten jumping rope. Even though we're in a combat zone, we still have to find the time to PT and stay in shape. The training will be intense when we get home due to the short turn-around time and I refuse to become an old, fat, lazy Gunny who leads with his mouth rather than his actions.

We decided to let the boys blow off a little steam this evening with boxing matches. I'm a certified boxing trainer and I brought 14-ounce gloves and headgear with me. We had smokers all the time when I first came in and they were great for building morale, blowing off steam and toughening up the Marines. The Goons worked hard all day, building the ring and setting up the fights. Everyone in camp was pretty excited about the whole thing and then the CO came in and reminded me once again how this new Marine Corps has changed.

**Letting off a little steam**

He wanted to know my thoughts on the subject of letting the Marines box. I told him I thought it was a great idea. Lt J, also on hand, is a Marine Corps certified martial arts instructor and it's not like we're going to let anyone get hurt. The CO told me there has to be neurosurgeon on deck to allow boxing matches. Since there are never any neurosurgeons hanging around when you need them, I guess the Marine Corps figured out a way to forever cancel the matches without saying we've gotten too soft for real boxing matches.

The CO is worried if a Marine gets hurt, he'll get fired. I guess it's a legitimate worry and another reason why I could never make it as an officer. When I look at it from my skewed viewpoint, I see a way for the Marines to build morale, have fun, get tougher, blow off steam and relieve a little built up stress. I guess I should look for all the reasons to say no instead.

I never thought the Corps would get to a point where we're afraid to let the world's toughest guys lace up the gloves and have a little fun. Where I come from, kids start boxing before they get out of elementary school. I realize there are inherent dangers associated with punching one another in the head but what are we supposed to do, play tiddly fuckin' winks? I heard a story last year where some schools in America make the kids jump rope without using the rope. They claim that an imaginary rope is better because when Lumpkins can't jump the real rope, it hurts his self-esteem. Imaginary jump ropes in our schools and now Marines who are too delicate to box. What in the Blue Hell is going on America?

02 Jan. 2005

I was asked to put the final touches on my words of wisdom for the Company Gunny who will replace me when 1/5 takes over in March. How do you sum up all the shit a Gunny needs to know in two to three pages? I guess I'll focus on the few things I wish someone had told me. I hope he gets this and applies whatever he can in his preparations. I hope it helps, brother.

SHIT THAT THE COMPANY
GUNNY SHOULD KNOW:

VEHICLES: We have (3) 7-tons and a five man team attached from the Motor Pool. They work out a schedule and mostly drive only the 7-tons when needed. However, one of them is a squared away Sgt and the 2nd Platoon Sgt commandeered him and made him his permanent driver. He didn't drive on the 7-ton rotation anyway so what the hell.

We have (9) gun-trucks; some are the hardbacks Weapons Company always runs with. 1043s is the correct nomenclature, I think. The other two types are 1114s and 1116s. These are the big armored Humvees you've probably seen or been in yourself. We have (6) ten-man Humvees upgraded with extra armor and all kinds of A-Team shit with the help of the Navy Seabees. There are a few other vehicles that run but never go into town and we use them for shit around the camp. I also have (2) 20 passenger busses that I signed for, with a fake name, from the Army. I let the platoons use them for runs to the chow hall or the PX, shit like that. I'll try to keep them for the turnover, if the Army doesn't catch on to me by then.

The way we operate is with four platoons and I'll explain how the vehicles fit in. By the way, we tried to operate as three line platoons with the weapons platoon Marines attached out, but that just doesn't work. The four-platoon rotation was the only solution and I wish we did that before we got here because going to four platoons once here became a fuckin' nightmare. Not just with the room assignments, but with the leadership, rosters, gear, and especially accountability. Trust me on this one; if you went to four platoons now, it would be much, much easier to change back to three later on, if the mission changes.

The vehicle breakdown is such: We have a Mobile QRF that supports the ONE OP we have and its main mission is MSR security, filling in gaps the OP cannot see. Secondary is supporting the OP for any reac's or for anything dealing with the logistics of the post.

Finally, they prowl around the AO looking for trouble, a kind of Ramadi 5-O. For this mission, we use (3) gun trucks and (1) ten-man hummer. The same platoon on OP mans the MQRF. This is a 24-hour post and they usually split the platoon and do 12 hours of OP and 12 hours of MQRF. There is a rest plan worked into the OP portion of post. The ten-man carries supplies or whatever and is used for a medevac vehicle, if the need should arise, which it will. The minimum amount of vehicles for a convoy is four, at least by our BNCO's order.

The QRF/A sled of vehicles is (2) gun trucks, (1) 7-ton and (2) ten-man Hummers. You can transport a max load of 49 bodies including drivers with this sled. QRF/A is on 10 minute alert at all times and stages at Hurricane Point every time the mission platoon is out for the purpose of a quicker response time.

The Mission Platoon has the same exact sled as the QRF/A. We run one or two missions (platoon-sized), planned by the platoon commanders, every day. Usually, the MQRF will satellite around the area of the mission. The platoon must figure out how to move its own vehicles in support of its own dismounted troops. This leaves one platoon back at the firm base. They are the QRF/B, with no transportation even if you wanted to get them in the fight. They have (2) ten-mans and (1) 7-ton and if the shit really hit the fan, you could get a Whiskey Platoon to pick them up and escort them where needed but we only had to do this once. Basically, that platoon has the day off.

That leaves the Command Sled of vehicles. For this you have the CO's vehicle, which has a double stack VRC mount radio and a blue force tracker, pretty much a big fuckin' GPS. The Company Gunny's vehicle has the same set up. These are both 1116s. Also, you have the ambulance, which is a modified Hummer (armored).

*The vehicles are your most critical assets. You are not walking where you need to go even if you wanted to.*

**Huge IED explosion, not a dust storm**

**These save lives. Trust me**

I can't tell you how to run your company or HQ section but I will tell you how I run mine and this has saved not only my ass but also my mind. I have 15 Marines and one sailor in the Company HQ. If you add the 5-man Motor T section and the two former Weapons Platoon SNCO's who run the COC and Intel cell, that makes 23.

- **Command vehicle** - Goes out on every Operation and consists of the CO, 1stSgt, CO's RTO, CO's driver (formerly asst. training NCO), and the CO's turret gunner (the training NCO). We have two radiomen from Comm. The CO keeps one with him and the other goes with the XO, or Gunny, on major ops. Otherwise, these guys stay busy. The training NCO is also my Ammunition NCO for the Company. Believe me, you'll need one. The Asst. Training NCO is also my Asst. Motor T NCO. Can't live without that either.

- **Gunny's vehicle** - Also goes out on every Operation and consists of the Gunny, Gunny's driver (Police Sgt), Turret gunner (formerly the Barracks NCO), and the HQ Plt. Sgt (A Sgt who checked in from the IRR one week before we left). I know there is no such billet but try managing all these different fuckers without one and you'll wish you had one. That leaves an extra seat in my vehicle and since some weirdo is always being attached last minute, like Combat Camera, ABC, NBC, CAG, USMC.mil, the seat comes in handy. Your Police Sergeant better be a hard fuckin' worker with an ass-load of initiative, and a good driver, or you're fucked, plain and simple. My Barracks NCO has no barracks to take care of so he is my Vehicle NCO. This guy should be a backyard mechanic and what I said about the Police Sergeant goes double for this guy.

- **Ambulance** – The ambulance is a four-seater, armored hummer with a double stack stretcher rigged inside. The HQ Doc obviously rides in here and his driver is one of the Company Armorers. This leaves two more open seats and this is for more last minute attachments, or you can squeeze in more of your HQ guys for vehicle security if you want. Also, if you have to evac casualties or ride around with a KIA, friendly or enemy, you really don't want them in a vehicle with all the troops.

The remainder of your HQ section is the XO, Company Clerk, other Armorer, and other RTO. On Company or Battalion-sized operations, the XO is either running the COC on base or running a Mobile COC with the other RTO. This leaves four Marines in camp to run your COC. Some Ops have lasted from twelve to fourteen hours so you need someone in the COC to run the show and that's usually whoever from HQ is left behind. Otherwise, you'll have to work out a schedule amongst the platoons but it's very hard to stick to a schedule with the nature of how we operate.

The next point is weapons, specifically heavy weapons. We did dick for training with .50 cals and MK-19s. One fuckin' day of familiarization fire with each Marine shooting like one fuckin' burst. Absolutely, the one thing I'd go back and change if I could. We have three .50 cals, one MK-19, six SMAWs and of course, our six 240s. These weapons stay mounted on the gun trucks, except the SMAWs and the 240 on OP. When we went to four platoons, we ensured we had an even distribution of machine gunners, assault men, and mortar men in each platoon. Everyone, and I mean everyone, especially the NCOs and SNCOs, need to know how to load, clear, unload, take apart, clean, fix, shoot, AIM, and perform immediate action on all of the weapons systems. Then teach them again and again, especially misfire and immediate action drills. You really don't want your heavy guns going down in a firefight and some numb-nuts who only knows how to load and pull the trigger on the gun. When we were at the Combat Outpost, we ran a gun line with an 81mm mortar and two 60mm mortars. At JC, they collect dust. We couldn't use them if we wanted to. But just because you start here, it doesn't mean you'll finish here.

- **Rosters and CMR.** You will get more gear over here than you have ever seen in one company. Your armorers need to be squared away and need to stay up with all the shit. You get new shit, Marines go down, shit gets evac'd, comes back, and dumb-asses lose shit. It's an accountability nightmare but if your guys are good, they can save your CO's ass. If one or both of them suck, you might want to fire their ass now and just get someone who's organized and has good computer and

> organization skills. All that bullshit, like in the rear, with the armory is non-existent here. You find a place to store your shit and then your people need to be able to keep track of it all. Remember this, in the rear you can get by with shit-heads that no one else wants in their platoons because you can do all the shit yourself. Out here, your ass is outside the wire all the time and your focus is, or should be, on fighting the fight and being what a Company Gunny needs to be, a gun fighter and duty expert with the weapons and tactics, not a fuckin' logistics pogue.

Also, for all the Gunnys, if your S-4 is good there, they'll be good here. If they suck there, you're on your own over here. Let's put it this way. Be prepared to politic, trade and make nice-nice with the Army, Navy and other units. When you're told you can't have it, and know you need it, and you know it's out there somewhere, you'll have to go get it yourself.

Finally, I would have done more training with radio procedures, especially calling in the medevac. As for your drivers, each platoon needs 6 or 7 of their own. We had about two per platoon when we got here and had to set up this bullshit course where drivers got 1 hour of practice and were on their own. Whoever your drivers are, they need to be well trained at driving with blackouts and IR covers with the PVS-14. Do not forget this; *DRIVERS HAVE PRIORITY ON PVS-14s.* You go from dark to light so often you need one eye night vision, the other regular. Otherwise, your driver gets whited-out when headlights, bright houselights or streetlights hit his 7-Bs. If this happens he crashes or fails to spot the IED that kills you all or destroys your vehicle. Believe me, both have happened.

03 Jan. 2005

It's 0100 and I'm having trouble sleeping. We were hit hard by an IED earlier. The MQRF were doing satellites around 4th Platoon during a mission. Somewhere along the way, our friends were able to dig under the ground near Buckeye and Hospital Road and emplace either an anti-tank mine or a very huge and nasty IED of some sort.

The MQRF rolls with three gun-trucks and one ten-man Hummer. On any normal patrol or operation, the ten-man would carry troops. When it rolls with the MQRF, it is used for logistics and for medevacs if necessary and therefore no troops ride in the back. Fortunately for us, the assholes do not know that.

1st Platoon was the MQRF for today's mission. When the ten-man rolled over the IED, they initiated the blast. A ten-man Hummer with all the extra armor and supplies weighs nearly 4,000 pounds. The blast from this IED went off underneath the vehicle, blew the back half and rear axle into the Habbiniyah Canal twenty yards away, and completely flipped the remainder of the truck. Everyone who saw the explosion agreed, neither should have walked away from this one. The two Marines riding in front, Oso received 5 stitches and a mild concussion and Dougy only a mild concussion.

I'm not too sure how religious they are, but if I were them, I'd be in church next Sunday.

**Before and after**

**Oso and Dougy walked away with barely a scratch**

The CO was ordered to recover the rest of the vehicle which is the reason for my unrest. Apparently, someone wants us to inflate a Zodiac, transport it to the canal, paddle out there, hook up the twisted hunk of metal to a Humvee winch, paddle back, and then drag it out of the water. For what reason in the world would we need to do this? The enemy can't possibly use it against us. We don't have a use for it. There is nothing, absolutely, positively nothing to be gained from this mission. On the downside, there is the fact we can be killed, hurt, drowned or possibly blown up again.

When the CO told me we had to do this I burst out laughing. I truly thought he was kidding and trying to get a rise out of me. But, he wasn't and now I'm left to contemplate the risk versus reward on this one. Oh well, "Ours is not to wonder why" and all that happy horseshit! "Yes sir, yes sir, three bags full."

OK, now it's morning and after a fitful night, it's time to go on our TROB mission. What's a TROB? A TRAP is an acronym for Tactical Recovery of Aircraft and Personnel, like what the Marines did when that O'Grady guy crashed his jet, but ours is a Tactical Recovery Of Bullshit. But orders are orders so we might as well just go do it and see what we're up against.

We went to the sight to do a recon and sure enough, about thirty feet out into the canal, was a hunk of armor from the truck. We went to HP and opened a boat locker that hasn't been used in over a year. All the parts were there so we got a Zodiac up and ready and loaded it onto the back of the 7-ton, which turned into this massive operation.

"Why don't we just pay an Iraqi $20 bucks to wade out there and hitch it up?" Bruce suggested.

No shit huh? Why go through all this elaborate nonsense to launch a boat thirty feet into the water?

"Fuck it, if an Iraqi won't take the money and do it, I'll wade out there and hitch it."

This led to an argument between Bruce and I as to which of us two idiots should wade out there since we both would rather do it ourselves than order one of the PFCs or Lcpls to do it. Plus, he's former Force Recon with the dive and swim quals that go with it, but this isn't exactly a high-skill swim or dive mission and he's over-qualified for this job. Rather than try to convince him, I just walked away to see if the CO's negotiations wielded any fruit.

After arriving back on the scene, we swept for more IEDs and secured the whole sector. Usually, whenever we group up in an area, the locals come out to gawk and rubberneck. This doesn't bother us in a normal situation but on this mission, we might have to go out in a boat without helmets and body armor. Therefore, we didn't want anyone eyeballing us. The usual crowd gathered 300 meters down the road so I launched a few smoke grenades their way. The locals get scared shitless when smoke spews, they run for cover and stay gone until we leave.

While I launched grenades and the CO negotiated with the local Muj, Bruce said "fuck it," waded into the canal and hooked up this "crucial" piece of scrap metal. Beeker drove off, dragging 200 pounds of useless, twisted metal out of the canal. We loaded it into a truck and the first-ever TROB was complete.

For last minute fun, Bruce, Swartz and I launched a few smoke grenades across the canal when a car pulled up and dismounted some Iraqis who ran behind the levee. We couldn't tell what they were doing, but it made no sense for a car to stop there, but the smoke grenades probably let them know we had eyes on them and at the same time probably scared them shitless.

If any Marine in this company gets killed on an operation, I can say with pride he went down fighting and played a vital role in an important mission. I'm thankful I will never have to tell some Marine's loved ones he died for a useless piece of scrap metal in a litter-filled canal of shit.

04 Jan. 2005

As part of the "winning the hearts and minds" campaign we are supposed to refrain from breaking any Iraqis shit when we enter their house. If it's a hard hit on a known terrorist or we take fire from the house or find weapons in the house then nobody gives a shit. But, if we have to use the house to gain an over-watch position, we are supposed to apologize for any inconveniences and be respectful of their property. This is only fair, as we would like the same courtesies in a reverse situation.

Since we have to search a residence if we occupy it, a Marine does not have the time to negotiate with a homeowner who has locked doors inside his house with no keys to get in the locked room. Maybe it's a cultural phenomenon, but this is the only country I have ever been to where people have locked rooms inside of their own houses with no keys for the doors. To the Marines, and any reasonable person, including myself, this is very suspicious and warrants the Marine way of opening a door without a key. Hell, in my mind, even if I break the goddamn door, I'm doing these people a favor. Now they have an extra room heretofore they were unable to enter. Unfortunately, if we do not find any shit to confirm our suspicions, we have to give the homeowner a claim form to pay for damages.

We went to a house to pay an owner for several doors he claims we broke. This was not too bad a deal because we were going to patrol that neighborhood anyway. This gave us the ability to do it under the guise of a payback mission. This particular guy works at the water treatment facility and lives right behind it. I think everybody at that joint is as crooked as a snake but we have our orders.

We were supposed to meet him at the treatment plant but when we showed up he wasn't there. The other employees told us he was at his house and gave us directions so we drove over there to take care of business. As soon as we arrived on the guy's porch, a huge explosion went off about two streets to our west, where 2nd Platoon set up their over-watch positions, right near the 7-ton. It was hidden in a pile of garbage and fortunately for us it didn't go off until all the Marines were well away from it. Only Clarke, the 7-ton driver, was injured and fortunately treated with band-aids.

While 2nd Platoon sorted this out, they thought they spotted another IED in the same area. We cleared the Marines and vehicles away and called in to EOD about the possible secondary IED. While we waited for an answer from EOD, a rocket landed inside the treatment plant and we caught a little small arms fire from the east. This was a straight set-up in my opinion. It could be a coincidence but believing in coincidences will get you killed.

As if this wasn't enough, the Ghetto OP reported they shot a suspicious vehicle parked at the side of the road. The driver apparently tried to lift something heavy out of the back seat and the locals who were in the area quickly ran away. Since there was no activity at 2nd Platoon's location, we left a portion of them there and the rest of us went to respond to the call from Ghetto. A car was parked on the side of the road and the Iraqi police carried a dead body out of it.

We went back to HP to report all of our activity and a call came in that the car had rockets and explosives in it. We had to go verify this information and if it was true, call in EOD to detonate the vehicle. As we pulled up, I figured since the IPs dragged a body out and the area locals were back, the likelihood of this being a remote detonate car bomb was pretty slim. Therefore, in typically stupid fashion, I took a deep breath, got out of my vehicle and went up to have a peek. When I got there I saw Fox 6 had the same idea. It would be very bad for business, not to mention morale, if both the CO *and* Gunny got blown up.

I took a quick peek and saw all I needed to see; a huge artillery shell on the back seat. I quickly hauled ass out of there, told Fox 6 what it was, and asked him to call EOD. We secured the area and waited for the bomb experts to show up. We obtained good strong-point positions on all the roads east, west and south of the car but we were still a little overextended without enough bodies to get any rooftop over-watch. Day was turning into night and I was in a hurry to finish risking my life for the day.

Finally, EOD showed up, I gave them a quick brief of the situation and informed them we really did not want to be hanging around much longer.

"There's an arty shell and explosives in that car. We've already been here way too long and I don't have enough ass for long fight."

"You saw the shell and the explosives?" asked the Gunny in charge of EOD.

"Yeah, I saw them, bigger n' shit!"

"That's good enough for me, let's blow up the fuckin' car and get out of here then," he said with a grin.

I never worked with EOD before Iraq but these guys are beginning to grow on me. They sent the robot up to the car with four pounds of C-4 in a neat little satchel. The robot placed the charge right under the rear passenger door and two minutes later we lit up the night with an explosion for your ass. This took place right across the street from a mosque and when the explosion went off, the imam or mullah or whatever the hell he is went ape shit over the loudspeakers. I don't know what he screamed, but it definitely was not the Star Spangled Banner.

We drove back to JC with the knowledge that business was about to pick up. After a few weeks of "routine" missions, today's actions made everyone realize these guys may lay low every now and again but they're surely here to stay.

05 Jan 2005

Even good news around here comes at a cost. In order for Marines to ever leave this fucked up country, two things have to happen: One, the elections need to take place and two, the Iraqis need to be able to police their own shit with their own military and police force.

Word from on high says 240 so-called special-forces, police commandos are coming to help with the election process. In order for the vote, and the entire election to be legit, the American Forces cannot be a part of the process. Therefore, Iraqi Commandos will secure the actual polling facilities and we will secure the outer cordon.

Vehicle traffic will be banned and after a thorough search by the commandos, only people on foot will be allowed through. We will enforce the vehicle ban and patrol the outer cordon and react when and where necessary. That way we can be responsible for securing the safety of those who come to vote without being present at the actual facility.

I guess this makes sense, at least as much as appearances are concerned and by now we realize perceptions are about all that counts. You never know when the TV people might show up. The last thing we want to portray to the world is Americans rigging an Iraqi election.

The bad news for us, since there is nowhere else to put the commandos, they become our neighbors, live in the same community of huts, eat in the same chow hall and shower and wash clothes in the same facilities as us. The Colonel gave us the big speech about how we need to make them feel welcome, not segregate them or treat them like hostiles and make them part of the team. I wonder if this is how they embraced these guys in Mosul?

In my opinion, a very, very conservative estimate, I estimate at least 10% of these guys are no good. As of tomorrow, we invite two complete squads of terrorists to come live with us and have access to our living and dining areas. I realize we train these guys and take them out on missions but at least then I'm armed and they're armed and if they feel froggy they can hop right on over. To put them amongst us while we sleep and eat unarmed in the chow hall and to give them access to our living areas while we are out on missions seems, not only foolish, but reckless.

Someday, sometime, somewhere there must be one, just give me one, fucking high ranking officer with some balls who is more worried about his troops than his career and let him raise the bullshit flag when it needs raised. The best part of this whole thing, the orders come from so high not even our colonel can effectively filter the bullshit coming our way.

I'm not going to hold my breath and wait for the politicians to realize our new best friends were the very same people shooting at us last year at this time. For now, we continue to adapt and put some security measures in place whether anyone likes it or not.

We conducted Operation Sling Blade to get a look at our area of responsibility for Election Day. The big wigs decided on ten polling locations in the town of Ramadi. We will be responsible for five and the Army, the other five. Since Fox has the sector furthest to the west, we are only responsible for one site. Golf and

Echo will get two and Whiskey will be the primary QRF for all three companies. Since Fox only has one site, we will also have a platoon on QRF. In addition, all the companies are still responsible for their primary OP sites, so we'll all be spread thin to say the least.

This does not frighten me as much as it probably should, 'cause I itch for these bastards to come out and fight like men. An infantry company packs quite the fuckin' wallop and I'm confident we would put a serious fuckin' hurt on anyone silly enough to attack our position.

As for our polling site, it is a fairly large, enclosed compound currently home to the Boys and Girls School. We know this area like the back of our hands and confident we can secure both the facility and the surrounding area. Our walk through today was without incident and the people not as hostile as in other places. We got a good look at how we'll set up security while trying not to tip our hand about why we were really there.

A key factor in all of this will be to not let anyone know where the polling sites will be until we're ready to lock down the areas. Our goal is to move in one or two days prior and stay until one or two days past the actual election date. Right now, I'm a lot more worried about the fox that's moving into the henhouse rather than the ones out in the forest.

06 Jan. 2005

Another mission with the MQRF, Operation Merlin, to get another look around the area of the proposed polling site. While we were at it, we also took a fresh look from a different angle at the area where we got hit with the IED and ambush the other day.

We're on the lookout for IEDs since the shooters are either hiding or scared to get behind their sights. It's really nerve wracking to drive around on vehicle patrols. Every sense is on such high alert and the anticipation of being blown up keeps the adrenaline pumping the entire time. This place has so much garbage and rubble strewn about an IED can be anywhere and everywhere. It's difficult when we get back to camp and try to amp down, relax, get some rest and prepare to right back out again.

Working with the Iraqis and planning for this election will be a great relief. We'll get a break from the daily grind while we focus our attention on a completely different mission. In our case, the harder work and the change in the routine keeps our head in the game.

09 Jan. 2005

January 7th was Operation Black Eye and January 8th was Operation Raven. Both were night operations that involved my truck reinforcing the MQRF. During night OPs, the curfew is back in effect and anyone we see is the enemy, or if not, at least, worth detaining, but if everyone has obeyed the curfew, you drive around for hours in a ghost town.

We drove to our areas and got into strong-point positions while the maneuver platoons patrolled their sectors, called in at the required checkpoints and patrolled back.

Those on patrol have senses on high alert, the NVGs light the way and behind every building, car, junk pile and structure they're sure the enemy lies in wait to ambush their ass. With live ammo and people trying, or at least willing, to kill you, they'll know a whole 'nother kind of adrenaline rush.

Unfortunately, as the Company Gunny, night patrols are no longer in my job description. As it stands now, my job is to lead the QRF for reinforcement, emergency extraction or medevac. My services were not required either night, mostly a good thing.

We had a Purple Heart ceremony earlier in the day and the Colonel told the Marines not to get discouraged by the lack of enemy activity. He told them lack of contact is what makes a mission successful in the first place. The fact we can go out on the streets night and day with impunity means we were successful in what we tried to accomplish.

This town is 100% better than the day we got here, maybe 200%. We went everywhere 2/4 told us not to go and we took the fight to these bastards and kept it up, with the help of the Army, to give credit where it's due. That's what it's all about over here and what I hope we keep doing for as long as we're here. We're Marines, trained to fight and fight hard. We're willing to try to keep the peace, but we're better suited for whooping ass and taking names, always have been, always will be. Anybody who tells you different, or trains you different has no business in this outfit. Plain and simple!

10 Jan. 2005

Another Purple Heart ceremony. Lt S received his second one of this war and for subsequent actions after being injured, he'll probably receive a Bronze Star. Cpl Paesano received his for being shot in the back and for subsequent actions after receiving his wound, he'll receive at least a Navy Achievement Medal with Combat Distinguishing Device. The third person to receive his Purple Heart got it by acting like a coward in the face of enemy contact and faking an injury. Somehow, that one just doesn't sit right with the rest of us and he disgraced and cheapened the whole ceremony by even being a part of it.

During one of our early engagements, this so-called Marine was about 100 yards away from an IED explosion. He was across the street and in a house no less, where several members of the platoon were closer to the explosion. Whereas everyone else was OK and able to continue with the mission, this guy curled up in the fetal and pretended to be unconscious. The Corpsman on scene called for an emergency medevac. They evac'd him and did all the things you're supposed to do when you think someone has a head injury.

Two weeks later, he needed to see a psychiatrist and claimed he couldn't take it anymore. Then he proceeded to continue faking symptoms long beyond the normal recovery period. When the members of his platoon came forward with stories of how he acted scared and talked about not wanting to be here in the first place, we realized we were duped.

By this time, the paperwork was already processed and even the Battalion Surgeon came forward and said he would change his diagnosis from concussion to panic attack.

Three times previous battalion told us to award him a Purple Heart because the original diagnosis was concussion and because he received an emergency *medevac*. Bruce, who received a Purple Heart in OIF 1 for being shot, with an enemy bullet, through the fuckin' forearm and triceps, flat out refused and did everything he could to get this thing revoked. The Battalion Commander absolutely refused to budge and there we stood, watching one of our own Marines disgrace the oldest award in the American Military.

We have Marines in our battalion who have lost arms and legs. I'll be damned if I'm going to stand next to them wearing a Purple Heart because I got a headache in combat.

After the ceremony, we conducted Operation Shakedown to use this lull in enemy attacks as an opportunity to really get to know our AO. We locked down an entire block, talked to every person in every house, saw who lived there and asked what they knew. Anyone not in a house got a real close look as to why they hung out in there in the first place. If someone didn't live there, and had no business being there, maybe we got us a troublemaker. We have ways of dealing with them that have proven quite effective. It's called getting detained, interrogated and sent to Abu Ghraib.

We passed out quite a few soccer balls, talked to a bunch of the families, figured out who lived in what house, detained one guy with a shit-load of bullets and a rifle and gathered decent intelligence about several different things.

One good example is the Muj hire teenagers to place their IEDs on the road. The teenager has a tough choice; either get killed for saying no, or chance getting killed while emplacing the IED. What are we supposed to do? If we catch someone placing anything on or along the road, we shoot to kill. But we're not killing the guy who made and can keep making the device. We're killing some kid who probably didn't have much choice in the matter. What a fuckin' country.

12 Jan. 2005

Operation Infinite Moonlight. In an ironic twist that had nothing to do with prior planning, there was no moonlight this evening. Either we're stupid or we just suck at naming operations. 2nd Platoon ran the show on this one and once again, my place was with the MQRF. Tonight we tried something different. We had an idea where these assholes launch mortar shots, so we set up an ambush position and hoped to get lucky. The odds on catching someone were not very good but if the enemy came out and tried some bullshit he'd get his ass handed to him. Every Marine would have an opportunity to unload a shit load of ammo and finally fight with and kill the enemy up close and personal. On the other hand, if he doesn't show up you silently lay in place for several hours in the cold ass Iraqi night.

As for Infinite Moonlight, we got Infinite Shit, went home tired and frustrated at 0200 and prepared to go right back out at 0600. Semper Fi, Mac!

13 Jan. 2005

Yesterday, we received intelligence from a supposedly reliable source that turned out to be accurate, which is pretty freakin' rare. Apparently, for a big comeback on the 14th and 15th of January, the Muj had meetings at several houses in our AO and planned a coordinated mortar attack on all of our bases. They supposedly have a tool or machine of some type that can drill through asphalt and plan on using this all along Route Nova to plant mortar rounds.

We received names and locations of the people involved in setting all this up. Rather than sit on our asses and wait to see if any of this panned out, we went on the offensive right away. We planned a very detailed three-phase operation named Operation Blackout with the goal of either arresting all of these bastards or at least throwing a monkey wrench in their plans. We refuse to lose our momentum and go back to reactive operations after the fact.

Phase One kicked off today at 1400 with two simultaneous raids on two of the meetinghouses. We have a target package with sixteen names of people wanted for apprehension, questioning and maybe a little jail time prior to the elections. I asked to go with 2nd Platoon on this one because I haven't been on a mission with Mikey in a while. Plus, his platoon operates well so I can get involved with the raid without having to worry about any of the logistical or planning details.

1st Platoon did the other raid so I expected two well-run operations with good results. As far as our AO is concerned, navigating to any house or area is never a problem and never will be again. This is an immense comfort and advantage that can't be explained.

When we got to our target house, I waited for the platoon to make the initial entry and then my goons and I entered. On every mission I have the same crew now, except this time Swartz asked Sgt D to drive so he could participate in the festivities. We had the right house but none of the four males present matched any names on the target list.

Across the way, 1st Platoon also struck out. We apprehended our four guys, just in case the interrogators could shake any info out of them, but this looked like another bum scoop mission from battalion. Tomorrow we will execute Phases Two and Three and we hope it turns out better than Phase One.

On the lighter side, one of the jack-offs we're looking for is named Turki. There are a few of them with either a first or middle name of turkey. Fox 6 grabbed a no-shit, live turkey at one of the target houses and had it detained and put in the vehicle. He called battalion to say he got one of the turkeys and was bringing him in. He had S-2, the Intel guys, come out to take pictures. They came out expecting to see a terrorist and instead we had a bird in flexi-cuffs on the front stoop of battalion headquarters. I guess you had to be there, huh?

14 Jan. 2005

Phases II and III kicked off this morning at 0500. 4th Platoon was tasked with raiding a house in order to find the real Turki and 1st Platoon had an area to sweep in the same vicinity. I was attached to 4th Platoon and we rolled up to our target house and the boys went flying inside in a good aggressive manner. We thought we had the wrong house again because when we asked for names, didn't get anything resembling Turki. We knew some of these people had to be around so we left and hit the houses to the right and left.

1st Platoon got lucky and grabbed two of the people from the shit list right off the bat. After a little more searching, we ended up with four of our own, then things got interesting. Sgt D and I joined up with Fox 6 and went over to see if we could help out 1st Platoon. They were in a house with an Iraqi Police

Captain who claimed his cousins across the street were big time Mujahedeen. Rather than wait for permission from battalion, we moved on their compound there and then.

Two squads from 1st Platoon, plus the contingent from HQ, rolled through the gate and immediately grabbed all the males from both houses, eight in total. We grilled them outside with the aid of our interpreter, Kabi. As usual, they knew nothing, loved America, wanted to be friends and thought we were all around great guys.

By now, I've developed a sixth sense with a lot of these situations and I was convinced these guys were no good and hiding something. Kabi said the same thing and Sgt D felt it, too.

While 1st Platoon tore the house apart and looked for evidence, I grabbed Sgt D and told him to come with me to search the outside of the compound. I went over to a stack of several bags of dates, which was not unusual because every house in Iraq had them somewhere. I moved them around and immediately found what I believed to be a mortar or artillery sight. I had Kabi ask them what it was and rather than have a reasonable explanation or any kind of excuse, they didn't know and claimed it wasn't theirs.

That answer means please tear this place apart and even look up my ass if necessary because I'm hiding something. They had a boat in the yard and Sgt D tipped it over and found a bag of ammunition, about 300 rounds, underneath it. This was enough to apprehend the four who lived in the one house, but not really enough to hold them for very long or send them to jail. As for the other four, we didn't have shit on them. Try as we might, we couldn't find any more evidence, even after Bruce chimed in with the funniest quote of the war. He walked beside the homeowner to where we found the ammo.

"You're coming over here with me and if you don't learn some English on the way there, I'm Whoopin your ASS!" he said.

He sounded so much like Stone Cold Steve Austin, and it doesn't hurt that he looks like him, I laughed until tears rolled down my cheek. We did all we could, even with the threats from Stone Cold, but we couldn't get anything from this guy. As we prepared to leave, Sgt D and I stood by a big stump hollowed out and filled full of dirt.

"Wouldn't it be funny if they filled this stump full of mortar rounds?" I asked.

Sgt D dug away a little bit of the dirt and fished his hand around in there.

"Holy shit, Gunny, there's a bag of something in here."

He pulled out his hand like a magician out of a hat and sure enough, he held a bag of something. We looked inside and BINGO! We have a winner! The bag contained 5 sticks of PE-4A explosive, a blasting cap and an M203, 40mm smoke grenade. Now we knew we not only had us some Muj, but also sneaky Muj, and now time to reexamine the area. We called in all the engineers, turned on the minesweepers, and gave the compound a real good once over.

Meanwhile, Sgt D had a brainstorm. There was a blue rag in a tree near us and in a nearby corner of the cement wall of the compound, there was another tree with a blue rag on a branch. He noticed a small, fist-sized hole in the wall right by the blue rag. Holes in these piece-of-shit, cement walls are so common that to have a wall without holes would be suspicious. Sgt D played his hunch and stuck his hand in the hole.

"Hey Gunny, look at this," he yelled again.

Once again the magician held up another bag. This one contained about fifty blasting caps. For the first time on our many searches, we took a real serious look in a heretofore-overlooked area, the outer wall of a compound. Sgt D was also smart enough to notice an awful lot of cheap patchwork done on the walls. He grabbed a hammer out of the tool shed, went around and busted open all of these patches. With thirty to forty holes in the wall when he finished, twenty of these had something in them like blasting caps, others had items ranging from cell phone batteries, walkie-talkies, cameras, cell phones, explosives, more blasting caps, and magazines with ammo.

This was a quality find by a Marine willing to look and think outside the box. Perhaps inspired by this thinking, Cpl. Reyno, another Goon, and Cpl. Licari, one of 1st Platoon's finest, called me over to a palm tree.

"Gunny, do you see a green bag up there or am I losing my mind?" Reyno asked.

I looked up and could barely see what looked like a green cloth. We couldn't climb up the tree so we decided to chop the fucker down. Here's where a great CO makes a great decision. He could have just said, "Hey, it's probably dates and I don't want my ass handed to me for chopping down palm trees," which had happened to other commanders or I wouldn't bring it up.

Fox 6 was all for it so once again we went to this asshole's tool shed and grabbed a few axes. After twenty or so minutes of chopping through a palm tree trunk with dull, piece-of-shit axes, the tree fell. Unluckily for us, it fell against another tree and got stuck. We volunteered our smallest Marine, Cpl. Aycock, to shimmy his ass up there.

Note to self: Next time you send a Marine up a tree, tell him what to do if he finds anything.

Aycock grabbed a bag, "You won't believe this shit," and dropped it 20 or so feet to the ground where it landed with a hard thud.

I looked inside and couldn't believe my eyes. The bag contained; (20) 1lb blocks of TNT, a bunch of propellant, several rocket boosters and blasting caps. Maybe it's just me, but I don't think it's a good thing to drop that shit twenty feet from the air to impact roughly on Mother Earth.

This wasn't even the bag we were originally concerned with. The "bag" was actually a well wrapped, brand new RPG launcher and a few rockets.

As common sense would demand, this caused us to closely examine the other trees in this compound. And what do you think we found? Another tree near the house had a few bags in it as well. As fate would demand, this tree had the biggest trunk of every tree in the whole fuckin' yard. The axes were dull as shit so Bruce tried to sharpen them with his Leatherman Tool in between whacks. The tree didn't go easy and about six of us worked in shifts to bring this fucker down.

Once again, it didn't fall exactly as planned, unless our plan was to have this huge tree fall on the house. However, it did work out nicely because the bags fell on the roof. In these we found more RPG rockets, boosters, and blasting caps.

At one point we were ready to leave with four detainees, one sight, and 300 rounds. Because of a little luck on my part and a smart Sergeant, we instead left with: (9) AK-47 mags, fully loaded, (2) AK-47 rifles, (1) artillery sight, (300) loose 7.62mm rounds, (1) RPK machine gun, (1) RPG launcher, (3) RPG rockets, (30) RPG rocket boosters, (4) cell phone batteries rigged for IEDs, (2) 120mm mortar increments, (1) motorcycle battery for IED use, (2) radio receivers, (1) 40mm smoke grenade, (1) cell phone rigged for IEDs, (1) 2-way radio, (1) 1lb bag of black powder, 5 lbs. PE-4A explosive, 20 lbs. of TNT blocks, (55) blasting caps, (1) pineapple grenade, (1) fighting knife, (25) crimped blasting caps, (1) disposable camera we hope has more evidence and four additional detainees, one of which turned out to be quite the wanted terrorist.

Needless to say, the Goons contributed well on this mission and 1st Platoon can claim another big score. We also exposed another secret of the Muj. Hopefully, intel fully exploits this knowledge and it makes its way around every unit over here. This may take away one of their last, best hiding places and result in huge cache finds all over Iraq.

Phase III of the operation consisted of emplacing two platoons in two separate OPs along with an 8-man sniper team in different locations along Route Nova. We waited in place at these positions and had two MQRFs ready to respond. We really hoped they would try to pull some shit with either mortar attacks or IED emplacement. We waited until the dark of night but had no luck on Phase III. Any way you slice it, their big attack never happened because we took the initiative, went on the offense and brought the fight to them. If I have my way, this is how we'll operate until the day we leave.

16 Jan. 2005

Yesterday, the CO, XO, 1stSgt, and I went over to meet the Iraqi Commandos that will be attached to our company from now until the end of the elections and possibly continue to work with us until the day we leave. I've already spoken my peace on the fact I cannot trust these guys because I am convinced some among them work for the enemy.

However, that being said, I am a professional military man and appreciate the bravery and sacrifice it takes to serve your country. For the most part, we're a respected profession. Even those in our own country who do not support the President or his policies still respect us and treat us with dignity. Hell, every time I'm in a bar and someone finds out I'm a Marine; it usually gets me a free drink or two. And when I go home to Pennsylvania, the greatest of all fifty states, fudgeddaboudit, people get insulted if I even try to pay for a beer. The last time I was home in the sprawling metropolis of Pittston PA, before I came to Iraq, I went out with my sister and had so many beers come my way, which I am obligated to drink, I had to be taken home in a wheelbarrow and trust me, I ain't no fuckin' lightweight. What I guess I'm trying to say is in America, being in the military is a pretty good life. For these Iraqis, most of their countrymen hate them and would very much like to kill them, if given the chance. It takes a pretty manly-sized pair of balls for these guys to suit up and serve, so for that, they have my respect, if not my trust and confidence.

We met the officers in charge of the two platoons that will be attached to us. Two things always strike me as odd whenever I meet the military leaders of damn near every other country on earth: One, they either cop this tough guy persona and attitude because they think they have to be tough and hard to impress us or they act like meeting us is the greatest day of their life. Two, and this the really strange part, there are never, never, never, any enlisted leaders among them.

If they recognize us as a superpower, and recognize our military as the world's finest, which we are and for many more reasons than technology and money, why don't they ever catch on to our system of leadership? Just about every other country treats their enlisted leaders like shit. Then again, maybe that's a good thing and a large part of the reason why we continue to whoop ass.

At this meeting we have a tough guy and a very happy man. My initial impression is both of these guys are leaders of men. They carried themselves like professionals and wanted us to know this isn't their first rodeo. They fought against us in the first go round and now they are on the same side as us this time around. I can't help but think how strange all this must be for them. Their former sworn enemies are now their benefactors and partners. I realize they want, most of all, for us to be gone from Iraq but I think they know they cannot gain control of this country without our help.

Another thing I contemplate is my own role in all this. I'm convinced we are one of the few, if not only, country on Earth so willing to quickly embrace and forgive our former enemies. I guess there is no way to just start all over from scratch with a completely volunteer military, certainly not if we want to remove our presence from this country in the next twenty years.

With that in mind, we agreed to start taking them out in squad-sized units and teaching them the skills they'll need to manage this place when we're nothing but a memory. If we're lucky, we'll do our jobs like the professionals we are, gain a fighting man's respect for one another and turn this place over to them for the rest of eternity. Or until they get another asshole dictator in charge who thinks he wants a piece of America or wants to fuck with our way of life. Then we'll be back and our new-found friends who were our former enemies will be our enemies once again and get the same ass kicking we gave them in all previous engagements

"No better friend, No worse enemy!" Your choice, Asshole!

17 Jan. 2005

A relatively quiet day in Ramadi. Now we realize the quiet of the past month has been due to these guys stockpiling and planning. There was too much intel coming in for all of it to be wrong and our finds of the past few days confirmed our suspicions.

When we have a lull, we collect our own information. This is a perfect situation for Snipers, if we can get them into a hide without being seen. We put them into position off of Route Michigan and Retard Road because of past reports of large groups of males hanging around in the area. If we're lucky, Snipers will develop some actionable intelligence or even shoot some terrorist in the head.

One of the ways our enemy operates is through locally sponsored terrorist cells. The basic breakdown is as follows: I'm Achnad, or Osama or any other Muj sympathizer. I am the known leader and/or financier of a cell of insurgents in Ramadi. Since most of the troublemakers are foreigners, or even Iraqis from another city, I have to arrange to get all my guys together to go over the plan, distribute supplies and get right to the heart of the real motivation, which is not allegiance to Saddam, hatred of America or service to Allah. That's right, I have to break out the money, American dollars, of course, pay my scumbags and send them out to do their thing. Therefore, we meet at a house somewhere and put our plan into action.

The ones with money are usually not willing to risk their own ass so they pay others. The dip-shits willing to do the actual dangerous or suicidal jobs aren't smart enough to either plan the operation or rig the explosives so others are needed for that end of the job. So a large group of insurgents meet at some point for any of their plans to go into effect. Ideally, if we could bust in on a meeting, we'd get somewhere between ten and twenty assholes taken down before they even have a chance to get outside and begin their attacks.

Snipers called in a report of keeping a close eye on sixteen males in four different cars entered a house on Retard Road. None of them brought in any supplies, bags, weapons or anything warranting being killed on the spot. Fox 6 ordered Snipers to continue to observe and report.

Just as I drifted off to sleep, Fox 6 mobilized the QRF. We drove to Retard Road, the very politically incorrect name given to the street the mental hospital is on, you gotta love Marines. When we arrived Snipers were supposed to use the PEQ-2A, an infrared flashlight beam we can see with our night optics, to shine a beam of light on the target house.

The Snipers thought we would be able to easily see exactly which house they illuminated, but from our vantage point on the street we could see about four houses lit up with the beam. We were right outside the houses, exposed and quickly losing our biggest advantage, surprise and speed. We made a decision to hit all four houses and hit them hard.

At one house, we could not breach the gate so we used the tried and trusty method of ramming it with the Humvee. All four houses went down quickly but we came up empty. There weren't sixteen males in all four houses combined so we either never got in the target house, the bad guys got away or the Snipers gave us bum scoop and brought us out here on a wild goose chase but option number three is unimaginable so it must be our fault. I've said before I love working with the Snipers but so far in this environment there have been so many more cons than pros, if it were up to me, I'd drastically reduce their role as far as intelligence gathering is concerned. Now we'll have to go back out there in a couple of days with some money to pay for the damages to property and to try and soothe the hard feelings these four households now harbor towards their "liberators."

If you ask me, which the Commandant does not, I'd tell you the longer Marines are in this country the more these people will grow to hate us. I wish this was not the case but it happens in the best of places even under peaceful conditions. With a raging insurgency well established within the population of this and many other cities, we must remain aggressive, defensive and at times violent and ruthless.

The bottom line is this: When the enemies of our country hear the Air Force is in the area, they go inside their houses. When they hear the Navy is around, they go in and close the door. When they hear the Army is coming, they go inside, close the door and lock it. When they hear the Marines are coming, they go inside, close the door, lock it twice, hide under the bed and piss their pants.

Marines never were, are not now and never will be a diplomatic force. We are what happens when diplomacy fails. Every American knows this and every American-hating piece of shit on this planet also would do well to know this. I just pray to God no battalion or regiment that has to come over here, ends up with some commander who is more worried about his own ass and political future than the lives of the Marines.

18 Jan. 2005

Today we did our first mission with the Iraqi Commandos, a pretty simple Vehicle Check Point (VCP) mission called Operation Lockdown. 4th Platoon were the lucky winners to take out the first commando squad. First, we locked down the North Bridge and then the South Bridge. The locking down of the bridges has never turned up anything of value. I think this is because unless someone is just plain unlucky enough to be on the bridge when we lock it down, they see traffic being searched and turn around. The bridge OPs get across the point and search at random locations, at random times on random days.

I hate VCPs. If a suicide bomber wants to kill Americans all he has to do is drive around and wait to be stopped at some point on any given day. When the Marines walk up to search the car, he initiates the device and Americans die, a tactic he has used not only in the past, but recently on Army soldiers here in Ramadi. There really is no way to tell if it's a SVBIED until it's too late. The explosives are either tucked into the door panels, under the hood or in the trunk.

But, orders are orders and there is a tactical purpose for doing this type of operation. I hope this doesn't sound too callous, but if someone actually has to go up to the cars to get the occupants out and do the search, then I volunteer the Iraqi soldiers. Meanwhile, we can get a safe standoff distance and provide protective over-watch. This seems fair to me and every other Marine and we'll operate this way until told otherwise.

For their part, the Iraqis are eager to get out there

and do their fair share and they don't seem too worried about their aspect of the mission. Maybe things will change if they finally find a SVBIED the hard way. In fact, I'm sure it will if I know the character of the Iraqi soldier. For now, I'm just glad we have a little time to do some operations with them prior to the election and I can only hope they can be somewhat professional and do what they're told. I guess we'll see soon enough.

19 Jan. 2005

We had a staff meeting to discuss two very important upcoming events. One, to devote 90% of our time and energy toward the election on the 30th. The other, our pending redeployment back to Camp Pendleton. It's hard to devote only 10% of your time and effort to something that consumes 90% of your thoughts. I think these elections represent our high water mark for this deployment. After that, we shift our main focus to get out of here and having a successful relief in place with Bravo 1/5.

We try not to give out our actual go home date because when you give the boys a solid date, they tend to lose focus on the daily grind. We absolutely have to keep everyone's head in the game and talking about ending this deployment would be bad for business. When the 1/5 advance party gets here, the boys will get real antsy. If we can keep the boys real focused up until then, we'll be okay. We're plenty busy with all other kind of shit right now so worrying about going home is low on the priority list.

We had a mission with the Commandos today but it got cancelled. As they pulled out of the parking lot, loaded up in the vehicles with 3rd Platoon, a youngster from 2nd Platoon flipped off one of them. This caused a complete uproar and they got off the vehicles and went home.

One thing about Iraqi guys is they seem very feminine to us. They like to hug and kiss, sit close, hold hands and are real touchy feely with one another. Maybe I'm a raging fuckin' homophobe. Plus, they get insulted very easily and when that happens you have to make nice-nice and apologize 500 fucking times and listen to them go on and on and on. Afterwards, you have to give them gifts or presents to say you're sorry. Sound like any American man-woman relationship to you?

They quit because they feel they aren't being shown any respect, think we hate them and will not look out for them on the missions. We tried to explain this was just one stupid, idiot youngster and did not reflect on the attitude of the whole company, but they weren't buying our story. That has always been another big problem for us wherever we go in the world. We are judged fairly or unfairly as a group by the actions of one or a few.

Bruce and the CO eventually smoothed everything over and Mikey gave his boys a good ass chewing and then I talked to them.

"I'll tell you right now, regardless of how any one person, or even all of us might feel about having to work with these guys, we follow orders, act professionally and give these guys the same respect we would want if the situation were reversed." I could tell they still weren't sufficiently upset, which prompted, "You made the CO and the company look like a bunch of jackasses." I shook my head disgustedly.

That really got to them. Regardless of how they feel toward this country or our new friends, they all feel very strongly about Fox Company. Most of them would rather take a bullet than let the company down or make us look bad.

I completely understand how they feel, but orders are orders. I don't fool myself that I'm working with a bunch of college educated, prim and proper bunch of pussies. These guys are some world-class tough guys and they've been hardened by training and now combat. If the worst thing they ever do to our so-called, non-enemies is flip them off, then I think we're doing okay.

20 Jan. 2005

Operation Blue Steel was an effort to find yet another cache along the banks of the Euphrates. HP has been hit more and more frequently by mortar attacks and for the past three days, IEDs were found near the hospital. Just short of the hospital, we split the northern part of the AO with Golf Company. For this morning's mission, 2nd Platoon dismounted the vehicles near Intersection 334, patrolled 2 clicks, 2000 meters, to an ambush site near the hospital and patrolled back along the riverbank at dawn.

When the enemy fires mortars or rockets, our artillery counter-battery registers the origins of the fire and records it in order to send counter fire. The main reason enemy mortar attacks are infrequent, inadequate and inaccurate. Along 2nd Platoon's route were a few of the locations used by the enemy this week. If they got lucky, they would either stumble along a cache or catch the enemy setting up IEDs.

I went with the MQRF but this time it was a little different than normal. This time we manned up two MQRF sections and staged in two different locations. That way we could cover more of Nova while 2nd patrolled to their ambush site and back. From 0200 until 0700 we tucked in our vehicles and waited to respond. Our MQRF went to this big house, owned by a pretty well to do Iraqi guy. The kids are friendly enough but Pops is probably getting pissed because we like to hang out there. Unfortunately for him, he has a house with a great view of Route Nova and the Euphrates. He also has a huge driveway we could park all of our Hummers on inside his compound. Provided we weren't seen going in, we could hang out there until sun up and no one would be the wiser. Things got interesting around 0730 when 2nd called in and reported finding artillery and rocket shells. At first, we told them to gather up whatever they found and use the engineers to blow the cache in place. That's a hell of a lot safer than transporting that shit around town in our vehicles.

A short while later, they called back to say they didn't have enough demo for that large of find, a total of about (7) 155mm artillery rounds, (10) 120mm tank rockets and (3) crudely built, improvised rocket launchers.

**Another Nova Cache**

We grabbed more demo and rolled out to meet 2nd Platoon. This time, they were hidden under large bushes that very closely resemble tumble weeds, and very hard to spot. I gave 2nd Platoon another big pat on the back for another excellent find.

After we scoured the entire sector, we decided to dig under the road that led down into the compound where we found most of the rockets. After we dug a nice deep hole under the road, we set off a bomb of our own. Needless to say, they won't be driving down that road any more. This actually turned out to be a highly successful mission. Sometimes you win, sometimes you lose and sometimes you do a little of both. Oh well, that's life in Ramadi.

22 Jan. 2005

Happy Birthday Janet. As I look back over our years together, I realize for one reason or another I wasn't home for over half of her birthdays. One of my favorite memories was her birthday and *very* pregnant with Danielle in 1992. We didn't know that Dani would arrive a few weeks early and show up exactly one week later. In our townhouse at Camp Lejeune, North Carolina, we spent the evening eating take-out Chinese food from our favorite restaurant and watching movies on the VCR. This may not sound very exciting or glamorous but for a married corporal with one child and another on the way, this was going all out. Sonia and I put the candles on a cake and sang Happy Birthday and the three, make that four, of us watched our movies. Maybe it's the separation, isolation, loneliness or the war itself but what I wouldn't give to be able to celebrate every birthday for the rest of my life just like that!

**The Love of my Life**

* * *

To celebrate this occasion, I went along on a neighborhood sweep with 4th Platoon. Once again, we cleared out the area of our sector's polling station. The sweep began like most other sweeps of this usually quiet neighborhood until we came across a guy who claimed he was a former Brigadier General in the Army and his friend. There was just something odd about these two. Sgt Dickson, the newest CAG attachment and honorary Goon, took down their information and I called the old man's name in to battalion and went through the whole phonetic spelling and since these guys all have five or six names, it's a painful process.

"Wrap this guy up. His name is on the shit list, and pretty high up at that, Gunny," came the callback from battalion.

We went back to his house to tell him the good news and to come with us and tell some war stories to our people. He starts getting uppity and asks me what they want.

"They need to ask you some questions," I replied.

"Find out what they want to ask and I'll answer their questions from here."

His tone and attitude irked the shit out of me.

"Hey asshole, I'm not makin' a fuckin request," I said and told the interpreter to translate exactly what I said, word for word.

He took offense and his little bullshit crony got

riled and stepped up to me. Through with the Mr. Niceguy routine, I prepared to get physical.

"Tell these two clowns there is an easy way and a hard way to do this, and in two fuckin' seconds, they're gonna' be on the wrong end of an ass kickin," I told the interpreter.

Luckily for them, they chose the easy way, came along quietly and we put them in the truck. Then things got really crazy. I had Sgt D, my wingman, on my left and Cpl. R., one of 4th Platoon's guys, on my right as we patrolled down the street. A taxi screeched around the corner. Recent intel from battalion reported several taxis have been used as SVBIED's lately.

I was right in the middle of the road and could only point my rifle and yell, "Halt!"

Sgt D and Cpl. R went immediately into threat posture, meaning they pointed rifles right at this guy and clicked off safe.

He didn't slow down, instead sped up, and as I clicked my selector lever from safe to fire, the boys were two steps ahead of me and each put a bullet in his headlights as a last chance effort to halt him.

Just like a dream, everything went slow motion as this guy gunned the gas, and now 25 meters away, Sgt D didn't hesitate, move or take cover. He put a round right through the windshield and stopped this guy in his tracks. He and Cpl. R quickly closed on the car, dragged the guy out and yelled to get everyone out of the area.

Unfortunately, he was not a suicide bomber but a complete dumb-ass who apparently drives at people standing on the road waving him off with guns.

"Jesus Christ! Give this fuckin' guy some first aid

and call battalion to get an ambulance down here," I told Sgt D and Cpl R.

I called in to higher and reported we had a guy with a bad gunshot wound to the face. Until right there and then, I never knew what a 5.56mm round could do to a human face. I've seen some bad shit and this is right up there. And I mean Fuckin'-A, major league, ghoul school bad. The round hit this guy in the right cheek and pretty much removed all of it. It tore up the flesh, most of his teeth and he bled like a running faucet. The Corpsman was a couple streets over so Sgt D and Cpl R did all the initial shit themselves. Once again, the professionalism and calm, cool demeanor of these guys amazed me. They had the wound dressed and under control in a matter of minutes and we evac'd the guy for treatment.

As luck, or lack of it, would have it, the guy lived nearby. His family was understandably upset.

"He shouldn't be driving anyway. He is nearly blind and probably didn't stop because he didn't see you," his wife said while crying hysterically. "He can't drive the taxi anymore with passengers and only uses the car to go to the market," she explained.

Now I've heard everything! A blind fucking taxi driver.

"How in the hell can he drive a goddamn car, if he's fuckin' blind?" I asked.

"Meestah, there are no rules here," she answered as if I was a dumbass for asking.

Sgt D felt bad afterward because none of us want to shoot at, hurt or kill anyone who is not trying, planning or helping to do the same to us.

Contrary to what many people believe, we are

not heartless maniacs who love to cause harm or hurt innocent people. But, he stood his ground beside me and fired to protect me. Any other course of action could have resulted in not only our deaths but also the deaths of other Marines and Iraqis in the area.

He and Cpl. R could have taken cover but they didn't. They were willing to go down with me if it turned out to be a suicide bomber. That's a hell of a thing. One hell of a thing! It humbles me to be around these guys. I guess you have to be a Marine to understand this brotherhood. All I can say, it's my life's honor to be around these men. I'd take them to hell for ice cream and the funny part is they would gladly go with me. Yes, it's a hell of a thing!

23 Jan. 2005

An early morning raid in a very nasty part of town kicked off at 0530 this morning. Operation Crusader brought Fox 2/5 to the intersection of Racetrack, Ice Cream and Tower. Fox 6 gets the credit for this one, even down to the name of the operation. I told him Crusade or any variation of the name is supposed to be a big no-no over here. Seems they're still a might bit touchy over the Christian Church's effort to eradicate them from the planet all those years ago. I wonder how many people know if not for the French fucking up yet another military operation, while, of course, trying to backstab their British "allies," maybe all the violence in this part of the world would never have materialized. Although, I'm sure over the centuries the people of this part of the world would have found something else to fight about but it does make one wonder.

Fox 6 refused to change the name for the cause of political correctness. I asked to be attached to 1st Platoon because they led the attack and started the whole show with a house raid. We quickly got to the target house, dismounted the vehicles, and banged our way inside. Nobody was home so we left a squad at the house to set up a rooftop overwatch, the rest of us remounted vehicles and set into a blocking position for 3rd and 4th Platoons.

4th Platoon entered a shop and found a huge cache tucked in behind a bunch of rice bags. They found several RPG launchers, boosters, machine guns, sniper rifles, ammunition and all kinds of bomb making material.

As soon as they reported their find, 3rd Platoon came over the radio to report they found several RPG launchers buried in a yard. 4th Platoon came right back on the net to report a vehicle rigged for explosion. SVBIEDs rate an immediate call to EOD 'cause we sure as shit don't even think about trying to dismantle those bad boys.

**Buffs at truck**

While we waited for EOD, 4th Platoon found another cache of RPG's, machine guns, rockets and bomb making material and 3rd found several more RPG's and rockets buried in the ground. The only bad news, no one was home at any of the houses or shops. However, this is by far the nastiest part of our AO and both Marine and army units have been heavily engaged here in recent weeks. Hopefully, we found their major stashes and put a serious dent in their munitions.

The "Wild Card," 3rd Platoon, kept things interesting by running over clearly visible spike strips that 1st Platoon set in place, and flattened all four tires. The Hummer has an amazing capacity to keep going on flat tires but this would really push the limits and my vehicles have taken an awful beating lately. The nature of the missions means the vehicles are going to be a constant maintenance nightmare but we really don't need to make things harder on ourselves.

For both the driver and A-driver to miss this obstacle shows a dangerous level of comfort, complacency and utter stupidity. If you really want to get killed or get others killed in this war, the enemy prays for that combination. When we got back, I had to go see the Motor Pool Chief and beg for four new tires. I am definitely not his favorite Gunny today.

24 Jan. 2005

About the elections: A big part of understanding the insurgency is understanding what's going to happen after the elections. It's a foregone conclusion the Shiites are going to take over as the power party in this country and the Sunnis become second-class citizens. Possibly, the Sunnis will be treated in at least as shitty a manner as they so willingly treated the Shiites under Uncle Saddam. Like any tyrants or former tyrants, they are undoubtedly much better at dishing it out than taking it.

You have to love their strategy and mindset. They cause all the trouble and then claim it's unsafe for them to vote.

The Mujahedeen have sufficiently terrorized enough of the population that I will be very surprised if 10% of the people of Ramadi come to the polls. Either way, if you ask me, and President Bush does not, the vote here in Ramadi is a joke. A whole lot of people will go to a whole lot of trouble to help a bunch of people who won't vote.

The actual polling site is a boys and girls school in a fairly secure, walled-in compound, known as the Inner Cordon. It has rooms, electricity and toilet facilities. The only people allowed in the actual facility are the IECI officials and for security, the Iraqi Commandos. Therefore, *NO American Presence* at the actual facility before, during or after the election and no one can say we influenced the vote. Like we give a shit!

The other companies will do more or less the same thing. Weapons Company will act as a MQRF force and go wherever there's trouble. Our entire battalion is out there at one time and for a common cause. We're doing so much work and planning and putting so much effort into this election, it's going to be a no-shit shame when no one comes to vote.

25 Jan. 2005

We conducted an early morning series of raids, Operation Tri-Force, aimed at mopping up some of the last bad guys in our sector. Now, with the elections looming, we gave it one last try and as usual came up empty.

I went with 1st Platoon as part of the raid force and we hit the target house with the usual brutality and had everyone on their faces in a matter of seconds. I love doing early morning raids. It's so heart pounding exciting to creep up in the dark and crash through a door. Plus, it scares the ever-living shit out of the occupants. Occasionally, I feel sorry for these people, but if they come up on a target list they are either Muj, support the Muj or, at the very least, knowledgeable of who the Muj are. Therefore, I no longer feel any remorse as we break into a house and drag their asshole men off to jail.

I know, I know, what if they're innocent right? What if someone gave bum scoop or if battalion has bad info? How about TFS and TFB, as in tough fuckin' shit or too fuckin' bad. It's not like we sit around and say, "Hey, I've got a great idea. Let's get up in the middle of the cold-ass night and go bust into some houses for no reason whatsoever. Won't that be fun?"

We go where we're told and do what we're told and if that takes assholes off the streets, or weapons and such out of the hands of the enemy, then a few hurt feelings along the way don't mean dick to me. This is not America; there is no Miranda, or any of the shit that comes with living in a free and just society. This is war; Marines are getting hurt or killed every day. If people don't want asshole Americans to cave in their houses, arrest their men and run roughshod in their country, maybe they should think of that the next time they decide to act with aggression towards Americans. How about when you mess with the bull, you get the horns. How about that?

29 Jan. 2005

Today is my baby's birthday. Happy Birthday Danielle! My little girl is officially a teenager. Fairly soon, I get to become the enemy and quite possibly the stupidest person she knows. I also get to be the middleman on all the upcoming fights she'll have with her mother for the next five to fifty years. I'm greatly looking forward to all that but for now, she's still my best girl and the light of my life. I'm sorry I'm not there, baby and I'm so proud of the person you've become.

**Dani and Me**

It really is tough to keep missing the big events in my family's lives but I think they know how much I love them. How much I miss them and, most importantly, how much I think about them every day of my life.

At every stage of Dani's life, I've either been going away or coming back. I remember giving her my poncho liner, when she was a baby in hopes it would remind her of me and give her comfort. I guess it worked 'cause she still has it at home.

**Baby Dani and me**

Tomorrow I can worry about the elections. Tonight I'm going to spend a little time thinking about my beautiful daughter and about what a lucky man I am to have such a special person in my life.

I have a great relationship with my baby. Just recently, I received a CD she recorded for me with the help of her guitar and singing teacher, George. I was absolutely blown away by the talent of her playing and the beauty of her voice. I'm sure the CO and Bruce are more than tired of hearing "Paper Moon" but I can't stop playing it. Much like the letter from Sonia, this begins and ends every day for me. I can't wait to get home and be with her and watch this amazing talent grow. Hopefully, she'll let me hang around with her and be a big part of her high school life.

I got through the teenage years with my oldest daughter and I'll get through them with Dani. Many people think the hardest thing I ever had to live through is this tour of combat in Ramadi, but try getting two beautiful and talented girls through high school and into college and you'll know the meaning of a combat tour!

30 Jan. 2005

Today is the great Iraqi election, the biggest political event during this deployment. We've done our part and then some, to make it safe, secure and simple. We knew coming into this deployment that we would be on the bubble during this time. Everyone and their asshole brother from Division on down take an active interest in how we run this show and the rest of the world is watching on TV.

I'm proud to say we pulled a Sneaky Pete and caught the Muj with their pants down. While they slept, we moved into position and put this entire neighborhood on lockdown. They may have planned something and so did we but we acted first. Now they either have to work out a whole new plan or stay home like scared little cowards.

As of last night at 2000, we finished our last

logistical convoy. I asked Sgt D how many convoys we ran in order to get the Marines, logistics, Iraqi forces, election officials and every other fuckin' thing under the sun out here and set up. We estimated somewhere between twenty and thirty and now we're probably looking at nearly as many to get out of here.

We came out a full 24 hours ahead of schedule and at first that really pissed me off. A Company Gunny does not want to find out about major changes to the plan at the last minute. If that wasn't bad enough, battalion sent us on a mission prior to moving in to the polling site. No one wanted to hear my complaints so I took a big drink of suck it the fuck up and made shit happen. The Goons earned their pay so far. I've come to expect great things out of these guys and they constantly show up big.

This neighborhood is as safe as possible. We have every road blocked, Marines on over-watch in eight different buildings, twenty seven Iraqi Commandos on the entry point, metal detectors on the walk through, two stations for body searches, eight gun trucks at selected locations for quick reaction and two interpreters on site. We did all this in one long night, and not a man in this company got more than an hour sleep.

Over the next three days, we did a massive campaign to clear all the houses and inform the population of what was going on and what they need to do in order to vote and be safe while doing so. To top it off, we got thirty four election officials and one more interpreter on site.

The polls have been open for three hours and the total tally as of right now is one. Yes that's right, one fuckin' ballot cast. The icing on the fuckin' cake for this one is the one ballot cast was by Ricky the interpreter, who came out here in my gun truck.

I have a few things to say about the election, Iraqis from Ramadi and the feeling in this room as I type this journal. I hope I can express this properly. Every person in this bullshit, whining, "what have you done for me lately city" can all line up and instead of voting for their own province, country and future, can kiss my Marine Ass! And the ass of every other Marine, who has spent one fuckin' second of his or her life away from home and in the midst of these sub-humans.

If the rest of this province or triangle or whatever this dump is called has the same bullshit attitude towards being free, independent and democratic, where everyone has a voice and a chance to be a part of their own government, what we ought to do is find the Shiite equivalent of Saddam and give this shit hole completely over to him with a caveat. If he ever thinks an anti-U.S. thought, we'll be back and operate this whole country like a drive-through gas pump. I have absolutely no time for people who stand around with their hand out and want every little thing in their life handed to them.

Please name for me, one group or culture in the history of history ever treated this kindly and fairly so soon after being defeated in combat. I'm not getting into the politics of the whole thing. My whole point; we work, sweat, bleed and die while these cowardly, lazy, shiftless, whiny bums don't even lift a finger to help themselves. This bullshit about being scared or intimidated is a bunch of fucking nonsense.

I'd like for someone to tell me what other people

throughout history haven't had to sacrifice for freedom and liberty. I can tell you in a nutshell the only reason none of these fuckers came out and voted is because they are like spoiled, pouting children who had their toys taken away. Ramadians had it good under Saddam. They were the privileged class, taken care of and catered to. Now, they have to step aside and watch as majority rather than tyranny rules their country. I heard John Kerry run his mouth about the unfairness of the process. John Kerry and every other Bush-hating liberal can also kiss my ass.

I read what certain groups had to say about the vote not being legitimate because certain Iraqis did not have the opportunity or security to cast a ballot. How about Bull Fuckin' Shit jackass? There is a very big difference between not being able to vote and *CHOOSING* not to vote. I busted my ass and risked my life so these *people* could vote in the election. They chose not to and they can kiss my ass!

I wish there was a politician somewhere with enough balls to come out and point the finger right where it belongs. Right at the same people who sit idly by and watch as terrorists destroy their town and hurt or kill innocent people.

The long day is over in our sector and the final tally is nineteen votes cast: thirteen by commandos, one by the interpreter and five by citizens who give a shit. The total tally for the entire town, 1600 give or take a few. That comes somewhere close to probably ½ of 1% of this town. FUCK YOU, RAMADI!

02 Feb. 2005

The last few days consisted mostly of recovering from the election week. The Marines had time to rest and I had a chance to square away a bunch of Gunny stuff; mostly vehicles and the maintenance thereof but also administrative stuff such as missing gear rosters and accounting for all of our shit. There are two things you have to flat-ass know to be a Company Gunny. One, Marines will lose shit before, during and after every operation and two, Marines will break shit either by accident, on purpose or merely on principle. There is an old saying if you put a Marine in a rubber room with a ball bearing for two hours he will either figure out a way to break it or he will lose it. Any way you shake it, the Marine and ball bearing are not coming out the same way they went in.

Therefore, once a month you have to line them up and account for every piece of gear on the company custodial maintenance receipt (CMR). The CMR lists *every* piece of gear the company owns, the serial numbers for each item, the price, the exact numbers you are supposed to have and most importantly the name of the responsible party, in our case, the Company Commander.

The CO doesn't have the time to sit around and waste his time counting every piece of gear. That bullshit is my job and it says a whole lot about our CO that not once has he ever looked over my shoulder and micro-managed the CMR accountability. We'll turn most of our shit over to Bravo Company 1/5 and it's pretty damn important to me it goes smooth and easy.

There is no way in hell I will do to them what was done to me. Not in this fuckin' lifetime.

The advance party leaves on the 11th of February. That's nine days from today. I should be on that flight and no one would think twice if I were. I came here three weeks earlier than everyone else, which means I should go home a few weeks early but I just cannot in good conscience leave until every Marine in my company is out of here. I told my wife and daughters I couldn't leave because SSgt Flammang is already back to take care of all advance party matters which is partially true. He is back there to take care of all the bullshit on that end.

Since I agreed to stay here until the end, I told Cpl. Swartz he could go with the advance party and help SSgt Flammang. After all, he also came here early.

"I'll leave when you leave, Gunny," was his reply.

Normally, I don't make suggestions. I give orders and they get carried out. Period. End of story. However, Cpl. Swartz and I have been on every mission together and there is something about keeping a good team together. I should order him to go but I learned long ago not to get myself into fights I can't finish. I told the Captain less than 5% of this company would voluntarily leave a month early on the advance party. He raised the bullshit flag and asked around and so far not one Marine he's asked said he would take the offer.

Imagine being in a complete shit-hole like this, having the opportunity to leave early with no shame, and still deciding to stick it out until the end. That's what separates being a Marine from everything else on this whole fuckin' planet. Enough said for tonight, my friends!

03 Feb 2005

The enemy finally got lucky with his mortars. It was really only a matter of time when one would finally land close enough to do damage. Counter battery does a great job of limiting them to one or two shots at a time. Anyone who knows mortar gunnery will tell you if you only have two rounds with shitty equipment, poorly trained mortarmen and no observers to correct your fire, the odds of hitting what you want to hit really is a matter of luck. But luck with mortars depends entirely upon where you happen to be standing. Unfortunately for Weapons Company, luck was on the wrong side today.

A mortar landed at HP either right outside where the Marines live or maybe even inside their building. It's hard to get accurate information when mass casualties come in. One Marine was killed, one an urgent surgical medevac, another a priority medevac and two were treated and released for minor wounds. I heard the KIA was a radio operator named Clifton, probably a young corporal or lance corporal. In an absurdly ironic twist, Clifton was attached to Weapons Company only because he had to replace the Marine killed by the SVBIED with Captain Rapicault.

I talked to my guys and we're all in agreement what really sucks is not just being killed, we all live with the thought every day but if it does happen, we want it to happen from being out on a mission. Let it be from an enemy firing a weapon or catching us along our route with an IED. To be killed when you are hanging out and bullshitting or having a smoke outside or something just plain sucks. It especially sucks because we all know this was not a well-planned hit by a clever enemy, but some cowardly jackass getting extremely lucky for the first time in five months.

I didn't know Clifton but it still hurts to lose a fellow 2/5 Marine. That's another strange feeling. I do know a quite a few of the Marines in Weapons Company and a few of them are Marines I consider my friends. When you hear that a Marine is KIA, you immediately hope it wasn't someone you were close with but then you feel bad for feeling that way. A Marine is a Marine and all hate to see a Brother go down. We all feel the loss on some level and all want to get a little revenge for our Brother.

Tomorrow morning I'm going on a raid with 1st Platoon and I really hope somewhere along the way we get contact and some son of a bitch with some kind of mortar system or something along those lines. But it's not that kind of war. It's not a matter of knowing where the enemy is and putting a plan together to go and kick his ass. It's a war where you hope to get lucky and be at the right place, at the right time. More often than not, we seem to chase ghosts, or even worse, our own tails. I hate to say this but before it's all over, there will be more casualties. All we can do is make sure to minimize the enemy's opportunities to harm us while maximizing our opportunities to kill him. At the end of the day, I still like the team I'm on a whole lot better.

04 Feb 2005

It started raining around midnight and still going strong at 0545 when we stepped off. Lt. Jones renamed the mission Operation Mudslide. Today, my assistance was needed to help set up a blocking position to the west of the target house. This is a sound tactic. If half the platoon is hitting the target house, the other half can seal off the area to make sure that no one can get in or out while the raid is in progress. This is right out of Combat Raids 101. Sometimes, the simple shit is simple for a reason. It's all good and well to be a tactical genius but sometimes less is definitely more.

1st Platoon hit the target house while my gun truck was one block west. Twenty minutes later, we departed with four detainees and no evidence of wrongdoing other than being in the target house. 1st Platoon got in, wrapped up the targets, got out, and mounted back up in a textbook raid.

We got back to JC and I went right back to the paperwork, rosters and lists that are becoming all important in the never-ending battle of the relief in place (RIP) with 1/5. I asked their Gunny to contact me if he has any questions or issues but so far he has not responded. Either he is too busy or he plans on coming in blind. In my opinion, this is not a very good move but he still has a few weeks before he gets here so maybe he will eventually get in contact. If not, he'll get what he gets and probably kick himself in the ass later on down the road. For my part, contact or not, I'll do my best to have my shit in one bag.

05 Feb 2005

Mikey came into my room this morning and talked about the operation we were doing later in the afternoon. He was MQRF today and my truck was going to join his crew while we supported 4th Platoon on their mission. He said he gave the guns an extra good cleaning and double-checked all the ammo. He claimed to have one of those Indian feelings about getting into some action today. Who am I to ignore that? Besides, he was out there on the roads and maybe his subconscious picked up something that was just too quick for his brain to register and transmit to the conscious mode. I'm not a psychologist and don't really want to be, I'll just stick to the Indian intuition thing.

Sure enough, we had five Marines wounded, two seriously, and two gun trucks destroyed. We didn't even have a chance to go on the mission yet when all hell broke loose. Gunny Betancourt, the H&S Company Gunny, came down to visit me and return a mortar system I loaned out. Since there is a standing order of having at least four vehicles in your convoy no matter where you are going or for what, Mikey escorted him from HP to JC and was in the process of taking him back when two IEDs hit the MQRF.

Our battalion operates out of three different bases. One is Hurricane Point, or HP. Golf Company, Weapons Company and about half of H&S Company live and work out of there. Just to the south and east of HP, prior to crossing the bridge, is the Snake Pit. Echo Company lives there by themselves. South and West of the Snake Pit, across the South Bridge and river is Junction City, or JC. Fox and the rest of H&S live there. JC is a huge base. It is home to us, 3rd LAR, Bravo Company 1/23, 2/11, several Army battalions, the Iraqi Commandos, a shit-load of civilian employees and other assorted units and who the fuck knows what else.

The army runs JC and we basically just live here. In order to get onto or out of JC, we have to go through the ARMY entry control point (ECP). They man this post with two Bradley Fighting Vehicles that double as movable roadblocks. From the ECP to Route Michigan is a distance of about 300-400 meters. It is a straight line from the ECP to the intersection of Michigan. The Army has sentries at the ECP, a guard tower and other armored vehicles with mounted heavy guns right there at the gate. Theoretically, no vehicle could ever make it down the road and onto the base unless the Army allowed it. There is also a serpentine barrier to negotiate prior to reaching the Bradleys on the way in.

They have a clear line of site down the road, known as Ogden Road, onto Route Michigan. When you reach the end of Ogden Road, you turn left to get onto Route Michigan northbound in order to get to the bridge, Snake Pit, HP or into Ramadi. If we were to turn right, which we never do because that is the Army's AO, we run into the first Army OP, which is only 200-300 meters away. This OP can observe most of Ogden Road and all of Route Michigan from where they are up to and including the bridge. At the very south end of the bridge, in fact on top of the bridge, is another Army OP that is responsible for looking south all the way down Michigan to the other OP. In other words, the entrance to Ogden Road is covered by no less than *three* Army OPs with direct, unimpeded, unhindered, unblocked and perfectly clear lines of site of the *entire* road, *especially* the entrance/exit point of Ogden Road and Michigan.

Therefore, it would be nice if some jackass in the entire Fucking United States Army could tell me why I had two vehicles blown up and five Marines injured right in the middle of Route Michigan where Ogden Road and Route Michigan meet. In fact, what I would really like to know is how in the Blue Hell the enemy had enough time to plant, not one, but *two* IEDs on each side of the divider we have to drive through to get onto northbound Michigan. I am absolutely furious at the incompetence and unprofessionalism of these mental fucking retards. And I'm very sorry to offend anyone out there who is, or is related to, or knows any retarded people for comparing retarded people with this Army unit. It's not fair to retarded people.

Bruce said it as eloquently as is his custom. "The Army is just a bunch of well-dressed Showanis."

While we were out there medevacing our Marines and recovering our vehicles an Army Colonel came up to Lt. J and asked him what happened. They were convinced it was suicide vehicles. Lt. J walked him over and showed him the holes and told him it was not a vehicular attack. Then he replied he just can't see how two IEDs could have been placed at that intersection. How about this for an idea? Go to your posts and take away the dvd players, lawn chairs, cots, radios, coolers, porn mags and every other non-military and unprofessional diversion and then make them do their fucking job. How about that?

This was one well-planned bombing. I gotta give credit where it's due. The part that bothers me the most, I know the enemy is a cowardly bastard who does not risk his life to plant his little surprises. He must have observed that area for a while, noticed the Army asleep at the switch and placed the IEDs exactly where they could hurt us the most.

When we go out the gate and onto Michigan, we occasionally run two vehicles out to the break in the divider. One vehicle blocks traffic from the south, another blocks traffic from the north and the rest of the vehicles shoot through the gap between the two blocking vehicles and head north toward the bridge. We do this because until yesterday we were convinced the biggest threat was VBIEDs hitting us broadside as we get out the gate and into convoy formation.

Where did the enemy place his IEDs yesterday? Right on both sides of the divider, exactly where the two blocking vehicles were located. The first IED went off right next to Mikey's vehicle and sent the vehicle spinning in a ball of flame. Van Brunt, the turret gunner, received a concussion and shrapnel injuries. Smalls, the driver, had his eardrum burst and a possible concussion. Everyone else was rocked but otherwise unharmed. Two civilian vehicles stopped to let the convoy out and they were as close to the blast as the Humvee. Neither of those guys lived. They were a gory mess of what used to be human bodies.

At the time of the explosion, everyone thought one of those vehicles was a SVBIED so the Marines lit them up after the fact. The drivers were already very much dead prior to any of the subsequent shooting and as Mikey called for a cease fire, some of his Marines got out of their vehicles to secure the area and help the wounded.

That's when the second IED went off. Right next to the other vehicle, just as Marines opened the armored doors to get out and help. Two Marines, Horton and Dunseith, received very serious leg and body wounds and even Gunny Betancourt, who tagged along for the ride back to HP, received a minor shrapnel wound to the leg. I can only imagine the chaos at this point but Mikey was all over it.

The Army showed up with their reaction force, thanks assholes, but at least they had a Medic who helped our Corpsmen stabilize the serious injuries. Mikey got those four patched up quick and had the ambulance back through the gate and on the way to Charlie Medical before we got out there and onto the scene. He put Cpl. Lundy, who was also injured and concussed, on the radio to get reinforcements out there and gave the SITREP back to the Captain. Next, he got the rest of his boys out of the danger zone and into position to cover any possible ambush sites.

Meanwhile, my vehicle and the Command Vehicle rolled out the gate and onto the scene to help get a handle on the situation. The Captain took over tactical control, 1st Platoon, the QRFA platoon, rolled out the gate and locked the area down and I began the job of recovering all of my vehicles and equipment. Somehow, the Battalion Commander and Sergeant Major were there too. I guess they were headed down to JC at the time.

Sgt D and Sgt Norman got to work on the recovery aspect and hitched up the vehicles and dragged them out of there. Unfortunately, there was no one to shoot or kill and no reason to hang around the Army because I seriously entertained the thought of shooting one of them, so we got all our shit in one bag and headed back into camp and over to medical to check on our boys.

**Big damage from IEDs**

**Shattered by IEDs**

I can't say enough about how well Mikey performed under those circumstances. Hopefully, he'll be recognized in the appropriate manner. Now I have to figure out how we're going to continue to run this Company with two less gun trucks. What should happen, but never will, the Colonel should call up the Army Jackass In Charge (JIC) and make that fucker give me two of his trucks. Yeah, like that's gonna happen!

07 Feb. 2005

I figured out how to continue doing business as usual with two less gun trucks and as is normally the case, the solution begins and ends with me taking it in the shorts. The loss of two gun trucks means the Mission Platoon does not have any gun trucks in their sled. Therefore, my truck and the Command Vehicle will substitute for the missing vehicles. I can give my vehicle to the mission platoon or I can staff it for them with my crew. The Command Vehicle will lose its battle-space mobility because rather than act as part of a beefed-up MQRF, the Command Vehicle will stay with the mission platoon. This is far from perfect but it's the best I can do until one of the vehicles gets back on line.

The biggest problem with this set-up, way too much of the command element is with the mission platoon. I don't like when we are all in the same kill zone at the same time and I'm sure the Platoon Commanders and Platoon Sergeants can do without me, the 1stSgt and CO in the middle of their shit on every mission. I talked to Fox 6 about switching one or the other of us out with one of the MQRF gun trucks. At least that provides a little separation.

Last night we tried this new set up with 3rd Platoon. I was not thrilled with the prospect of escorting their Platoon Commander around but I guess we all have to make sacrifices when vehicles get destroyed. The mission went surprisingly well with the new vehicle scheme and we didn't have much trouble moving in support of the dismounted squads.

It's been a while since I traveled close enough to 3rd to see how the platoon shoots, moves and communicates. I was pleased with the growth and *much* improved movement and communication. We shot a shit load of cars! The funny thing about shooting at cars, before we came here we had this big brief about the ROE concerning when you could or could not shoot. "At no time are warning shots allowed." What a crock of shit! If the biggest threat is VBIEDs, and if Marines have been hurt and killed by VBIEDs, what Marine in his right mind is going to allow a vehicle to come through our lines as we strongpoint an intersection or if we're halted in a particular danger zone?

Add to the mix most Iraqis cannot seem to figure out burning flares, chemlites, orange cones and a Marine pointing a rifle at him means "Stop The Fucking Car" and we have the ever popular Catch-22. The Marine has two choices. Option one is to shoot a warning shot near the car or at a headlight. Option two is; kill the driver and neutralize the car with extreme force. I guess the bleeding heart, hippie, safe at home and not ever in a life or death situation piece of shit Jane fuckin' Fonda wannabe would say we should add a third option, let the cars pass and hope it's not your unlucky day.

We use remarkable restraint if you ask me. We shot several warning shots, didn't hurt or kill anybody and didn't disable any vehicles. Most importantly, we didn't get blown up and killed by some brainwashed nitwit who thinks Allah is waiting to greet him in paradise with a hug and kiss and 72 virgins.

The mission was a day/night movement to contact that did not result in any contact. We apprehended three assholes when we used their roof for over-watch and one of the Marines found Al Qaeda-made DVDs with helpful homemaking skills such as how to construct bombs in your house to kill the infidels and other similar fun-filled activities. Maybe these assholes can lead us to other assholes and we can eventually find the assholes responsible for blowing up my vehicles. Tomorrow marks the one-month mark for our replacements to arrive in country. Please Lord, let my Marines stay safe and my vehicles stay running until then.

08 Feb. 2005

Very early this morning, we went on a series of raids aimed at houses where IEDs are made, stored and at three houses of suspected IED makers. For once, the intel seemed credible. I thought we were a long way from finding shit in people's houses. These boys are not stupid when it comes to figuring out we have this area pretty well buttoned up. The supposed IED factory we hit in Phase One of the raid was an abandoned house in one of the nicer parts of town.

I guess we got this information from more than one source but they had it nailed down to a general area rather than a specific house. 1st Platoon was in charge of this one and Lt. J broke it down into three separate squad-sized searches. Each squad got a few houses to search and we brought two military working dogs to assist us in sniffing out the bombs.

As we rolled out Ogden Gate, the Army was hard at work setting up a serpentine barrier on the Ogden Gate side of the South Bridge. Word has it they will close down that part of Route Michigan for all civilian traffic and re-route them along a frontage road a little to the east of Michigan. Trust the Army to close the barn door *after* the cow gets out. I guess this is their way of dealing with the problem of sleeping sentries. If you eliminate the ROAD the sentries are supposed to watch then the problem goes away. Personally, I like the idea of re-routing the traffic.

We got to the target area without incident and the searches began. There was one small, piece of shit looking, half-built house just to the west of one of the target houses so a few of the guys and one of the dogs decided to check it out. There were several holes dug up in some of the rooms and the dog was suspicious of the holes. SSgt D came up with the "Holy Shit!" of the night. As he stumbled around the rubble in the dark at 0300, he felt some looser than normal dirt under his feet. He kicked some of it away and discovered to his surprise he stood on an anti-tank mine. That'll wake you up in a hurry, boy! I don't know how many pounds of pressure it takes to set one of those fuckers off, but I can tell you we're all real thankful SSgt D is a skinny bastard.

It looks as if we had the right house but a day late and a dollar short. Someone got there before us and dug up all the shit and got it out of there. I'm no expert tracker or any of that horseshit but even I could spot freshly dug holes.

We took the tank mine with us and moved on to Phase Two which was a double raid on the other two target houses and two squads would hit the houses simultaneously. We had the names and descriptions of the guys in the target houses but did not turn up the insurgents.

3rd Platoon raided one house prior to us getting to our houses and they bagged four individuals who fit the right description so hopefully something good comes of that.

We got in at 0600 and went right to our racks. Mikey came in my room at 0830 and yelled 3rd Platoon just got hit with an IED on Route Michigan where the serpentine barriers were just put into position by the Army. Luckily, no one was injured and no vehicles damaged. This time the IED was on the southbound traffic side of the road and even closer to the so-called South Bridge OP, less than 200-300 meters away from these jackasses and right where they had a roadblock set up all night to put the serpentines in place.

Fox 6 called the Colonel to complain once again and offered to either take over the OP or emplace our snipers to protect the road. Truthfully, something has to be done before someone gets killed due to this unit's negligence. How many times are we going to get bitten by this same worthless dog? I know many Army soldiers and I'm sure there are great Army units over here doing their part. Unfortunately for us, the group watching Ogden Gate and Michigan just don't seem to give a shit.

09 Feb 2005

Last night one of our lieutenants got himself relieved from his duties as Platoon Commander. In other words, he was fired. There are many ways to get fired but this one will go down as one of the stupidest acts ever. How ridiculous that the lieutenant in question got fired because he drove a vehicle to the PX without wearing a flak jacket?

The Army is allowed to drive around the base in tactical vehicles without flak jackets. Their only rule for gear, they must wear a helmet. We started out following this Army rule until the Commanding General of the division said all Marines will wear full body armor and helmets whenever they are in a tactical vehicle. Marines will always challenge those orders they deem silly, especially since they are the only ones who have to follow that particular order on this whole base.

More than once, I had to remind the lieutenants they are no different than the enlisted men when it comes to following orders and, in fact, they should be setting the example for the men. I spent three years on AMOI duty, training future officers how to act like officers. If there was one thing that chafed my ass above all other things it was when those aspiring officers thought this so-called higher status somehow made them a better class of Marine than the enlisted man.

A Marine is a Marine and we all live by the same code and follow the same rules and regulations. If anything, the Commandant expects the officers in our Corps to hold themselves to an even higher standard than our already high standards of order and discipline.

This is why I was so pissed off when a seemingly stupid little thing like riding to the PX without body armor occurred. In addition, this officer was not carrying his weapon, 100% non negotiable. EVER! For God's sake, even though we are on base, we are in fuckin' Combat here.

The worst part, how many Marines saw this officer breaking two of our flat ass orders? I told the Captain without even mentioning names he needed to have a talk with his officers concerning this behavior. It could have ended with a talking to by the Captain. Instead, this jackass of a lieutenant decided to get in the Captain's face and challenged him because apparently he thinks he was being picked on.

In a perfect world, the Captain would have beaten his ass to a bloody pulp. I know I would have. I can't imagine how many surgeries it would take to repair a junior Marine if he ever got in my face and challenged me in my own room when he was clearly wrong. But, that's probably another reason why I would never make it as an officer.

In this case, the Captain exercised remarkable restraint and professionalism and simply told the lieutenant to go pack his shit because his services were no longer required. Another thing about the officer ranks; shit happens fast. Two hours later, our company had one less lieutenant.

Deep down, I hate to see this kind of shit happen. We all came here together as a company and after a long hard fight we should all go home as an even tighter company. Nothing brings Marines closer together than shared hardships during combat. Personality differences get put aside because if the Marines in the company don't like one another on a personal level, they respect and trust one another as fellow warriors and brothers. Then again, if ever there was a case of someone making his own bed and now having to sleep in it, this young lieutenant epitomizes that cliché.

12 Feb 2005

Yesterday was one of those wild days in the wild west of Ramadi. It all started with an early morning wake up QRF. 4th Platoon was on the MQRF and came across an IED on the intersection of Hospital Road and Michigan. This was the most obvious IED in the history of IEDs and made Lt. S think it was a set-up. Rather than just call EOD to detonate in place, he called a QRF to lock down the whole area.

As we rolled onto the scene, Lt. S had the immediate area around the IED blocked off and 3rd Platoon should have established a wider cordon, cleared and locked down an even larger area. Instead, they turned off Michigan and disappeared for a while. This left my vehicle alone on Michigan. Since I had my ass hanging in the breeze, I decided to lock down Retard Road and prevent any traffic from rolling onto Michigan, but I couldn't stop any eastbound traffic from coming down Michigan and right into both the IED and our gun trucks. The only way to stop traffic was warning shots and I was not at all happy. I tried to call 3rd Platoon to get them to put a vehicle or something on Michigan, but, as usual, they did not respond to the radio.

I talked to their SSgt and he told me the lieutenant continues to fuck up and not listen.

"Gunny, he never asked where we needed to go. He just took off when I told him we needed to stay on Michigan."

"Look, if he's still this fucked up, you need to go to the CO. This fuckin' shit is getting' real fuckin' old. I'm out here with my shit hangin' out and you fuckers are off joy riding," I yelled.

"Gunny, he took the lead vehicle down to Buckeye and I spent ten minutes trying to tell him we needed to get back to Michigan."

"Then you need to get on the horn and let the rest of us know what the fuck is going on, Goddammit."

I felt bad for the Platoon Sergeant but this shit has to fuckin' stop. The lieutenant placed the platoon in one small area and they were better off not being a part of the mission.

At one point, a car came eastbound on Michigan and all four of the Marines in my gun truck opened fire in order to prevent it from going right into the IED intersection. First, they shot the headlights, then the wheels, then the back windows as the car came abreast of us and lastly the doors.

Finally, the jackass realized we wanted him to stop and he saved his own life as he put on the brakes and came out with his hands held high.

I praised my guys for their remarkable restraint in firing to stop the vehicle and not kill the driver and passenger. 4th Platoon came to the rescue with some traffic cones and a gun truck further up Michigan and no one else tried to drive through our lines.

As we prepared to detonate the IED and get the hell out of there, 4th Platoon yelled "fire in the hole" and a motorcycle came out of nowhere, or from

3rd platoon's area of responsibility, and drove right through the detonation. I couldn't believe what I saw as a motorcycle flew through the smoke. Even more amazing, he didn't get blown up or fall off the bike. However, his luck ran out as he drove at the EOD vehicle. I'm sure he couldn't hear the shouts to stop or the warning shots fired at his bike tires. Plus, the adrenaline he must be pumping after driving through the explosion made him drive head-on at our vehicles at a very high rate of speed.

I actually felt bad for the guy as the Marines lit him up. I'm pretty sure he wasn't strapped with any explosives but how can you be sure in this place?

That's what really sucks about this place and the situations we face on a daily basis. We absolutely, positively, unequivocally do not want to kill anyone who absolutely does not have it coming. We want to fight armed insurgents who mean us harm.

I once sat in a philosophy class at the University of Colorado and had an interesting discussion on collateral damage in a wartime environment. The discussion was on the Law of Double Effect. None of those people had a remote sense of what a combat environment was really like but it was easy to take the moral high ground when sitting in a safe, secure, protected college classroom. All of the people in the class, except me, said they could not engage in any activity that could kill innocent people no matter the reasons.

In this case, the professor was using the example of bombing an ammunition factory located near civilian houses. Bombing the factory would save thousands of lives in the long run because it would help win the war and stop that particular ammo from killing friendly forces. On the downside, bombing the factory would surely result in killing some of the civilians living nearby.

I was the only person among the pot smoking, tree-hugging hippies who gave the bombing mission the thumbs up. Many of my classmates felt it was *OUR*, as in the U.S. military's, responsibility to take these things into account. For my argument, I stated the enemy was at fault for putting these people at risk in the first place and it was more his fault than ours if they got killed.

Let's just for the sake of argument maybe make believe the people living nearby are not complete retards and understand that living next to a bomb factory during war might be a good reason to go on a fuckin' vacation. Maybe that's the curse of living in such freedom and democracy. We get so wrapped up in how good we have it, we have to find fault within our own system.

Let me ask the philosophers this question. If a car bomb impacts within 10 feet of your vehicle, it will kill you, everyone in your vehicle and destroy the vehicle. So, if a vehicle is coming toward you, and does not understand warnings or indicators to stop, do you let it get within ten feet? Don't answer this from the safety of where you are. Try as hard as you can, to imagine for some reason you are at that point and place in time. The Marines will not shoot unless you say so. You have maybe three seconds to give the order to fire or not. You have already been subjected to suicide bombings and friends of yours have been killed by this very tactic on this very road in nearly the exact same spot under the exact same circumstances.

Even if you are willing to take the chance with your own life, do you take that chance with the lives of the Marines around you? Also, take this into account. If you do not act very aggressively and decisively then you subject yourself to many, many more suicide attacks. What do you do, smart guy?

13 Feb 2005

The perfect mission for the Goon Squad presented itself on Route Nova and illustrated the need for a Goon Squad. In the great game of hockey every team has a goon. His role is not to score, but to beat people up.

My goons perform a myriad of roles in the day-to-day operations of the company; however, they were born and raised to whoop ass when the situation presents itself. We went out with 2nd Platoon's MQRF to provide an extra bit of muscle while they ran security operations for 4th Platoon's dismounted patrol.

The patrol proceeded along without contact so we raided a house to see if this one particular asshole was home and searched a suspected abandoned house or two to see if any weapons or IEDs might be stashed for later use. Although we didn't find anything at first, we certainly provided a menacing presence in the area, which is half the battle.

Eventually, Mikey decided to drive up on Route Nova and do a Snap VCP. I'm a big fan of the Snap which works great with the MQRF. We put a little extra space between our vehicles and at a point determined by the convoy leader, Mikey, he suddenly stopped the lead vehicle and blocked all on-coming traffic. The rear vehicle, me, did the same thing for any trailing traffic.

We made everyone get out of their vehicles and moved them to a personnel search area. When they were safely away with arms up and hands in sight and free of trigger devices, the vehicle search began.

The first vehicle in the row of six had a nice surprise in the trunk.

"Holy shit! There's two 155's in this trunk!" SSgt D yelled.

Immediately, all the people went onto the pavement and we asked who the first car belonged to. Although none spoke English, the question was very clear and four immediately pointed at this fat bastard, who damn sure didn't volunteer himself. He was dragged away from the others while Swartz and one of Mikey's guys searched him in earnest.

For some strange reason, he wanted to fight. Swartz landed a few punches, put the guy down and I came over and put a knee on his neck.

SSgt D, Sgt D and myself went to work tearing asshole's car apart while Swartz and Barlow went through his pockets. SSgt D found a bunch of wires and I found a little bag containing two sticks of PE-4A explosive, all the ingredients necessary to make one very nasty IED. The strange thing about the two 155 rounds, they were American ammo.

**Makings of IEDs**

A big part of every detainment is getting a ten-digit grid and a picture of the terrorist with his toys. I went back to get fat-ass and brought him over by the vehicle to get the picture taken. Once again, he tried to get tough with me and jerked out of my grip and chest bumped me.

Swartz knocked his legs out from under him with a textbook leg sweep followed by a nice bit of jolly stomping. I guess Swartz took exception to a terrorist disrespecting me. Luckily for this piece of shit, I tempered Swartz's enthusiasm.

Meanwhile, Sgt D and Sgt Norman went to work on what has become a Goon Squad specialty, disabling motor vehicles. After a little handiwork with the appropriate sharpened instruments, the car looked like modern art.

All in all, the perfect Goon Squad mission. We found explosives, captured and roughed up a terrorist who had it coming and vandalized a vehicle beyond repair. Once again, I have to hand it to Mikey, that boy has a nose for bombs. Hopefully, we get good intel off this guy and send him away on an all expense paid vacation to Abu Ghraib.

15 Feb 2005

We did a fairly large operation that could have had the coolest operation name yet. It was supposed to be called, The Saint Valentines Day Massacre. The Captain worried a name like that could only lead to some seriously hard to answer questions at the investigation sure to follow if we did in fact have to massacre some upstanding citizens.

As a compromise, Operation Heart Breaker and Operation Heart Punch were thrown into the hat.

"What do you do in the Marines?"

"I name Operations. Ever hear of Operation Can of Whoop Ass? Yeah, that was me!"

What came out? Operation Gas Crunch, since the raid would take place at a fuel refinery, but still I continue to hate the creativity or lack thereof in naming our operations.

We were all pretty pumped about this operation.

There is always a shit load of cars there, we've been shot at by snipers and hit by IEDs. I went with 2nd Platoon as part of the raid force. Our first objective was to get into the fuel refinery and look for weapons or explosives. Next, we searched every car near the place and every person in the place. From there, we moved to the outdoor market adjacent to the oil refinery and searched every person and vehicle trapped inside of our cordon.

After 50 cars and nearly 200 people, we got exactly jack and shit. We used three working dogs to sniff everything. On the positive side, we shook up a whole bunch of citizens with our presence. If any were terrorists, we made them nervous and put them on notice. The Blackhearts are still around and still looking for a fight.

I truly believe the reason we have had very little no-shit firefights since early November is because we were tested early and whooped some serious ass. I think the enemy got rocked so bad and hit so hard, he decided it was not in his best interests to ever come out again and fight like a man. They couldn't even muster a decent scare tactic during the election and if the Muj ever wanted to make a political statement on a worldwide level, that was his last best chance.

Another big factor was the assault on Fallujah. Pictures circulated of what went down during that offensive that make me cringe. I guess those boys who stayed thought they could stand up to a full Marine assault. They hung around the streets, waving their guns and rocket launchers and really believed their own bullshit. The results have shown our friends over here the USMC does not fuck around.

We've accomplished all we set out to accomplish and I can state with absolute certainty this town is much, much safer than when we got here. I don't really know how we can measure success against an insurgency but a lack of getting shot at and blown up seems like a great indicator to me.

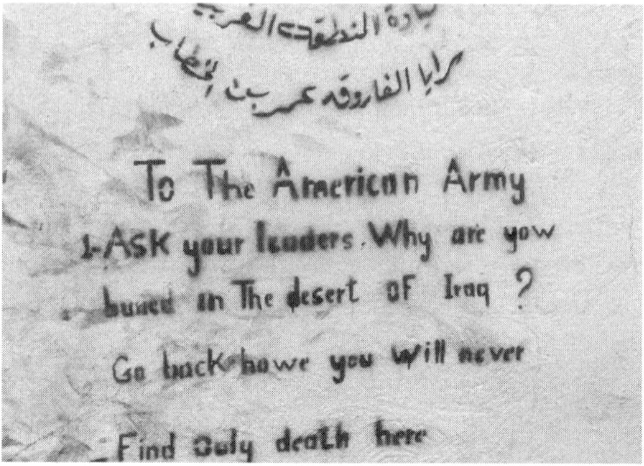


**Love Letter**

After seeing shit like this, I think of my family and one of my favorite memories come from the one place we swore we'd never return, Camp Lejeune, North Carolina. Sonia, not yet a teenager, Dani, just a toddler, and Molly, still a puppy and we didn't have two nickels to rub together. I was a corporal and Janet didn't work because we decided against day care for Danielle. Being poor meant we spent a lot of terrific time together and I loved it.

We spent many weekends at the beach with a picnic lunch and made funky castles in the sand. Most nights we sat together and watched TV or played games with the kids. Back then, I wished we could have more than we did. Now, I wish I could go back to those days.

16 Feb 2005

I spent a half hour of my life, writing the missing gear statement. Over three months ago, when we first came to Junction City, the S-4 shop asked me if they could borrow a Humvee trailer registered to my account. I hadn't used it since the war began and didn't envision ever using it so I told them to take it for as long as they like. Here is the part where I am a true idiot because I did not make them sign for it and never really bothered to get it taken off my account. As is usual in my dealings with the S-4, I took it in the short pants.

The trailer is lost and they vehemently deny ever even seeing it, much less using it. In fact, they claim that they are not even quite sure what a Humvee trailer is or how they might ever use such a device. So, I get to turn in a missing gear statement to battalion. I shall include my statement as another example of some of the bullshit a Marine Gunny might have to deal with from time to time. If this appears sarcastic or disingenuous, well, you can be the judge of that.

* * *

## STATEMENT OF GUNNERY SERGEANT P. M. TRACY

During the move from the Combat Outpost to Junction City on or about 01 Nov. 2004, Fox Company, and therefore Gunnery Sergeant Tracy, was in possession of a Humvee Trailer, the nomenclature and numerical identifier to which I cannot recall. I will bear witness to the fact I was under the impression it was Fox Company's equipment and therefore my responsibility. Upon arrival at Junction City, I positioned this trailer by the quad-cons located near the newly constructed laundry facility. I used the trailer to store ammo dunnage, as I was unaware at the time of where to dispose of said dunnage.

On or about 07 November, I was asked by a representative of the S-4 shop if Boxcar could borrow this trailer. Since I am an agreeable and gregarious fellow by nature, and since I had no need for the trailer, I told the S-4 representative they could empty the dunnage and borrow, or better still if it took their fancy, keep the trailer for their own nefarious purposes. The next day, the trailer was not where I had last seen it or accounted for it and I assumed that the S-4 acted upon my generosity and spirit of cooperation and borrowed the trailer or indeed kept it as their own. After this fateful day, which will live in ignominy if not infamy, I thought of this trailer nevermore. As if to prove the axiom of no good deed going unpunished, I was asked recently to account for the whereabouts of the aforementioned trailer.

Alas, to my everlasting shame and torment, I cannot. In fact, I cannot in good conscience recall

with whom I had these discussions, concerning the woebegone trailer. And I am sure, since there is now a culpability issue concerning the chain of custody of this trailer, there will not be any volunteers or admissions of guilt forthcoming. As I have affirmed previously, I did convey the trailer to Junction City in the early days of November and I can account for its whereabouts only until on or about 07 November. I will accept full responsibility for the absence of the trailer and can only cite my previous outstanding and unblemished record of never losing a piece of gear in my proud tenure as the Company Gunnery Sergeant for Fox Company, Second Battalion, Fifth Marines.
End of statement.

I expect to see someone, concerning my statement, but I have had about all I can take as far as the S-4 is concerned. Now that I think about it, I'll add a post script.
P.S. S-4 can take the trailer, turn that sum-bitch sideways and shove it straight up their candy ass.

But I'm sure quotes from The Rock, however appropriate, would go unappreciated or even worse unrecognized

17 Feb 2005

A giant kick in the balls came down disguised as orders from division. We lost an ongoing battle to do what is perhaps the most dangerous long-term operation since our arrival in Ramadi. At our end of town there are two bridges that control access into and out of Ramadi, the North Bridge and South Bridge. Someone from the division level thought it would be great good fun to set up a permanent VCP, to be manned 24/7 by Fox Company from 20 Feb until 05 March on both bridges. However, they did come up with a cool mission name: Operation River Blitz.

The first lesson we learned at March Air Force Base, where the USMC has sent the war-fighting lab to conduct training for all I MEF units who deploy to Iraq, is VCPs must be short in duration and non-permanent, so you are not an easy target for a SVBIED bomber or if you ever want to catch anyone with anything.

Once again we must follow an order that makes no tactical sense just to say "Yes, Sir" to some planning jackass who doesn't know shit about our AO. The only possible reason to do anything even remotely like this would be if we were 100% sure the city was cleaned up of all insurgents and cleaned out of all weapons and explosives. Even then it wouldn't make much sense considering we've found our biggest caches on the riverbanks. Now, I'm no strategic genius, but this seems to suggest, at least to an uneducated idiot like myself, maybe the Muj gets the shit in via the *river*.

The real kick in the nuts, we have broken our asses in our AO. We have it locked up so tight, every time a Haji turns around, he sees one of our gun trucks and our Marines patrolling around him and his neighborhood. Now, we'll abandon our AO to sit our asses on the bridges non-stop for two weeks.

The part that really, really sucks and that really,

really pisses us all off, this is a recipe to get someone hurt or killed before we get the fuck out of here.

If I had to design a plan with the goal of getting a few more Marines hurt or killed, this would be it. In order to guard against complacency, we tell our Marines not to establish patterns or do things in a way that will make us easy to figure out. Although cowardly, our enemy is a very clever opportunist. We preach this to the Marines over and over and then wrap up our deployment with the biggest bit of jackassery and buffoonery to date.

I wonder if the person who came up with this plan would think it was such a great goddamn idea if his ass had to sit on the fuckin' bridge VCP and wait for some misguided asshole to cash in his ticket to Allahland.

18 Feb 2005

Four more of our Marines earned the Purple Heart at the hands of an IED today. It always pisses me off when Marines get injured but it really pisses me off if they didn't need to get injured. I don't know why this is always the case but the person who makes the bad call or bad decision is never the one who gets hurt. Hopefully, someone learned a lesson and this shit won't happen again.

**Purple Hearts Ceremony**

This was a dismounted day patrol but due to slowness of movement, day turned to night. I hate dismounted night patrols in this fucking town because they serve nearly no purpose. There is nothing a Marine can see in this town at night until it is way too late. There is just way too much garbage, debris and clutter to be able to spot the hidden IED. We occasionally get lucky when we see them by day and that's usually due to bad emplacement.

If we get hit with an IED while in the vehicle then that's just the way it goes. Usually, no one gets killed and lately we've done real well on not getting too badly hurt. In the blast that took out Mikey's boys, the Marines who got out of the vehicles got the worst of it. Everyone in a vehicle is still on full duty.

The lieutenant submitted his patrol plan with the checkpoints and it was approved. He went out to do the patrol and while they moved, the MQRF screened his route with their vehicles and gave him the green light to carry on. Or, they certified it as safe as far as they could tell. Normally, this tactic works because if you have an IED and trigger-man hanging around, he usually tries to take out a vehicle in the convoy and waits for the first thing to come by because he has no way of knowing about a foot patrol.

Therefore, lesson number one, stick to the route you submitted and the MQRF cleared. Not only did the lieutenant not do this, he decided to continue past his final checkpoint and go up near a Main Supply Route (MSR). Not just any MSR, but Route Michigan, at night, on foot.

Whatever the case, he fucked around up by Route Michigan when Army vehicles moved onto the road. That should have been the clue it was really time to get the fuck out of there because this had to be as sweet as it gets for an IED trigger-man. His Platoon Sgt, Platoon Guide and Squad Leader told him this was not such a good idea but he decided not to listen and the IED was triggered.

The platoon had three casualties and only because of sheer good luck, no deaths. Two of them were pretty bad and an immediate medevac was called. In order to push a medevac you need four vehicles. He had five on this patrol but refused to put the remaining two squads in the trucks. He told the Platoon Sgt he was going to look for the triggerman in the nearby houses. Meanwhile, the Platoon Sgt loaded up the medevacs, moved with the four vehicles and initiated a QRF.

At this point, he took two squads and continued to move down this same road the IED was on with no medevac vehicles or gun truck support. He was actually looking for the guy and must think he wears a sign that says, "I'm an IED triggerman.

We got out there with the QRF and after linking up with 3rd Platoon we found five guys sitting in a car. It was after curfew so we could detain them on principal. Almost as an afterthought, I busted out my gunpowder test kit and decided to see if I could get any hits. The kit is pretty unreliable because it can give off a lot of false positives but if the suspects are guilty of handling explosives, they think we've got them and usually they come up with some bullshit story or try to make a deal.

In this case, two of the suspects tested positive. They denied having anything to do with the IED but they gave up info on some of their Muj buddies. I don't know if these guys set in the IED or not, but I do know that Sgt C, Cpl. B, Lcpl Y and Lcpl M are now out of the fight. Not because they went down fighting or the enemy outsmarted us, but because after six months of combat, a Second Lieutenant still doesn't know how to listen.

19 Feb 2005

Tonight we occupied the bridges and higher HQ wants us to run this shit right up until the 5th and turn it over to 1/5. I really hope I'm wrong and the Muj doesn't get his shit together in this two-week span. We joked around today in the morbid way Marines have of finding the humor in any situation. We took bets on when an SVBIED would kill a bunch of us.

My bet was for the 27th of February. I figure it will take our Muj buddies a couple days to figure out we're in this position for the long haul, a couple days to get good and pissed, a few more to formulate a plan and then, on the 7th day… BOOM!

Many times I've had to shut up and follow orders but this is by far the hardest pill to swallow in a long time. I will also make another prediction: although the Iraqis I have apprehended qualify as the stupidest group of people I have ever been in contact with, I am predicting we do not find one car with enough contraband or anything else to justify a long-term detainment. We damn sure won't get anyone from the big-time shit list and we won't catch any insurgents with bomb making material, unless we catch them the hard way.

I am a professional fighting man and I've been around long enough to know when something is being force fed from way on high that makes sense to some so-called tactician who probably sees the loss of a few Marines as an acceptable and inevitable result of his brilliant fuckin' strategy.

26 Feb 2005

Well, we've sat out asses on the bridges for a week and at least we haven't been blown up yet. My prediction was for tomorrow and I still hope to be very, very wrong on that one. We haven't gotten any detainees of note because no one has been so shit-all-stupid as to drive up to a checkpoint with a trunk full of shit.

**River Blitz**

As for my pain, this mission has become a logistical nightmare to rival the elections. Every day I get up at 0400 and roll out by 0500. The Iraqi Commandos are supposed to show up at 0430. So far they skipped one day, came at 0430 the next, 0445 the day after that, 0500 the next day, 0530 the next day and for the coup de gras, produced the longest wait yet as we departed at 0600 this morning.

Two Marines are assigned to get these guys there on time but they feel their responsibility lies in telling the Commandos where to be and when, and trust them to make it happen. I am disgusted and ashamed with the non-grunt NCO Corps I've dealt with. One would think a sergeant and corporal could wake up forty or so Commandos but, as usual, only grunts are held accountable for being squared away, diligent and professional. If an infantry corporal or sergeant was continually late and lazy to a near criminal point, they would be dealt with harshly, summarily fired and their evaluations would prevent further promotion and retention. I've given two legendary ass-chewings, the magnitude of which was so spectacular, the XO logged them in the Operations Logbook.

The Commandos are also a giant pain in the ass. I can understand the language barrier thing but everyday they act like it's their first time on the job. Today, I had their Captain try to tell the Marines he was in charge and would pull in only what vehicles he felt needed to be checked. I guess I should explain the complexity of the operation in order for one to understand this moron's jackassery.

We have a position directly off of each bridge the Combat Engineers built for bringing in vehicles and doing all of the processing. Inside of the vehicle checkpoint we have a high-speed BATS computer system that takes digital pictures, fingerprints and retinal scans. Our Marines trained in how to run this machinery because no pogue will come out here and do it for us. We also have the Commandos inside to search the personnel and vehicles. When they finish the searches, we have the military working dog teams sniff around to see if the Commandos missed anything.

We also have Intelligence Marines to question suspicious characters, Information Operations Marines to hand out propaganda, Interpreters for the obvious,

Civil Affairs Marines for who knows what the fuck they do and Army females to search selected women. What I have is a four-service operation. At each VCP, I have the Army represented with the Lioness search teams, the Navy Corpsmen, Air Force dog handlers with dogs and of course the USMC overseeing the whole goddamn circus.

As if that's not enough, we go international with Iraqi National Guardsmen A.K.A. (Muj), the illustrious Commandos and the assorted IPs who are there for civilian traffic control on the other side of the bridge.

We can't stop every vehicle just because of the sheer volume coming through. Therefore, we get specific targets from the intel weenies that match descriptions of suspect vehicles and we unabashedly profile those we think look suspicious. For instance, the past two days we were told to pull over commercial vehicles, all vehicles containing three or more military-aged males and all gray Opels. Apparently, we have intel coming in on suspects in gray Opels and commercial trucks.

Now, fast forward to today where some jackass Iraqi Commando who couldn't show up on time decides he was in charge of the whole shebang and states he knows who the terrorists are and he will decide who gets pulled in and who does not. I had to go down there and explain to this asshole he was in charge of jack and shit and if he kept running his pie hole, I would shut it for him.

Of course, I had to do this in a way that would not make him quit because if these weirdo's quit, which they do once or twice a week, then the Marines are the ones who pull in and search the vehicles. If and when we get unlucky, it would be mostly Marines instead of mostly Iraqis who get blown the fuck up. So far we haven't even had a sniff of an IED threat from any searched vehicles but we have had sporadic sniper fire, one very close rocket impact, a few IEDs in our AO, and one discovered by the MQRF under a suspicious box at an intersection.

Although the MQRF can't really patrol our entire AO, they patrol a small section of it just to keep these fuckers honest. Today, when the sniper took his fourth shot near our compound, we went out with the MQRF and looked for someone on a rooftop but nothing turned up. A little while later, we discovered the Iraqi National Guard (ING) compound took potshots to clear cars off the street. We told them to cut that shit out and they said they would be willing to stop if we gave them some soccer balls. I shit you not! Can you believe a Marine would ever have to deal with something like that? Only in Iraq!

27 Feb 2005

Today we took the 1/5 advance party leadership on a tour of our AO. We added my gun truck and the Command Vehicle to the MQRF which gave us five heavy gun trucks and one Ten-man Hummer. This seems like a lot of ass for a vehicle tour but considering we have no company back-up and one Whiskey Platoon for MQRF, we needed all the ass we could get. Our goal was to hit just about every intersection in our AO and breeze past some of the trouble spots.

It's weird when you take people out on a tour. The last thing you want is contact because it defeats the whole purpose of the tour. Then again, a part of you really wants contact because without it you just ride around the same old streets. We gave them a very good brief followed by a well-run tour and dumped as much information as we could. They asked a lot of questions and seemed like good, eager lieutenants.

There is one aspect of their advance party that troubled me. All of the companies sent their XOs as their sole representatives. I don't know what kind of battalion they run over there but if the Company XOs are the go-to guys, this battalion is out of whack if you ask me. I don't have anything against any young lieutenant or his abilities, but I'm not about to tell him how I make my deals and who I make them with. There are many ways to get things done and often you have to be willing to walk in the gray area between the black and white. Every Gunny worth his salt is a master of how to get things done one way or the other. Lieutenants are not experienced enough, or trusted enough, to be let in to this secret handshake club.

It just seems very strange to send over the most inexperienced leaders in the battalion on advance party and leave the Gunny's home. I've never heard of an advance party with no SNCOs. I guess they run things differently and quite frankly I couldn't care less. This is their fight to fight in three weeks and I'll be home with my family enjoying much needed leave. I just hope the young enlisted guys aren't the ones who pay the price because there aren't any SNCOs taking care of them in advance.

02 March 2005

It's March and hallelujah, holy shit and amen, I can say I'll be home this month! No one alive that hasn't been deployed to combat can possibly know how good it feels to say that. The end is definitely in sight and if I didn't believe it when I woke up this morning, I damn sure started believing it when I saw five truckloads of 1/5 Marines with all their gear in my parking lot.

Getting this close to the end is a very weird feeling. Up until now, I played it hour-by-hour and day-by-day. I stayed focused and kept my Marines focused on what's going on and tried not to think ahead to the trip home, but it gets harder and harder. It was easy until our replacements actually showed up. It wouldn't bother me if they took over right now. Going on missions and driving around have always been a bit of an adrenaline rush. I've never had to do it while thinking about how bad it would suck to get hurt with only two weeks to go.

I wonder how I'm going to feel when I go out for the *last* time. I can already bet I'll count the minutes until that one is over. For now, I still have to concentrate on the turnover. There are goddamn mountains to move and, as usual, not a whole lot of time to do it. At least, our battalion eased the burden on us. We kept our OP on the North Bridge and Echo took over the South Bridge. Now we'll only turn over two OPs to Bravo 1/5, which makes life a whole lot easier.

We can train each platoon on how to stand our two OPs and probably go on a few platoon-sized missions and maybe one company-sized. I have a feeling they'll want to take over the battle space sooner than the 17th of March. We took over from 2/4 earlier than our deadline date. No company wants another company baby-sitting them. They trained hard and have the right attitude for coming in and taking over. That's on the positive side.

On the negative side, they have this attitude of already knowing everything there is to know because they were in Fallujah for the first Fallujah Assault. That's a dangerous and reckless attitude because this isn't Fallujah and they could learn a lot from us. We've been in Ramadi and know this place very well. We know things our Marines learned from operating here, not somewhere else in Iraq, during a previous deployment. But, to be honest, they can do what they want and if they prefer to learn their lessons the hard way, there is nothing I can do to stop them. I'm glad they're here and even more so that we're getting out of here. That's all I have to say about that!

05 March 2005

The Company Gunny for Bravo 1/5 has finally arrived. He came in with the last group to arrive, which made my life more difficult but he's here and that's what counts. Tomorrow, I will take him out and introduce him to the North Bridge OP and probably swing past the Ghetto OP. I'll start with the gear and equipment of each post and explain how we operate and let him get a feel for what's going on in our AO.

I think their battalion will run very differently than we are right now and I don't think Bravo will end up staying in our AO. Who goes where will be decided later down the road for them. Any changes could be for the better. Maybe a new approach and a new attitude is what this place needs. We took a completely different approach than Echo 2/4 and we made a hell of a difference. Maybe they can pick up where we left off and finish cleaning up this shit hole.

Today we drove around Junction City and I showed him where all of the services and facilities he will need to deal with are located. By now, he's probably suffering from information overload but we have a very short time to accomplish a whole lot of different things. I'm going to focus on the vehicles and OPs for starters and then the nightmare of gear turnover. I hope he's a quick learner and comes in with an open mind and a good attitude. So far, he seems like a guy who's willing to look and listen and make his changes later on down the road.

I don't care where he's been or what he's done up until now. The funny thing about this war is you can't say, "I've been to Iraq so I know what's up."

Each town and city is completely different from the next. Although the basics of shooting, moving and communicating are always the same, one must learn from those who have experience in that particular city. I'm sure there are ways to operate and do business here that are completely different than in Fallujah.

Hopefully, the SNCOs and officers know this and can communicate this to the youngsters. Like all good, young, hard-core Marines, these guys want us to shut up and get out of the way so they can commence to whipping some ass. I love that attitude because that's what makes a Marine a Marine. I just hope they don't let their eagerness get in the way of their common sense and at least take the time to learn a little from the guys who have been here for seven months. I guess time will tell. As for me, I'll do my part and work my ass off to give these guys a professional, informative and complete turnover.

07 March 2005

Tomorrow we launch Operation Stone. Fox Company will patrol through our entire northern boundary from Smash to Give Me Street and then 2nd Platoon will cross Nova and go foot mobile from there to well past the hospital. From there, Golf will take over and sweep through the hospital. Since the hospital is covered by the Geneva Convention and a protected site, I'm sure the cowardly, chicken-shit, Muj bastards use it as an operating base.

Hopefully, Golf comes across some good shit in there and we close down another weapons storage facility. Whiskey will screen our flanks and an Army Engineer Company will once again sweep the entire Euphrates riverbank in our sector. This will tell us if they've gotten anything across while we've been doing VCPs. Our job is to keep pace with the army, patrol through our entire AO, search every abandoned building, public facility and most importantly bring all the leadership of Bravo Company along with us.

The idea is Bravo not only learns the AO but also how we shoot, move and communicate. I'm not sure how much of this they did in Fallujah. I know they were part of the build-up and siege. They rolled in on the first attack, which was halted so the Iraqi Army could go in and reinforce the "Freedom Fighters." For some of these Marines, this is their third time over here.

Another aspect to tomorrow's mission is this will be the last time the majority of the company operates out in town. For a lot of our boys, the war pretty much ends for them as of tomorrow. We have two more days of training with 1/5 and then they take over and only our leadership, squad leaders and above, will go out with them for the next four days. I'll hang around with their Gunny until he tells me to shove off and my combat tour will come to a close.

It's hard to explain what this feels like. Recently, General Mattis got into a little trouble with the liberals and politicians both in the Corps and out because he said combat, especially shooting and killing people, is fun. Well, it' crazy, ass-puckering, a complete adrenaline rush and a wild, wild ride. Maybe fun is not the best word but for us, that's how we see it. The only part that isn't fun is the intense worry you have for your Marines. Tomorrow, I will worry my ass off because I just won't be able to handle it mentally if one of my guys gets hurt or killed this close to the end, but you have to force yourself not to worry about those things.

You can't get overly cautious and careful because we've made it this far with an aggressive balls-out attitude and it's way too late in the game to change tactics now. I told the Goons, we would be even more physical and aggressive and if the enemy shoots even one round, we would unleash hell back at them. This lit up the smiles on their happy little faces and I think we're looking forward to our last mission as the Goon Squad.

08 March 2005

We rolled out at 0530 after a busy morning of swapping out the North Bridge and MQRF platoons. I'm no stranger to getting up early or working hard but I woke up at 0400 or earlier for three straight weeks. I haven't been this bone-tired and mentally ass-whipped since my first cycle of working lights to lights as a young Drill Instructor.

Everyone was keyed up to go out and finish off on a high note. We rolled out with our heavy hitters, 1st and 2nd Platoons, in order to show 1/5 how to operate on an extremely coordinated and professional level.

Lt. J requested my presence and that of my .50 cal gun truck in order to put a little extra punch with his platoon. The plan called for his platoon to sit in place and hold tight in a very bad part of town for several hours while 2nd platoon swept north and east of the hospital. I was more than happy to oblige because I started this war by going to a big fight in a bad part of town and 1st Platoon whooped ass then and we'd whoop ass again if it came to that.

My truck was given the honor of being lead truck. First of all, I wanted to be right up front in case anything went down and secondly, Crazy Mike has been dying to shoot his .50 cal and this is his last best chance. The movement out was a bit slow and methodical because we kept pace with the Army engineers who swept the riverbank. This was good for Bravo 1/5 because it was a lot easier to observe and learn at a slower speed. We made it to our limit of advance, which was on Fire Station Road, between Racetrack and Nova, gained the high ground, blocked off all avenues of civilian traffic, and commenced to wait for the enemy to come and get a taste.

As usual, the boredom factor had to be fought off. It's real easy to get bored, and then distracted, and then killed. Fortunately, my vehicle never has that problem. My guys were so eager to get into a fight they never rested, dozed off, took a break and damn sure never slept. Crazy Mike is without a doubt the most dedicated .50 cal gunner on the planet. No matter how long the operation or how many hours he had to stand behind the gun, he never took his eyes off his sector or took a rest. When someone asked if he wanted a break, he answered with an emphatic "NO" even before the question was finished. After six hours, he never even got out to take a piss.

After being in place for a few hours, 2nd Platoon linked up and reported they found a cache right up the street from us. I thought this would be a great opportunity to show the 1/5 Gunny how we exploit a cache site and how we separate the weapons and explosives and evaluate whether or not to transport some items or blow them in place. As I left, Lt. J warned me the shit would hit the fan and I would miss out. That would be just my luck but I felt this was important enough to take the chance.

We hustled our asses up the street and linked up with Mikey, who is the undisputed heavyweight champ of finding cache sites. The engineers uncovered a plastic tub buried in the ground with a nice little collection of toys. The total haul: 2 RPG launchers, 1 AK-47, 1 PKC machine gun, 5 RPG warheads, 10 boosters, 2 frag grenades, 10 armor piercing boosters, 3 Mujahedeen ski masks and a shit-load of ammunition for the AK-47 and PKC in very good condition, as well as being armor piercing. All of this equipment was in very good condition and recently used.

The Captain was worried about transporting the grenades and boosters and called in for EOD before I could get there. He didn't want to blow it in place because we were near a Mosque and worried about damage to the windows. My answer was "fuck them," once again, demonstrating why I will never be a Captain.

As the Gunny and I arrived, they looked for

more weapons and I showed him what the possible clues might look like. In this case, the tree near the buried bucket had blue wire wrapped around it. I told the engineers to look out for more types of this wire marking on some other trees but unfortunately for us this was all we could find.

As we waited for EOD, we heard incoming rounds. There are three unique sounds of gunfire. One is this loud SNAP, which means you are close enough to hear this tiny piece of lead breaking the sound barrier and it's fairly close by. Second is this whining ZIP! This means you are even closer than you were when you heard the snapping. The third, and definitely scariest is the FFPPT! This sounds like darts hitting a board and means you are in the kill zone. Today we heard the least formidable of all three, which is the snapping of rounds traveling overhead.

The Gunny and I headed in the direction of the gunfire. As we moved, he was right on my tail, looking for a target to shoot and that told me all I needed to know about this guy. It seemed the sniper shot from in between 1st and 2nd's position. For an inexperienced unit this could have been disastrous but 2nd stayed disciplined and obeyed their geometries while 1st unloaded on the target.

Just as I gained over-watch in a nearby house, I heard "Mike" go buck wild with the .50 cal and knew I'd never hear the end of it from Lt. J. Sure as shit, I left, the enemy grew balls and my boys went ape shit with the guns. Even the Captain busted my balls because I missed my last chance to get some. Prior to the enemy sniper taking his chances, there was a lot of activity in the souk (marketplace) but as soon as we opened up, that place became a ghost town. I, for one, prefer the ghost town because only bad guys come out and run around during firefights.

By the time the Bravo 1/5 Gunny and I got back to our vehicle, the fight was over. At least the Goons got to finish their combat tour on a high note. We didn't get a no-shit slugfest but action is action and the goal of showing Bravo 1/5 what the streets of Ramadi are all about was met and then some. After our little bit of fun, we sat in place for a few more hours and then retrograded back to the firm base. No Marines hurt, a cache found, a few enemy killed and a well-run operation spells success any way you shake it. If that was my last mission, I'll go out happy.

10 March 2005

Happy birthday Sonia! Today is my oldest daughter's birthday. I always thought I wanted a son until my oldest daughter grew up and became my best friend. She's one of the smartest, kindest, most independent and good people I know. Plus, she's a complete and total Daddy's Girl and that's all right with me. There is nothing on this earth that feels better than having a daughter who loves you. Her birthday also marks my final milestone of this deployment. I figured if I could make it that far, I'd be home in the blink of an eye.

**Sonia and me in Las Vegas, Nevada**

Like any responsible father, I took Sonia to Las Vegas for her 21st birthday. I may not have been able to teach my girls how to play football, wrestle, box, or fight, but I'll be damned, if they didn't know how to throw the dice and play poker. Unfortunately, Janet had to stay in the room to watch Danielle.

Sonia and I went down to the casino and after a warm up session on the slot machines. I decided to give her a lesson in roulette. My strategy, and that of countless others, is to cover about half the board with lucky numbers and birthdays. Sonia did likewise and beginner's luck blessed us. In the first five rolls, we hit all five times and twice on the number 29 and since that's Dani's birthday, we added a few extra chips.

We had a nice little stack when the waitress came by.

"Would you like a cocktail?" She asked ever so sweetly.

"Is a pig's ass made of pork? Today is my daughter's birthday. How about a couple of margaritas," I cheerfully exclaimed and waited for the waitress' comment. I must admit, I love to hear it every time.

"This is your daughter? You don't look old enough to be her father."

"Did you hear that Sonia? I'm a handsome, young-looking fella."

"Oh shut up, Dad."

After the waitress came back, Sonia prepared to pay her and I taught her the best lesson about the greatest city in the world.

"Uh, Sonia, this is Vegas. The drinks are on the house."

For the rest of the night, I took my beautiful daughter around the casino and taught her to play all the games of chance. Every now again, I think maybe I'm not such a great father. But on this night, I taught my girl how to throw away her money and drink for free. Father of the year is locked up, Baby.

She'll kill me for sharing this but I have a letter from her that I keep in my wallet and read every day of my life.

Dad,

> You told me in Las Vegas that I was more like you than anyone. It was the best compliment I've ever received. I wish you didn't have to go to Iraq but I know you'll be all right. It's just that we'll all miss you. I'm glad we got to spend time together in Ireland even though

it was so chaotic. I love you so much and will think of you all the time.
I love you, Dad.
Sonia

Many Marines carry mementos from loved ones at home. Some in the form of letters or poems and nearly everyone has a religious or good luck medallion or trinket. My letter from Sonia goes with me everywhere and constantly reminds me of what I have at home and why I'm among the luckiest men on Earth. It's hard to believe that one little letter can be such a powerful force in my life.

* * *

I thought I was finished with operations but apparently my dope was off. Tomorrow morning we are going on a series of raids on three different targets and that, my friends, will be my final operation in this shit-hole town. Now I go back to worrying about my boys all over again but not too much. These assholes have never been up and alert and ready for action before sunrise and I see no reason why tomorrow will be any different. Hopefully, we can finish by taking a couple more assholes off the streets of Ramadi. I guess that would be a good enough ending to a long seven months of combat operations.

11 March 2005

If there were any doubts this was my last day of combat operations, those ended as I cleaned my M203, took off my ACOG sight and turned it over to Bravo 1/5. The only weapon I have left is an AK-47 I confiscated a few months ago and I was told to turn that in also. It seems war trophies, in the form of automatic weapons taken from dead insurgents is frowned upon at customs.

**Fox 7 with a '47**

The morning raids went well with five detainees captured, to include one fucker we've been after for quite some time. There were no rounds fired in anger as we caught them all asleep and unaware their lives were about to turn to shit in a hurry.

Once again, we had a somewhat rocky start because the steering rod broke on one of the MQRF vehicles. I am so happy to be finished with goddamn vehicles. That has been the biggest headache and pain in the ass of my entire time in this country. I had no idea this monster was over here waiting for me. Nevertheless, we didn't let that ruin our fun. We carried on with one less vehicle and each element made it to their target house.

Fortunately, I traveled with 2nd Platoon because I wanted to end on a high note and I wanted to enter the target house with the breaching element. Unfortunately, 2nd Platoon was the only unit to come up empty. Either they had the wrong houses or the bad guy was just not there. Either way, they still did a solid raid and once again Bravo 1/5 saw how we accomplish a raid package.

* * *

As I sit here and contemplate everything that happened during my time in Ramadi, I can't help but feel a little sad it's all coming to a close. It's a very weird feeling now that the time is actually here. Every Marine begins a countdown from the day he leaves home until the day he gets back. We all want to leave, are ready and glad to leave. I guess it's just such a weird feeling to know I am not going back out into the town on any more combat operations. You have to force yourself into a groove where the insanity that makes up the daily schedule seems normal. The fact it is so far beyond normal is the crazy part.

There is no way to explain the ups and downs, the peaks and valleys of emotions you live with from moment to moment. I had my highest of highs and certainly my lowest of lows. I remember being in firefights and being so pumped up, scared and excited, I didn't know whether to shit or go blind as the saying goes. I remember the sensations that can only be called out-of-body experiences as I saw an enemy firing at me and as I fired back and came out the victor. I've never been overly anxious to kill someone just for the sake of killing someone because I believe that's pretty much the definition of insanity but killing someone as they shoot at you is like connecting on that Doug Flutie, Hail Mary pass as the clock winds down.

I also remember the lowest of lows. I still remember looking at Folmar as they brought his lifeless body into the Aid Station. I can't shake that image from my mind and I'm not sure if I want to because as much as war is fun and sexy and exciting and all that, it's also about young men dying. My young men, I would be proud to have as sons if I had any sons.

The next few days will be a bit of a winding down period and a bit busy as I turn all the gear, equipment, vehicles, bombs, guns, bullets, radio's and every other fucking thing under the sun to the Bravo Company Gunny. I hope they have a good tour and all come out OK. I hope they appreciate how much we tried to give them everything we had and everything we learned.

Saint Patrick's Day is on the 17th and the day when 1/5 officially takes over. Until then, my squad leaders, platoon sergeants and platoon commanders will continue to operate with them in an advisory capacity. The next time any of my boys leave the gate after the 17th is when we leave this shit-hole for good. For now, I'll continue the turnover and try to find a way to score some beer for Saint Paddy's Day.

12 March 2005

I guess Bravo's story can start right where mine ends. We sat on the porch smoking cigars when the North Bridge took fire. It's been a while since the Bravo Marines have been in action so it came over the radio sounding like the OP was under a full-on attack. Bravo's guys were on the OP and our guys were on the MQRF. It's still our fight but I stepped back to let their Gunny go out and do his thing. It was a very weird feeling to watch a QRF roll out the gate. The only QRF I was not a part of during this war was the one where 4th Platoon took all those casualties.

I sat in the COC and listened to the action, glad not to be a part of it yet wishing like hell I could be. This just made me want to go home even more so than normal. Much like when I first arrived at the outpost seven months ago, I cannot stand to hang around another unit and not run my part of the show.

The "attack" on the North Bridge turned out to be a few poorly aimed potshots but there's nothing like a little unfriendly fire to make you realize that you're in a combat zone. When the Gunny got back I told him to get used to it because today and tonight was a small preview of what his next seven months will be like in wonderful Ramadi.

15 March 2005

Today we finished for good. Bravo Company took over all aspects of this mission and we are completely out of the fight. We have a convoy to Al Asad on the 22nd, a flight to Kuwait on the 26th, and a flight back home on the 28th. The next week will be spent doing jack and shit. This is supposed to be our "decompression" period. I guess some Sigmund determined we need a week or so of sitting around with our thumbs up our asses in order to really be ready to go home. As for me, I can teleport from this shit-hole to my living room and I'm pretty sure when I get there I won't kill my whole family because of some latent homicidal urges left over from combat but who am I to argue with the wizard community.

Today will also be the last day of writing my journal until I get home. I had to turn over my computer and I won't have anything to type on until I'm back in my office at Camp Pendleton. I'm pretty sure by the time I tune back in I'll have gone through the long wait and long flight and write my final chapter from the comfort of my home.

**Victory Cigar**

Other than the long trip home, my combat tour has ended. It may sound crazy but all career infantrymen want to be tested in combat. "Why" is a question for the wizards. I don't know why I had this need to be put in the worst of all situations where every day could be my last or where every decision could be life and death for me or my Marines. I doubt any Marine could fully explain why the lure of combat is so strong. Maybe we're all crazy. We probably are. But I do know in the profession of arms there is a big difference between those who have been in combat and those who haven't. I guess in the end, I've seen what I was made of and answered questions about myself all of us probably wonder about. I know I love the Marine Corps, especially the young Marines that make us what we are. I've seen this company grow from a bunch of untested boots to finely trained and very fierce war fighters. I'm glad to be on this team and really fucking glad this team will never kick in my door and look for me.

I began this journal by mentioning I've read

hundreds of books about past conflicts and the men who fought in them. I always wondered if any of my stories or actions would measure up or if I would ever be a part of the story of Marines in battle. Well, I've been there and back and I'm damn proud to say Fox 2/5, the Blackhearts, are more than equal to any Marine, who ever laced up a pair of combat boots.

01 April 2005

The journey home consisted of a three hour convoy in the back of Army-driven 7-tons to Al Asad air base followed by a short flight to Kuwait three days later. All we had to do was eat chow and wait for our flight home. We flew to Germany, then Newfoundland, then Maine and finally March Air Force Base in Riverside, California. From there we got a bus ride to Camp Pendleton, retrieved our bags and turned in weapons. This long, long journey ended with all of us reunited with our families in the same spot we said goodbye.

The excitement and happiness more than doubled the sadness of that dark and dreary day over seven months ago. Hundreds of friends and family members cheered and waved flags as I marched the company on to the parade deck. Whereas the excitement and patriotic fervor of the average American is by now much dampened by the longevity of this war, for our families it was very much at fever pitch.

**Welcome Home**

There are many emotions and experiences I said couldn't be imagined or explained by those who haven't been deployed to combat and this homecoming is at the very top of that list. Many thoughts were going through my head as the cheering began and the band played the Marines Hymn. Mostly, I was happy to be home and in a state of near disbelief I was finally there. I'm pretty sure everyone else felt the same way. Many times I thought I might never see my family again and to actually hug and kiss my wife and daughter ranks right at the top of the greatest and happiest moments of my life.

Homecoming is always a little awkward. We have to readjust to being home and away from combat and our families have to readjust to us. Despite this, it's such an amazing feeling to be in *my* house with *my* family with a cold beer in my hand and my dog at my feet that I can't help but wonder how I ever overlooked the absolute joy of this experience. Combat has changed me, it's changed all of us, and the remarkable thing, the changes are for the better.

It's time to spend some *quality* time with my family and then a long relaxing thirty days of leave. And then guess what? Fox 2/5 will re-deploy in the winter of 2005 as part of the 31st MEU. We're not scheduled to return to combat but with operations ongoing in Iraq and Afghanistan, the only thing that's a sure thing is we will go where we're told, when we're told and do what we're told. If that means going to Iraq or Afghanistan, then that's where we'll go. Even though it's a very short turn around, we'll be ready. Marines have been ready for 230 years. Marines will be ready for the next 230 years. You can bet your ass on that.

# ABOUT THE AUTHOR

Patrick Tracy was born in 1967 and raised in Pittston, PA. A career infantry Marine, he has been stationed in Scotland, Japan, North Carolina, South Carolina, Washington D.C., Hawaii, Colorado and presently resides in San Clemente, California with his wife Janet and daughters Sonia and Danielle.

He reported for duty at Camp Pendleton in September of 2003 and deployed to Iraq in August of 2004 as the Company Gunnery Sergeant for Fox Company 2nd Battalion 5th Marines.